thegentleanarchist

For John Burns
with thanks and best wishes

thegentleanarchist
a life of George Woodcock

Douglas Fetherling

Vancouver
March 98

DOUGLAS FETHERLING

Douglas & McIntyre
Vancouver/Toronto

University of Washington Press
Seattle

By the same author:

Travels by Night: A Memoir of the Sixties
Way Down Deep in the Belly of the Beast: A Memoir of the Seventies
The File on Arthur Moss
Selected Poems
The Dreams of Ancient Peoples
Variorum: New Poems and Old 1965–1985
Moving towards the Vertical Horizon
Rites of Alienation
Chinese Anthology
The Blue Notebook: Reports on Canadian Culture
Notes from a Journal
The Five Lives of Ben Hecht
The Crowded Darkness
Some Day Soon: Essays on Canadian Songwriters
Year of the Horse: A Journey through Russia and China
Gold Diggers of 1929
The Gold Crusades: A Social History of Gold Rushes 1849–1929
The Rise of the Canadian Newspaper
A Little Bit of Thunder
The Other China
Documents in Canadian Art (editor)

98 99 00 01 02   5 4 3 2 1

Douglas & McIntyre Ltd.
1615 Venables Street
Vancouver, British Columbia
V5L 2H1

Canadian Cataloguing in Publication Data

Fetherling, Douglas, 1949–
 The gentle anarchist: A life of George Woodcock

 ISBN 1-55054-606-6
 1. Woodcock, George, 1912–1995. 2. Authors, Canadian
(English)—Biography. 3. Anarchists—Biography. I. Title.
PS8545.O6Z65 1997 c818'.5409 C97-910514-5
PR9199.3.W58Z7 1997

Originated by Douglas & McIntyre
and published simultaneously in the United States of America by
The University of Washington Press
PO Box 50096
Seattle, Washington 98145-5096

Library of Congress Cataloging-in-Publication Data

Fetherling, Doug, 1949–
 The gentle anarchist: a life of George Woodcock / Douglas Fetherling.
  p. cm.
 Includes bibliographical references and index.
 ISBN 0-295-97701-9 (alk. paper)
 1. Woodcock, George, 1912-1995—Biography-. 2. Authors,
Canadian—20th century—Biography. 3. Anarchism—Canada—
History—20th century. 4. Periodical editors—Canada—Biography.
5. Historians—Canada—Biography. 6. Anarchists—Canada—Biography.
I. Title.
PR9199.3.W58Z67 1998
818'.5409—dc21
[B]   97-45568
                    CIP

Editing by Deborah Viets
Jacket photograph courtesy of Queen's University Archives
Jacket design by Isabelle Swiderski
Typeset by Brenda and Neil West, BN Typographics West
Printed and bound in Canada by Friesens
Printed on acid-free paper ∞

Frontispiece: George Woodcock panning for gold at Leach River, near Sooke, B.C., in 1949—"One foot still in Central London and the other in a remote stream on Vancouver Island."
QUEEN'S UNIVERSITY ARCHIVES

The publisher gratefully acknowledges the assistance of the Canada
Council and of the British Columbia Ministry of Tourism, Small Business and Culture.

For Don Stewart
at the corner of Pender and Richards
next to the Hotel Niagara

CONTENTS

PROLOGUE: GEORGE WOODCOCK AND THE NECROLOGISTS

GEORGE WOODCOCK DISLIKED being photographed. Canada's most prolific man of letters usually demurred when asked for a recent likeness to use with one of his new books, of which there were sometimes four or five a year during his most productive periods in the 1970s and 1980s. Sometimes he cited an affinity with indigenous peoples who believed that the camera steals one's soul. At other times he pleaded shyness. Some suspected him of vanity in this matter but kept their suspicions to themselves. Didn't one such failing in a person so generous, gentle and good-hearted serve only to make him more human? But the proof of their intuition was the way Woodcock held to his position as advancing years changed his physiognomy. In 1984 he replied this way to an anthologist seeking a picture to accompany a piece of fiction she was using: "Since my story is a dream story, standing in its own time, I don't think it is necessary to keep our time frames precise, so I am sending a photograph from another time, another life, taken in 1946."[1] He wanted it returned.

For a public figure—which is what he became, albeit a somewhat reclusive one—there are, then, surprisingly few photographs of Woodcock, so that each must carry more interpretative weight than would photos of most other authors of his stature. One photograph in particular seems to me to speak with special meaning. It was taken in 1949 near Sooke, British Columbia, where the Woodcocks, George and Ingeborg, had come to homestead after leaving England the previous year. It shows him panning for gold, using a handle-less spade as his pan. His hair is unkempt, he hasn't shaved in a day or two, and the stub of a cigarette, possibly of the roll-your-own variety, dangles from one corner of his mouth. He wears what must have been cheap corduroy trousers, which he has rolled up to his shins, and what appears to be a thin, well-worn pullover. He is also sporting a necktie, fully done-up, black wing-tip shoes, and a shirt that could be from Turnbull & Asser of Jermyn Street. Purchases made in the New World have not yet completely supplanted his original British wardrobe. The image calls to mind the awful verse by the nineteenth-century Scottish poetaster William MacGonagall: "Hail Queen Victoria / In all her regalia / With one foot in Canada / And the other in Australia." Except that Woodcock, in what remains of his regalia as a young English literary gent, has one foot still in Central London and the other in a remote stream on Vancouver Island.

This seems to me to encapsulate the major change in George Woodcock's life: his emigration/immigration, with the steady shift of perspective that the solidus implies.

Obituary notices, particularly those in the Fleet Street necrological tradition (which is less telegraphic and gestural in its language than its American counterpart), are especially useful points of entry into a career, releasing a collective judgement that has been building up pressure just below the surface during the decedent's lifetime. They often present one means of inquiry. Certainly this is the case with George Woodcock.

The first duty of the obituary is to report the death as news and to provide a sketch of the person's career and achievements, quickly assigning him or her a tentative place in history. On 30 January 1995, news of Woodcock's death was the top item in the news summary on the front page of the *Globe and Mail,* and that evening the story was reported on both the *CTV National News* and *Prime Time News* on CBC Television. The following morning, the *Globe and Mail's* obituary, by Chris Dafoe, the paper's arts correspondent in the Canadian West, itself began on page one immediately below the fold and jumped inside for a total of thirty-one and a half column inches. This was in addition to a seventeen-column-inch eulogy in the arts section, written by George Galt, the editor of *The Purdy-Woodcock Letters: Selected Correspondence 1964–1984* and a board member of the Woodcock Trust, the charity set up by George and Inge for the relief of Canadian writers in distress.

There was a panel that same morning on CBC Radio's *Morningside,* with contributions from Alan Twigg and Doris Shadbolt in Vancouver and a miniature anthology, patched together from the archives, of Woodcock reminiscing. The following day Jeffrey Simpson, the *Globe and Mail's* national political columnist, devoted his space across the bottom of the editorial page to Woodcock and

> his tremendous impact on Canadian writing in English.
>
> Few people in postwar Canada contributed so much to expanding the understanding of Canada, or more properly of English-speaking Canada, and to promoting what was the fragile flower of domestic writing in English.
>
> Mr. Woodcock would have been, I suppose, a hero in other countries as a prolific man of letters. (His politics were a trifle bizarre, although he lived what he perceived the truth of his principles.)[2]

The parenthetical statement was the only discordant note and, coming from so conservative an institution as the *Globe and Mail,* was tantamount to a ringing endorsement.

More puzzling was a column the next day by Trevor Lautens of the Vancouver *Sun.* Lautens challenged Woodcock's competence as a writer, stating "that I find his writing lifeless. Sterile. Bloodless. Uninventive. Unoriginal. Riskless."[3] This was more than the stunning example of poor taste for which it was subsequently denounced in letters to the editor. It was a statement on the transitional position Woodcock occupied in the progress of Canada's English prose. His earlier writings might almost have been examples from his friend Herbert Read's still useful 1928 guidebook *English Prose Style.* As Woodcock discusses in his memoirs, he tried to make his writing more colloquial once he set up shop in Canada, where the American influence, in this as in all other aspects of culture, grows stronger each year. But he never fully abandoned English prose-rhythms for the paratactic and heavily caffeinated American journalese (indeed, this was among the many reasons to admire and love him). Lautens was unwittingly representing the statistical majority of Canadian readers who somehow believe, without ever quite articulating the distinction, that what does not share the diction of speech heard on television is therefore poor writing.

The liberal Toronto *Star* was generous in its own obituary: "The failure of his 82-year-old heart was the only thing that could put a stop to the astounding career of George Woodcock, one of Canada's most honored men of letters."[4] The utilitarian Canadian Press was only slightly less declamatory. *Maclean's* came out in turn with a page of generous tributes, followed by similar outpourings in the book review media such as *Books in Canada* and *Quill & Quire*.

The prominence and number of the reports in the British press were similar to those in Canada, but the tone was generally much different.

In his memoirs, Woodcock tells how, in the 1940s, a favourable review of one of his early books, by Harold Nicolson in the *Daily Telegraph*, helped to change his life by making it possible for him to write books for a living. Almost fifty years and more than a hundred volumes later, the same newspaper recalled in its obituary how, "much to the amusement of his friends, Woodcock moved to Canada" and that while "he never modified his English accent, [he] became increasingly Canadian in outlook."[5] The anonymous obituarist (the staff writer David Twiston Davis) meant that Woodcock gradually increased the percentage of his work having to do with Canadian literature and Canadian history, making himself in time an elder statesman of the discipline but also limiting the outside world's interest in him.

In his column in the *New Statesman & Society*, Woodcock's former protégé Colin Ward interpreted Woodcock's Canadian outlook in terms of his very Canadian concerns with regionalism, decentralization and nationalism—issues that in Woodcock's case amounted to the principles of anarchism made universal by application to his own backyard. Ward wrote: "Among his vast range of interests, one of the endlessly topical issues, both in Canada and here, was his interpretation of federalism and decentralization. He never told me his views on the current debate on a federal Europe. I suspect that he would simply have despaired at the crude level of understanding among British politicians."[6] Ward also composed the *Guardian's* obituary for Woodcock.

In the *Independent*, Nicholas Walter wrote bluntly that Woodcock "divided his life between two worlds"[7]—which indeed is what a comparative reading of the obituaries in the two countries tends to confirm.

The British acknowledged his Canadian writings but tended to give less weight to his philosophical anarchism than did the Canadian press. The exceptions were the anarchist paper *Freedom* and, in time, *Peace News*, the pacifist monthly. *Freedom* was co-founded by Peter Kropotkin in 1886. Woodcock once helped to edit it and contributed to it down through the years. Now it ran two full pages of tributes, including affectionate ones by Colin Ward and Nicholas Walter and harsher ones by Robert Graham and Tony Gibson, dwelling on old internecine squabbles in the movement. I believe these are worth quoting to show the dichotomy—it is practically a seismic fault line —that runs across Woodcock's career.

Gibson, for example, stated that when Woodcock departed for Canada few people in the British anarchist movement "were even aware of the departure of the shy, sly and secretive figure of George" who became "very highly regarded as an intellectual in Canada where he was something of a big fish in a rather small literary pond."[8] Gibson also quarrelled with Woodcock's own recollections of the anarchist movement. "His inconsistencies were not due to the failing memory of an old man," Gibson wrote, "for as he had been publishing continually for over forty years one could trace how his account of things had altered from time to time. I am not charging him with being a deliberate liar, for I think that he believed what he said at the time of saying it, but not only has he been a creative writer but had a very creative memory."[9] Yet Gibson had to conclude that Woodcock's was "a life to be proud of, and I wish there were more like him."[10]

Walter, a former member of the *Times Literary Supplement* staff, was altogether more charitable without ceasing to be frank: Woodcock, from Walter's perspective, "saw himself as an intellectual and as an autodidact, an independent man of letters rather than a professional scholar or journalist. He was an elegant as well as a prolific writer, and never wrote an ugly or unclear sentence."[11] No other line in the British obituaries speaks so strongly about the transatlantic polarization of prose, the matter raised unconsciously by Lautens in Vancouver. Walter continued: "He was inclined to be rather vain, but then had a lot to be vain about. He was impatient with what he saw as the pedantry of academic scholarship, and rather careless with facts and references; he might have replied that he preferred what he did to what other people didn't do, and he did more than anyone else of his time to make anarchism familiar and friendly to ordinary people. He was also a courteous controversialist, a loyal comrade, and a valued colleague. He and his wife had no children but a large family of friends all over the world, including many people they never met."[12]

This left only the press in the United States (where Woodcock was not well known and had little wish to be) to wrestle with the puzzle: the *New York Times* ran a brief Associated Press obituary notice on

1 February, rather than one by the paper's Canada correspondent, Clyde Farnsworth. It makes no mention of the fact that Woodcock was barred from the United States and forced to give up his early teaching job at the University of Washington by the provisions of the notorious McCarran Act, which was enforced against him for more than three decades.

Despite a marked difference in perspective and interpretation between the Canadian and the British (and the American) reviewers of his life, there was general agreement on the basics, leading to a quick sketch that can be easily fleshed out. Woodcock's father, Arthur, whom George idolized and perhaps idealized, was intellectually and physically adventurous, much at odds with his humble position in the Great Western Railway, and went out to Canada in 1907, where he took part in the Cobalt silver rush in Ontario and later tried farming in Manitoba. Gertrude Lewis Woodcock, George's mother, was a difficult personality who would do much to refine the patience for which her son became famous. George was born at Winnipeg but when he was still an infant the family returned in failure to England, where George grew up in genteel semi-rural poverty, first in Shropshire and then in the market town of Marlow in the Thames Valley. Too poor to attend Oxford on a half-fees scholarship, and too honest to accept the offer of a more prosperous relative to study at Cambridge in return for a promise to become an Anglican clergyman, Woodcock became the third generation of his family to endure lowly employment in the Great Western. This, the darkest period of his life, was also, paradoxically, the time of his intellectual and literary awakening. He laboured for eleven years in an office above Paddington Station in London (as a clerk like his father—not as "a ticket-sorter",[13] as Colin Ward had it in the *New Statesman*: a clerk for the railway, not a railway clerk).

In London, Woodcock began to carve out a literary career for himself, at once imaginative, historical, critical and political. He represented neither the aging establishment with roots in Bloomsbury nor the young Turks of the Auden generation. Rather, he was part of a third force in English writing whose members were younger than the former and politically more sophisticated than those of the latter. Chronologically and ideologically, their world-view was shaped by the fighting in Spain but put to the test only by the Second World War, which they responded to variously, Woodcock by becoming a conscientious objector.

Certain elder writers on the fringe of this group are canonical today, particularly George Orwell, an antagonist whom Woodcock made into a friend; but also, in a sense, Graham Greene (Woodcock wrote the first assessment of Greene's work between hard covers). Some members retain a place in pop culture, such as Julian Symons, the mystery writer, and Alex Comfort, who would rise to celebrity in the 1970s as the author of *The Joy of Sex*. One reason this grouping is forgotten now is that the members pursued their individualism in such different ways as these. But another reason, some believe, is that the group lost its focus when the Woodcocks removed themselves to Canada. In his memoir *Inside the Forties*, the poet Derek Stanford remarks that "the English literary scene lost a lot" when the Woodcocks left London.[14]

Stanford does not speculate on the complicated components of their decision to quit at a time when, it seemed, Woodcock was poised to achieve much wider public acceptance. Nor does Woodcock himself go into great detail about his thinking in the appropriate volume of his autobiography, *Letter to the Past*; instead, he concentrates on the abiding pull of Canada, as the place where his late father had failed to attain independence. In fact, emigration, undoubtedly the major decision of his life (more important even than the glide from socialism into anarchism) involved a tangle of motives.

During the war, Woodcock was involved in highly charged personal and political relationships. These came to a head when all his colleagues on the ad hoc journal *War Commentary*, including his close associates Marie Louise Berneri and her husband Vernon Richards, were arrested on charges of urging British troops to mutiny. Woodcock was not arrested (he went underground), though police had evidence that his typewriter had cut the mimeo stencil used to reproduce the offending article. And charges against Berneri were dropped. But the others, after a sensational trial in 1945 that is part of the contested folklore of the British anarchist movement, were convicted and served prison sentences.

After the war, it must have been difficult to have been a conscientious objector. Having a German wife probably didn't make life easier, though the surviving members of the Woodcocks' circle cannot recall specific instances of discrimination against Inge. Certainly it was difficult to reconstruct the mood of pre-war London which had vanished in a trick of fundamental change. Roy Porter captures the atmosphere of the late 1940s in *London: A Social History*:

After the doodle-bugs the sigh was for 'business as usual', the cry was for peace and quiet and cosy, familiar routine, and Londoners resumed their old lifestyles as if the clock could be turned back. Demobbed majors dusted down their brollies; wives left munitions work and went back to the kitchen sink; cricket enjoyed the golden age of the Comptons and Bedsers; the Olympic Games came to London in 1948. [This was] London's Indian summer, when the docks still thrived and the trams sailed majestically through pea-soupers. [But the] postwar years proved difficult, of course, with their fuel shortages, power cuts and ubiquitous queuing. Rebuilding proceeded slowly. With money short and a certain LCC puritanism in the air, reconstruction was cautious and visions rationed ...

Population leakage was both a cause and a symptom of emergent postwar economic troubles. Inner London had long been thinning, but now even Greater London was becoming less great. Greater London contained about 6.25 million people in 1938 [but would lose five hundred thousand in each of the next four decades].

Globally Britain became a loser, as her industries—overmanned, undercapitalized, and obsolete, their success long dependent upon imperial preference and soft markets—failed to meet the challenge of the USA and the reborn postwar economies of Germany, France, Italy and the Low Countries ...

With the decline of protected imperial markets and with hot world competition, many of London's traditional employers collapsed.[15]

Woodcock would recall in *The Crystal Spirit: A Study of George Orwell* how Orwell seemed to relish the poor post-war diet. This was either a brave front born of the egalitarian dream or poor taste. For people of Woodcock's generation, London was never the same again, certainly not even the resurgent Swinging London of twenty years later, which was the property of a different generation. Although Woodcock did maintain many professional contacts with London until the 1970s (when his London wardrobe, so to speak, finally became threadbare), his personal contacts fell off more sharply. Two factors were the deaths of Berneri and Orwell shortly after Woodcock's arrival in British Columbia. He would avoid visiting Britain if possible while travelling much of the rest of the world with easy enthusiasm.

And so one finds George Woodcock, approaching forty, living on Vancouver Island, building two cabins with his own hands and at one point reduced to shovelling manure for seventy-five cents an hour, starting over again as a writer, making for himself, ultimately, a career of such breadth, and perhaps singularly Canadian character, that it eluded the understanding of his former British colleagues.

The obituaries demonstrate that there were two George Woodcocks, the Briton (up to thirty-seven) and the Canadian (thirty-seven to eighty-two). To Nicholas Walter, writing in *Freedom* (commenting less formally than he had in the *Independent* and signing himself with the initials NW), Woodcock "was largely forgotten in Britain, except among students of anarchism and other survivors of his literary generation, but in Canada he became a grand old man ..."[16] The status puzzled British observers, such as the more plain-spoken Tony Gibson, who, appearing in the same issue, posited that Woodcock "was really very pleased by such adulation, and what may seem to some people his rather ridiculous naive egotism of his later years may partly be attributed to all the flattery he received in Canada"—a place where, nevertheless, he produced works which "have probably made more people around the world aware of anarchism than any other twentieth-century writer except perhaps Kropotkin."[17]

One further perspective was offered in *Freedom* by Robert Graham, doing the opposite of what I am attempting here: looking at the Canadian obituaries and tributes through British eyes. He wrote: "It was amusing to hear national media personalties try to treat his 'anarchy' with some understanding and respect, but there is no doubt that those who knew him as a Canadian literary figure had some difficulty dealing with his political beliefs. Nevertheless, he did more than anyone else in Canada to popularise anarchist ideas and to promote anti-authoritarian approaches to politics, even is [*sic*] he was not a consistent anti-statist."[18] Graham continued: "No doubt he will remain a figure of controversy in England, but in Canada it appears his reputation as a 'lifelong anarchist' is secure. That is how he will be remembered and, perhaps, even revered."[19]

This also makes clear the task of a Woodcock biographer: to arbitrate between two views that are more conflicting than complementary, explaining the young British Woodcock to Canadians, explaining the older Canadian Woodcock to the British. Such at least is what I have tried to accomplish in the following pages.

1 A DREAM THAT FAILED

IN THE WORLD in which George Woodcock grew up, the old feudalism, symbolized by the great houses of the land-owning aristocracy, was still alive, at least in the Welsh Marches and in Shropshire, where the snow was slow to recede under the sun of change. At some point in their lives, two of his grandparents and various of their siblings had been "in service". But even in these thoroughly rural parts of Britain the system of nobility based on hereditary privilege and ownership of land had long ago started to give way to what might be called feudal capitalism. Giant companies, formed by Victorian entrepreneurs, controlled whole towns and counties and oversaw the lives of thousands of employees, spawning similar feelings of dependency and deference among the people. The Woodcocks and, on the maternal side, the Lewises, who were Anglo-Welsh and Welsh respectively, were among the victims of this system. Three generations of Woodcocks, down to and including the one who is the subject of this book, were employed by the Great Western Railway, sometimes more than once.

From Paddington Station in London, the Great Western's lines fanned out through Reading and Bristol to the Bristol Channel. They spread southwest through Cornwall all the way to Penzance and northwest to Liverpool by way of Birmingham and Shrewsbury. And of course they permeated every exploitable path into Wales, both the Rhondda Valley and other mining areas in the south and those in North Wales as well. The routes were punctuated with bridges, tunnels and viaducts built by Isambard Kingdom Brunel, the greatest of the Victorian railway engineers, who also laid 1600 kilometres of track

before turning his attention to the sea and designing the *Great Western*, the first ship to cross the Atlantic under steam, and the *Great
Eastern*, the largest vessel built up to that time.

The GWR had a bigger share of the market than the other three of
the so-called Big Four railways because it transported an immense
volume of English holiday-makers to the seashore and an even greater
tonnage of coal from the Welsh mining districts. In the words of one
of its modern historians, the GWR's

> tradition was established early and very powerfully. There was always a
> clear-cut Great Western way of doing things, from selecting typefaces
> to making sandwiches, from sending messages full of the company's
> own code abbreviations to the care of the stations. When change took
> place, it happened consciously and was well-publicised, the new way
> immediately becoming the accepted law.[1]

There were many famous trains on the GWR, including one called the
Merchant Venturer. The name seems to recall the so-called companie
of merchant adventurers of the Hudson's Bay Company in Canada.
Like the HBC, the GWR was a publicly traded monolith, a blue-chip
enterprise that made its backers wealthy by exploiting the resources
of the vast areas to which it had been given licence. The stationmas-
ter at the lowliest stop on any of the lines occupied a social role not
unlike that of the humblest Hudson's Bay factor, who could be a lord
at the most remote trading post:

> Stationmasters were the local upholders of the tradition and the expec-
> tation. To talk to them was an honour, but they did their job ... They
> met the important trains, helped if there was a queue at the booking
> office, canvassed for traffic, and ensured that important customers
> received their copy of the timetable ... But then the trains were
> seldom late, or so memory tells us ... To delay the Bristolian was a
> disgrace so great that nobody risked it. And while many trains on lesser
> routes plodded slowly on their way to identical schedules decade by
> decade, making leisurely breaks for water on branch lines, it was the
> deities among the trains that gave everyone expectations.[2]

Most of George Woodcock's childhood and adolescence took place at
two dots on the railway map: Market Drayton in Shropshire, on the

line that terminates at Liverpool far to the north, and two hundred miles to the south, at Marlow, in the Thames Valley in Buckinghamshire, west of London. Marlow was the only town on a spur of a branch line that connected the two great arteries of the GWR, those running northwest and southwest from Paddington, the loudly beating heart.

George would always remember that a pall of gloom and failure seemed to hang over his family. His great-grandfather Thomas Woodcock established himself as a small farmer, but his prospects were ruined when the repeal of the Corn Laws flooded Britain with cheap wheat from Canada and America. Decades later, George would memorialize him, explaining how, like John Hanning Speke, the African explorer, Great-Grandfather Woodcock had walked out to the hedgerows with his shotgun and killed himself. He did so "to avoid facing / a roomful of daughters / without dowries" and in such a way that no one could say with certainty whether the suicide was not in fact an accident: "Juries of sportsmen / returned appropriate verdicts. / They knew in those days / that life also / is mainly accidental."[3]

Creditors foreclosed on the farm, and Thomas's wife, to avoid the work-house, moved to a cottage and took in washing. So when Samuel Woodcock, the half-brother to all those unmarried sisters, worked as a footman to one of the local squires he was actually coming up in the world, a process that would continue when he entered the service of the GWR. Later still, he married a ladies' maid, much older than himself, who had saved a bit of money—enough to allow him to set up as a coal merchant in Market Drayton. He became a respectable member of the minor gentry in this quiet, conservative West of England community, whose best remembered historical event had occurred in 1827, when a murder case revealed the existence of a secret band of local thugs. When George Woodcock was a boy, the gang and its crimes would be recalled for the British public by Sir Arthur Conan Doyle in a *Strand* piece, "The Bravoes of Market-Drayton".[4]

Samuel Woodcock the coal merchant had two sons who survived childhood. Harold followed his father's path both temperamentally and professionally so that the coal company became known as S. Woodcock & Son. But the younger, George's father, Arthur Woodcock, was interested in music, the theatre, literature and art. Such pursuits shocked and saddened his family. To lure him back to the path of righteousness, Samuel Woodcock offered Arthur a partnership in the business if he would give up this artistic nonsense. But as George

Woodcock would write: "With a characteristic combination of weakness and obstinacy which I recognize that I inherited, my father chose a third alternative. He left for Canada in 1907."[5]

By then he was already engaged to Margaret Gertrude Lewis, a grim and sickly young milliner's apprentice in the nearby village of Little Drayton. She was one of three daughters of a bitter, tempestuous Baptist radical, who was a signalman on the Great Western but kept his ties to the land by raising pigs on a three-acre freehold with a brick house called Runneymede, in Maer Lane, Market Drayton.

Canada seemed a promising possibility. In these years the Dominion government and the Canadian railways managed huge immigration schemes in an attempt to fill up the North and the Prairies, a propaganda effort that reached even Market Drayton. Arthur Woodcock embarked at Liverpool for New York and thence for Montreal, where he took one of the migrants' trains to Manitoba. There a Shropshire-born rancher gave him work in his stables. Later, he did farm labour for another man from the Old Country, who was homesteading. But Arthur Woodcock was not strong physically, as events would prove. He drifted to Winnipeg, where there was plenty of indoor employment and even a circle of bohemians with whom to spend time. Still infatuated with the theatre in all its forms, Arthur made the acquaintance of a vaudeville comedian, Charlie Chaplin, who was performing locally. Also, he became friends with a former prize fighter and future Hollywood actor, Victor McLaglen, with whom he forged the idea of moving to Cobalt in northern Ontario to seek their fortunes in the silver rush that had captured international attention. But in fact the rush was nearing its peak at about the time of Woodcock's arrival in Canada, and they came back to Winnipeg empty-handed. With railways part of his genetic endowment, Arthur found employment in the office of the Canadian Northern line. Later he went to work for Imperial Oil as a bookkeeper. When he was elevated to the position of accountant early in 1911, he felt he could send for Margaret to join him.

She had been to North America once before, spending a brief unhappy period in New England, and she had a less romantic, perhaps even a jaundiced view of the New World. But she made the long journey to Winnipeg, where she and Arthur were married in May 1911. In later life she was given to repeating an old Shropshire rhyme, "Marry in May, you'll rue the day." Their only child was born a year

later, on 8 May 1912, at Grace Hospital, and the family lived in a flat
on Portage Avenue. In North American style, Arthur Woodcock
wanted to give his son a middle name, Meredith, in homage to one
of his favourite authors, George Meredith (whose most famous work,
The Egoist, George would edit and introduce for Penguin many
decades later). But the new father was overruled by his wife, and
George Woodcock would have only an unofficial middle name, which
he almost always kept to himself, a secret souvenir of his father.

George would have no memory of these places, because his mother,
having experienced her first Prairie winter, vowed not to endure
another. In October she and her son returned to England, where they
stayed with her parents. Her husband tidied up their affairs in Canada
and left the country, never to return, as soon as possible after the
spring break-up in 1913 brought shipping in the St Lawrence back to
life. Once reunited, the family moved into a cottage in Long Lands
Lane, the name a relic from the age of strip-farms, before the Enclo-
sures in the nineteenth century. The next year they stepped up to a
semi-detached house in Frogmoore Road (named after the Royal
Mausoleum at Windsor). The next-door neighbour was a giant of a
man, Kent Godwin, who became Arthur's best friend and whose son,
Lance, became George's.

By now Arthur Woodcock had acquiesced to his father's repeated
offer of a partnership—the junior partnership—in the family business,
which thus became S. Woodcock & Sons, plural. But his improved
circumstances were proof of his own failure to make a new life on his
own. Before the end of 1916 he quit the coal company and took a
bookkeeper's job with a flour mill at Altrincham in neighbouring
Cheshire, just far enough away to be out of his father's shadow. Their
rented house in Altrincham's High Street was "advanced enough to
have a bathroom",[6] George recalled decades later. The arrangement
proved only an interim one. In 1918, George's father went south and
"through pull"[7] got a job as a clerk at the GWR at Marlow, taking out
a mortgage on 82 Station Road, one of a row of nineteenth- century
worker's houses. Officially, the job was temporary because his poor
health (he would prove to have Bright's disease) disqualified him for
the railway's superannuation scheme, but he would hold it until he
died in 1926 at only forty-four. George was fourteen and still a pupil
at Sir William Borlase's School when the death of his father, the first
of two great tragedies in his life, befell him.

Sixty-four years later, towards the end of his own life, George would confess to a fellow Canadian author: "I suppose I am a man whose psychic arrangement is Jungian rather than Freudian; I loved my father and always disliked my mother."[8] He loved his father's outgoing and creative personality and sense of adventure. As he grew increasingly ill, Arthur would talk to his young son of Canada and promise that they would return there one day and go even farther west and even farther north, perhaps to the country beyond the Mackenzie River. He gave voice to these dreams outside the hearing of Mrs Woodcock, who cursed Canada as an impossibly inhospitable place and later took to blaming the climate there for her husband's early death.

George loved his father for his intuitive interest in the arts, and came to a sad understanding of how much Arthur Woodcock might have been able to accomplish if circumstances had freed him to do so. Perhaps young George even resolved silently not to allow himself to be trapped as his father had been. George somehow knew, understood and was in harmony with the jaunty musical fellow who

> had been quite a different person from the sick and rather weak recluse with the lost values whom I knew. The literally hundreds of men in their forties who turned out [for the funeral] to mourn their youths knew another Art Woodcock who, with Lance Godwin's father Kent, ran a lively band and came back from North America to teach ragtime to his friends and to tell tales of Chicago and the Canadian West. An extrovert who turned inward with misfortune is how I see him. [He is part of] my mythology in a way my mother never was. I've always defended her virtues—straightforwardness, loyalty, lack of snobbery— but these nonetheless were the possible sides of her self-righteousness with its often unwilling recourse to tyranny and its appalling dependence on men ...[9]

Until the end of his life, George was haunted by the benevolent and protective spectre of his father. His last book of verse, published in 1994, contains "Envoi: Arthur Woodcock", one of the series of what he called memorial medallions.

> What do I owe you? Love and care?
> You left so soon and lived in echoes.
> Perhaps most of your failures,

your lost ambitions,
the lacunae I
felt forced to fill.
You were too sick to come
back here to Canada. You
failed in your art of music.
My way was clear. I came
to Canada, succeeded
in my art. What I did
was what you intended
and so our account
with the Gods has been balanced.
I can speak your name proudly.[10]

Woodcock was fortunate to live in a town with such a solid if minor (and affordable) public school as Sir William Borlase's (named after the eighteenth-century antiquary who served fifty years as the vicar of Ludgan, near Penzance). There he felt out of place and lonely, but he achieved academic distinction, as a plaque at the school still attests. When he matriculated at sixteen, he had been educated to a standard equivalent to, if not superior to, a B.A. from a top North American university of today. But except for some later courses in German and other subjects at Morley College in London, one of the crammers where one was prepared for university, 1928 marked the end of his schooling (in time he would receive honorary doctorates from four Canadian universities: UBC, Victoria, Winnipeg and what was then Sir George Williams in Montreal, later renamed Concordia). Grandfather Woodcock, the now solidly middle-class coal merchant, proposed sending George to Cambridge if he would agree to enter the Anglican clergy. If not, he would leave the cash equivalent in trust with George's mother, to go to George on his mother's death. George, already an earnest young rebel, felt he could not commit himself to the church. Instead, he too used the cumulative pull from both sides of his family and became a clerk at the GWR's headquarters above Paddington, commuting between London and Station Road in Marlow, looking after his mother until her death in 1940. These were George Woodcock's dark years, darker even than his time at the sport-obsessed boys' school, years he could scarcely bear to write or speak about in later life. There is, however, some documentation from the time that gives the flavour of his existence, including his relationship with his widowed mother. It also shows what a precocious young literary fellow he was.

Lewis Cooke, who would become a vice-president of the National Westminster Bank, was George's young cousin: George's mother was his Auntie Mag, his own mother's older sister. The two boys grew up together in Market Drayton, before the Woodcocks moved to Marlow and the Cookes to Lewisham in southeast London, where Lewis's father was a manager with Boots Chemists. The lads spent a great deal of time together but, in Cooke's words, "I have to say that our worlds were not the same. I loved the games and all that sort of thing and George loved poetry and the literary side, but we never fell out over it."[11] He would recall also, "I was always a great trouble as far as his mother was concerned. She was a very, very strict lady and brought George up very tightly. Whatever George and I did always seemed to have a great flair for getting him into trouble and me also."[12]

In Marlow, George spent much of his time with Lance Godwin, the son of Arthur's friend and musical collaborator. The Godwins lived in the other half of the semi at 82 Station Road. Thus Lance, who shared George's literary ambitions but became a teacher rather than an author, enjoyed a privileged position from which to observe the Woodcock household. He would remember Mrs Woodcock as "a rather tall, thinish person with a ramrod backbone and principles to match. She had white hair and she didn't look terribly happy."[13] George by contrast "was friendly and very good-natured. I don't think he ever really quarrelled with anybody to my knowledge, but at the same time he was capable of making critical remarks."[14] Although "George was not physically gifted",[15] he would urge Lance to join him in tramps of ten miles and more, to towns as distant as Newport, during which they would discuss life and letters. When he was about thirteen, George began sending Lance poems he had written at Sir William Borlase's. "Your letter seemed to me rather outspoken and even dangerous," he wrote Godwin from school at sixteen, "but my mother has never yet opened a letter from you (although she did another with disasterous [*sic*] effect)."[16] The reference is to a letter in which George had revealed one of his adolescent sexual fantasies.

The correspondence with Godwin continued after George began

work in London. Indeed, George's letters to him, the earliest ones in the Woodcock Archive, are the only extant source of important information about his work for the Great Western.

> You will no doubt be surprised and glad to hear that I have now started work [George wrote from London in summer 1929, age seventeen]. I have now been working for a week as Junior-Clerk to the Docks and Steamboats Section of the Chief Engineer's Office. I find the work quite interesting, and have got to learn shorthand and typing. I am getting on well with the typing, and have to-day started to make copies of letters for official use, instead of practising. Besides typing, my duties consist of filing papers, answering the phone and taking messages from various offices. I am really glad to be started, although, of course, I shall not be able to visit Drayton so often. I have had to be vaccinated, and shall soon have a very pretty arm. I have also to get glasses, but many people wear them now, so that I shall but be conforming to fashion.[17]

He also professed eagerness to begin study of the violin. But optimism about his new life was quick to fade. A mere five months later, Woodcock was writing: "I get frequent fits of depression nowadays, especially when I think of Monica [the subject of his fantasies at the time]. The other day I was walking in the Park, feeling very spirited with life, when I saw a girl who reminded me of her, and felt awful all day after that; couldn't settle down to work or a book or any thing."[18] This was during January, "the hardest month at the Office, with the Annual Audits and Reports in addition to the Ordinary work."[19] The office system turned out to be rigidly authoritarian. Someone tried to pay a surprise call on Woodcock at the office one day; the visitor was told that the person he sought was out; later, Woodcock "was accosted by the Chief Messenger, who gave off sundry rumblings from beneath his massive and heavily drooping mustaches ..."[20]

These letters reveal Woodcock's growing interest in literature as well as his close attention to questions of the day, both domestic and imperial, and to politics generally. They even contain early suggestions of his later interest in Buddhism. What's more, the accompanying poems, often written in bouts of depression which are sometimes difficult to distinguish from youthful envy of his elders' nostalgia, become increasingly sophisticated and disciplined, particularly from about 1934 onwards. Godwin would offer his own poems in response; for one of them Woodcock was "stricken with admiration".[21]

Woodcock would observe one day in his book on the British Empire that it reached its zenith in 1930. In that year he commented to Godwin: "flag days and flower days are becoming one of the greatest plagues ever conceived in London ..."[22] The observation is cast in the diction of the premature curmudgeon but also in that of the world-weary cosmopolite, for Woodcock was gorging himself on the attractions, both cultural and romantic, of the capital of the world: "Miss P. met me yesterday afternoon (Saturday) and went round to the National Gallery with me, after which we had lunch."[23] The letters also reveal him as the talented observer of the pulsing life around him of which he was not a part, a skill that would be his hallmark as a travel writer. They show his gift for language and for sketching personalities. He comments, for example, on the seemingly unique style of profanity practised by one of his superiors at the office:

"Dash my Joseph if it isn't ..." an oath used by a certain interesting individual in my office [though] I am not quite sure, and the gentleman himself is rather hazy, as to the identity of the Joseph. Some say that he is Joseph of Arimathea, some say Joseph father of Jesus, and still others Joseph surnamed Conrad, but I hold, with great steadfastness, that he is Poor [*sic*] Black Joe, that notable figure whom I have never been able entirely to dissociate with Campbelltown [*sic*] races and its bob-tailed nags.[24]

But far and away the most remarkable letter concerns another unnamed individual in the young commuter's life, one who clearly showed the way Woodcock was leaning politically.

There is a very interesting man going up on our train from Marlow now. He also comes down on my train of a night, which is fortunate, for he is well advanced in years, and was one of the first band of English Socialists, the Idealist band who preceded Trade Unionism. He knew William Morris well, and also Annie Besant, Hyndman, Wells, Shaw, Snowden, Carpenter, and greater than these, the Russians Kropotkin and Sergei Stiplick, and the Germans Engels, Bebel and the great Karl Marx himself. In his youth, too, he attended meetings of the old Ethical Society and heard the farm debate between Huxley and

Charles Bradlaugh. Although an ardent Socialist, he denounces Trade Unionism as a blight and a retarding influence on progress. He is also an agnostic, like myself, although at one time he was Materialist. His knowledge of literature, history, the religions of the world, science and life itself, is very wide. He also knew Zangwell and Conelly, the writers of the socialist song "The Red Flag". He has a fine brow, a clear skin for his age, fine white hair and the bright, clear eyes of an enthusiast. I am very glad to have met him, for he is one of the relics of that age whose glory was her great rebels. Few ages have produced so many great men as the latter half of the 19th century, yet all of them were striving against the spirit of the age. What giants they were! These were Darwin, Huxley, Bradlaugh, Lyell, Ruskin, Matthew Arnold, Meredith, Winwood Reade, Spencer, Carlyle, Stevenson, Henley and half a hundred others. I doubt if, thinking to fourty [*sic*] years hence, men will find so many great ones as we can in that age.[25]

The author of those words was only eighteen.

Lewis Cooke remembered once meeting a man who had worked at GWR headquarters when Woodcock was there. Cooke told me that he asked whether the fellow remembered a young clerk by that name. Yes, the man had replied, but all he could recall was that Woodcock always wore a pin or badge on his coat—a pin from the Canadian Pacific Railway. If true, the story is a small bit of evidence about how Woodcock kept alive the memory of his father and his father's failed dream, and his own birth in a country he was free to romanticize because he had no memories of it. But when I put this to Woodcock he said that he could not recollect wearing such a pin and that, furthermore, if he did indeed wear a pin on his lapel in those bleak years, it was likely that of the Peace Pledge Union. Woodcock was becoming a radical. One of his early letters to Godwin is signed with the hammer and sickle, but fascination with the Soviet Union was only a phase. Before the decade was over, it would be the old man on the train's memories of Kropotkin that Woodcock would hold most dear, not the ones of Marx or Engels. Woodcock was ripe to become a radical, a literary radical to be sure, but an anarchist in particular and specifically.

2 A PREFERENCE FOR PARADOX

TO SAY THAT George Woodcock led a double life sounds melodramatic, but he was certainly the kind of person who always leads parallel and, on the surface at least, contradictory lives. He was English yet he was not, as he would go to pains to inform people. His colleagues at the railway did not seem to know that he was a writer, nor did many of his literary cohorts know where he worked. In any case, he was a creative writer but likewise a purely political one. In later years, he would be an anti-academic within the university and a Canadian cultural nationalist who didn't believe in borders. Perhaps this preference for paradox had its origins in his situation at home, his need to tiptoe through the minefield of his mother's personality. He may also have had to play games with himself to keep from becoming bored by the steel-grey realities of daily living. In later years, typically, he would cite conflicting reasons for the evasiveness that many recognized as part of his make-up; he would say variously that this was the Welsh side of his heritage rising up to dominate the English or that caution was a necessity of survival that he had learned in wartime, in his days on the dodge as a conscientious objector.

He began writing poetry when he was thirteen, with the ardent encouragement of his dying father. At eighteen, alone in the world as he must have felt himself to be, he commenced a novel. At that same age he started to keep

a diary in which I wrote indiscriminately and with enthusiastic prolix-ity the trivia of daily life and the impressions—impressions of the physical world—were intense to the point of ecstasy, and I could apprehend Blake immediately and understand him slowly, whereas now [more than forty years later] I understand him quickly and apprehend him laboriously. In that diary I recorded the books I read; I tried to square off the ideas they set going in my mind. It was a kind of autodidactic substitute for the university training I never had. I filled a tall pile of notebooks, and then, when I was twenty-four, extracted what seemed the redeemable parts—they were actually the pretentious pseudo-philosophical passages which would now interest me least—and burnt the rest with the manuscript of my first novel. Later in disgust with its presumptuous juvenility, I burnt even what I had salvaged, along with my second novel. My third and last novel went unfinished in the same way; after I had destroyed it I knew everything about how a novel should not be written, and found I had no desire to continue. Yet in the process I had acquired the primary equipment of a critic: to know the pains of creation, the reasons for failure.[1]

His obstacle was provincial isolation. He began to overcome it in 1935, however, when he decided to go to France during annual holidays from the GWR. This, his first visit to a foreign country, was a banquet for the senses as well as a much-needed change for the body. The part of him that was a poet was drawn to Provence just as Ezra Pound had been. But something in that land of troubadours also awakened Woodcock's latent anti-authoritarianism. Woodcock would note how in Britain, with its restrictive laws about pub closings, the streets were full of drunkards, whereas in France, where people could buy liquor and wine at any hour of the day or night, the only inebriants appeared to be visiting Americans or Swedes. "You saw what free manners meant to people: that they didn't have to behave excessively once they could do anything they wanted to do and at any time. The temptation to become excessive vanished."[2] A belief springing from this realization would become part of Woodcock's practical anarchism.

That same year—whether before or after the trip abroad isn't clear—Woodcock discovered Charlie Lahr, who kept the Blue Moon Bookshop in Red Lion Street, a narrow arcade-like lane connecting Holborn and Theobalds Road. Woodcock was walking past and noticed what appeared to be a newspaper placard displaying a headline, in thick bold type: PROFESSOR JOAD'S DAUGHTER ELOPES WITH POPE! This was a reference to the philosopher for the masses, C. E. M. Joad ("the agile, mellifluous and quodlibetarian Joad", in Max Beerbohm's words). The typography looked authentic, and Woodcock required a few seconds, as any other startled passerby would, before realizing that the poster was a clever fake. Such salacious forgeries (of the *Evening Standard* according to Woodcock; others would say of the *Daily Mail*) were the personal art form of Lahr, a German anarchist who had fled his native country in 1905 and whom the British would intern as an enemy alien during both world wars. The literary editor Walter Allen would recall Lahr's shop as

> a resort of rebels and eccentrics [including] the Count Potocki de Montalk, who claimed to be king of Poland but, according to gossip, was a New Zealander. He had long hair down his back and wore medieval robes of scarlet and an apparently heavy chain of what I cannot believe was gold. He referred casually to 'my cousin the Count of Paris' ...³

Lahr told the story of being part of the huge crowd watching Kaiser Wilhelm pass along the Strand. When Lahr absent-mindedly scratched the back of his head, four Special Branch goons pounced on him, assuming that he was reaching for a weapon in his hat. At that time, Lahr eked out his living as a bakery roundsman, propelling his bread cart up and down the streets and squares of Bloomsbury, with a detective following his every step. When he reinvented himself as a bookseller, it was as one whose incisive taste in writing sometimes seemed at odds with his eccentricity in other departments of life. In the 1920s he had published a series of limited edition pamphlets by the writers who patronized his shop. These included Aldous Huxley, H. E. Bates, Liam O'Flaherty, and Woodcock's fellow Welshmen, T. F. Powys and Rhys Davies, some of whom based fictional characters on Lahr. In addition to these Blue Moon chapbooks, Lahr had put out a quarterly, *New Coterie*, best remembered for publishing D. H. Lawrence. Yet he was a figure of fun because he wore sandals and rode a bicycle both winter and summer. Perhaps for Lahr as for the society in general, the Great War had been a watershed, signalling, in his case, a long decline from rebel to eccentric. Woodcock was instantly attracted to Lahr and his shop not only because of his former publishing activities but also because they appeared to represent the heterodox side of literary London.

The war and its immediate aftermath had swept away one genera-tion of readers and brought new writers to prominence. By 1935, when Woodcock had assembled his first book-length manuscript of poetry (later destroyed), the people who had once pounded on the gate for admittance were now the entrenched post-war establishment, deny-ing purchase to a new wave of barbarians. Particularly objectionable to Woodcock and other like-minded and politically conscious young writers were Virginia Woolf and her circle, the youngest of whom was John Lehmann, once an apprentice at Woolf's Hogarth Press, soon to be in charge of *New Writing*, the first of his many important editor-ships. This was also the early heyday of the group associated with a much younger figure, W. H. Auden, a writer of whom Woodcock was almost equally at odds: "I resented him, his bogus Marxism, his per-verted Oxbridge snobbery, but I was fascinated against my will by his poetic skill, and how he gave new life to traditional forms."[4]

Woodcock's own success as a poet had been spotty. In 1932, A. R. Orage, the famous editor and disciple of Gurdjieff, who had published Shaw, Wells and Yeats in the *New Age* a generation earlier, had accepted a poem of Woodcock's for the *New English Weekly*. The coup filled Woodcock "with an indescribable joy and [I] danced a fantastic elephantine dance of triumph, chanting the whole (for God only knows what reason) opening verses of the 'Ballad of Reading Gaol'."[5] Other, less important acceptances followed irregularly amid the world's general outpouring of rejection. It was at that juncture that Wood-cock asked Lahr if the Blue Moon might publish his manuscript. Lahr would try hard to interest magazine editors and literary agents in the young man's work, but Lahr himself no longer had the stamina for book publishing. His activities in this area were now limited to an annual Christmas keepsake featuring the work of some new young writer. After Woodcock had been a customer for two years, Lahr asked him for a poem for the 1937 edition that he might print and distrib-ute to his preferred customers. Woodcock, who was already publishing verses in a Manchester periodical called the *Serpent*, wrote a new poem, "Solstice", which Lahr had printed in an edition of one hundred copies on one folded sheet of pale yellow card stock: Woodcock's first "book" publication, the start of an avalanche of publishing that, by Wood-cock's death, would total approximately 150 pamphlets and books either written or edited. Lahr would choose Woodcock's work for each of the next two Christmases as well, in editions of the same size. In

1938 came the more ambitious *Six Poems* and in 1939 a curious work entitled *Ballad of an Orphan Hand*, redolent of the sexual starvation from which Woodcock was apparently suffering. The last of these was by "George Meredith Woodcock" and would be Woodcock's only publication to include his unofficial middle name: a bibliographical curiosity that Woodcock was hard pressed to account for in retrospect except as the result of "pure caprice [though] for a period from 1940 to '41, there was one person who called me nothing but Meredith—the Welsh poet Lynette Roberts."[6] By that time, of course, the world, and Woodcock's role in it, had been turned upside down.

During this period Woodcock began his lifelong practice as a book reviewer. Significantly, perhaps, in view of the romantic notions at the back of his mind, notions revived or strengthened perhaps by the coming war, one of his first reviews, published in *Life and Letters*, was of a Canadian work, *French Canadians To-day* by Wilfrid Bovey.

In retrospect, it would appear to Woodcock that this was also the stage when he finally found his voice as a poet. Certainly it was during this period that he started to become a fixture of the literary magazines. Julian Symons, the younger brother of A. J. A. Symons, the bibliophile, gourmet and aesthete, who wrote *Quest for Corvo*, was not yet a mystery writer but rather a poet and the editor of an important magazine, *Twentieth Century Verse*. In 1938, Woodcock sent him some poems and in accepting them Symons admitted Woodcock into his circle. Following the editorial practice he learned from Wyndham Lewis (who made a famous portrait of him), Symons "used at that time to invite contributors to come and have tea, not in my rather dingy flat, but in an ABC, a chain of pretty cheap teashops, which no longer exists."[7] Woodcock also found his way into the rival magazines such as *New Verse* and, a little later, *Partisan Review* in New York, where one of the editors was Dwight Macdonald, another anarchist in the making. Woodcock would always look back to this brief period of calm before the outbreak of the war as a sort of poetic idyll, though it could hardly be said to have marked the end of his political innocence: the civil war in Spain had already done that for Woodcock and his entire generation.

This was Woodcock's position on the outskirts of literary London when the war came on 3 September 1939. He was twenty-seven. He had not yet declared himself an anarchist, but anarchist tendencies in his personality were obvious. He had voted only once, in 1934 (and would do so only once more in his life, decades later, in a local ref-erendum in Vancouver). Yet in 1939, as if preparing for an apocalypse of unknown nature that seemed to await the entire population, he went to Canada House in Trafalgar Square and claimed his right to a Canadian passport, just in case.

His breakthrough, his acceptance at last as a member of youthful literary London, had come in 1938, the time of the collapse of the anti-fascist fight in Spain. A decade later, not long before leaving for Canada, Woodcock entitled his first collection of essays *The Writer and Politics*. For in that decade certainly, and in different ways and to different degrees for the rest of his life, literature and ideology would always go together naturally. He did not feel himself a mem-ber of the 1930s generation, though biologically he was. He felt rather that he was part of a 1940s generation that lay round the cor-ner, shaped in some measure by the shambles of the immediate past: the war in Spain.

> The writers I was associated with in the 1940s kept the faith in their individual ways, but *all* were disillusioned with the Communist role there. We salvaged the Spanish communes for history, and I wrote about them, but as events in the past. Books like [George Orwell's] *Homage to Catalonia* were really denunciations and threnodies combined. No one in my circles "kept faith with the left" if by that you mean the CPGB [Communist Party of Great Britain] which bemused so many writers of the 1930s. The only statement I can make is that the major tragedy of Spain was that the anarchists let themselves be talked into joining the government and thus made themselves vulnerable to the manoeuvres of the Communists. What did Auden call the Thirties? "A low, dishonest decade." I agree. That realization in the 1940s helped to shape my whole philosophy of life.[8]

Gertrude Lewis Woodcock died in May 1940, leaving George with mixed emotions and all the money given to her for safe keeping by his Grandfather Woodcock, the coal merchant. The final sum amounted to £1,398, an extraordinary windfall for someone who was accustomed to getting by (thanks to his railway pass) on only 20/ a week pocket money and whose favourite restaurant served a full-course dinner for only 7*d* (or an extra large one for 9*d*). With characteristic generosity, Woodcock gave away some of the inheritance to writers even poorer than himself. The remainder was still enough to allow him to quit the GWR to devote himself to literature and politics full time, which meant devoting himself to London as well. He took up residence at 38 Queen's Avenue in Muswell Hill, North London, a flat in what had been called a London merchant's home when it had been built, in 1910 or so, in what was then a suburb. The flat, with its high-ceilinged airy rooms, belonged to Tom Earley, a poet and teacher, and his wife Elizabeth. They had it free to lend to Woodcock because Earley and his school had been relocated to Brighton as part of the evacuation of the cities. "Sometimes the Earleys would come home for a weekend, and sometimes Elizabeth only", Woodcock would recall.[9] Julian Symons, who thought Elizabeth "a very pretty woman", didn't know "whether George actually went to bed with her [but] he was very keen on her, and she, I think, to a certain extent, on him."[10]

Tony Gibson, a member of the circle, who would one day turn to collecting oral histories from British anarchists of the time, would volunteer this a year or so later:

> From George's autobiography one might assume that Elizabeth was, for a time, his mistress—not that he actually says so. This was not the case; he was in love with her for a time, and indeed wrote her poems (some of which she may even have kept!), but she just didn't fancy him sexually. This caused him to be very hostile to me for a time, for she became my mistress for many years, and had a daughter by me— proudly boasting of it to her friends when she was pregnant. George doesn't know this (but you can tell him now it will no longer matter) that our daughter Kathleen was actually conceived in George's caravan, which he generously lent to Elizabeth for our little holiday.[11]

What broke the silence between the two men was a chance meeting at a party when Gibson saw George sidling up to the drinks table and quipped, "Now is the Woodcock near the gin" (*Twelfth Night*, act 1, scene 2). "This trivial joke caused George to roar with laughter, and henceforward he was friendly towards me. This is a sidelight on George's character; in human relations he is very impressed by fun and wit, even if the joke is on him."[12]

More than fifty years after the period when he lived in the Earley flat, neither of the Earleys would discuss Woodcock with me, despite interventions on my behalf by Woodcock and other survivors.

As for his literary career, which a residence in London could only facilitate, Woodcock made the acquaintance of R. A. Caton, a colourful and mysterious figure in English publishing, the proprietor, since 1924, of Fortune Press, which had published the first book of Dylan Thomas and would go on to produce a remarkable list of important new British writers. This empire of taste was subsidized by pornography, both that which Caton published himself and that which he distributed from his shop, where he sold what were politely called rubber goods. *The White Island*, Woodcock's first true book of verse, appeared under the Fortune Press imprint in 1940, a year of chaos for Britain and for Woodcock personally. It was the year he would be forced to act on his principles.

Young men were called up for service, those who were not volunteering first. Most members of Woodcock's literary circle enlisted. Symons went into the army after his claim to being a conscientious objector was refused; he didn't seem to mind, he would say, as he was only "a mock conscientious objector [who didn't] have a lot of sympathy with [real COs] on pacifist grounds", whereas Woodcock was "a much gentler and kinder person than me."[13] Woodcock, too, filed for exemption as a CO. "This caused a considerable rift with the other senior members of the family", George's cousin, Lewis Cooke, who had already joined up, recalled. "My parents were horrified, I have to say, and I think the sisters [of George's mother, two in North Wales and the third in South Wales] referred to it as one way of ducking out ... He never seemed to warm to the family at all ... and he gradually drifted outside their circle and hence outside my circle."[14]

As Woodcock would write later in an entry on conscientious objectors for the *Encylopaedia Britannica*, the CO objects to military service on religious, philosophic or political grounds. The earliest recorded conscientious objectors were Christians who refused to enter the Roman legions, for which some were put to death. As for the nineteenth century, refusal to bear arms became a tenet of sects as different as the Society of Friends in Britain, the Mennonites in Germany and the Doukhobors and Molokans in Russia. Various societies dealt with the question differently, but for at least short periods during the nineteenth century both Russia and Prussia, as well as the United States and Canada, made some provisions for religious non-combatants. The test came in the Great War, when the United States granted CO status only to members of recognized religious sects that included pacifism among their core beliefs, not those with merely philosophical or ethical objections to taking human life. Such too was the case in Britain, where writers such as Bertrand Russell and Lytton Strachey were among the objectors in this second category. Another CO, who joined a field ambulance corps rather than serve as a combatant, was Kingsley Martin, who in 1931 became editor of the *New Statesman & Nation*, but he reversed his position on war the next time; Woodcock always denounced him as a hypocrite, though that didn't prevent him from contributing to Martin's magazine.

Britain was more liberal on this issue in 1940 than in 1914. Some men were permitted to perform only non-combatant roles in the armed services and two categories were created for those who refused to don a uniform: unconditional (given to those meeting the strict religious criterion) and conditional (given those with ethical objections who would agree to perform alternative civilian service, often in agriculture). Woodcock applied for and was granted the second of these on condition that he join the War Agricultural Committee and work the land. Towards the end of September he went to Langham Community in the Essex marshes, on the edge of Constable country, to a Victorian house that had once been owned by a cavalry colonel. Woodcock always recalled that the bathtubs were of such size as to suggest "complex orgies";[15] Edward VII had once been entertained there. The estate had dormitories, three labourers to a room, and common areas for meetings and meals. Another literary objector was Max Plowman, the editor of the *Adelphi*; he lived apart from the house, in a separate building; he offered Woodcock the use of a private room for writing.

The manual labour was onerous. When Woodcock was almost killed by a major heart attack in 1966, he supposed that the strain to his heart during the Langham period had done permanent damage. In fact, though, as his health worsened during the 1980s and early 1990s, more sophisticated diagnosis revealed that his cardiac problem was congenital and would no doubt have kept him out of military service.

By the spring, Woodcock had had his fill of Langham and went to live with his friend, the poet and critic Derek Savage, a Christian positivist, in his medieval daub-and-wattle cottage at Dry Drayton, near Cambridge. Conditions were impossibly cramped. Woodcock and two acquaintances from Langham, an aspiring actor named Peter Brent and a High Church ritualist named Jonathan Edwards, who later became a monk in a Benedictine-like order of Anglicans called the Society of Sacred Mission, took accommodations together—two rooms on the ground floor and another on the first—at 66 Huntingdon Road in Cambridge, intending eventually to establish a farming commune of their own. The middle-aged landlady was eager for boarders, as she had lost her licence to rent to students at the university. Woodcock thought this must have stemmed from her untidiness or from the fact that "her rather unsavoury son was in fact a spiv, as we called them before we started to call them Teds, and was in some slot machine racket."[16]

In Cambridge, the three young men remained members of the War Agricultural Committee, which turned out to be an implausible and perhaps unworkable coalition, rather like the Loyalists in Spain. During the summer of 1941, a revolt was brewing among the WAC workers. When "a couple of harmless Commies were sacked as agitators",[17] Woodcock, Brent and Edwards called for mass resignations, a call that was taken seriously by the anarchists and the secular pacifists as well as by those resisters who were homosexual. After that, still clinging to his membership in the WAC, Woodcock returned briefly to London and then spent a couple of months on a commune in Surrey before joining another man in running a small market garden at Ashford in Middlesex. At one point in this period of shifting addresses he lived in the attic of a house in Richmond. The landlady, a pacifist, had a husband who was a dispensing chemist in East Ham and a lover who was a Labour MP, whom she entertained in a separate house elsewhere. In somewhat the same spirit, Woodcock rented an additional room from a widow in Belsize Park Gardens for use on weekends, when he went "boozing in Soho".[18] On one such occasion Woodcock and Dylan Thomas "went arm in arm, barking like dogs, through the blacked out streets of Soho, and were nabbed by the police in Golden Square for committing a nuisance [only to be] let go by a fatherly sergeant who seemed to recognize the errant boy that survived in Dylan alongside the maturing inner vision that enabled him to write his score of great poems."[19] The room in Belsize Park Gardens was a high-ceilinged affair. Half of the window pane was missing—shattered by the concussion from a German bomb or rocket—and had been replaced by a thin sheet of wood. So Woodcock sometimes had to burn unwanted review copies of books in the grate, for it was a "cold place when one slept alone ..."[20]

3 NOW

BETWEEN PAPER RATIONING and the fact that many editors went into uniform, the world of literary magazines began to shrink. Those rivals *Twentieth Century Verse* and *New Verse* both suspended publication, for example. So did T. S. Eliot's *Criterion* (whereupon Cyril Connolly, with some assistance from Stephen Spender, rushed to fill the void for established writers by founding *Horizon*). Another notable venture at the time was Woodcock's magazine *NOW*, begun in 1940, as his embrace of anarchism grew tighter. Woodcock

> felt a journal was needed for young writers and for writers who went against the grain of the times: pacifists, anarchists, dissident socialists. *NOW* ran intermittently until 1947, and if *The White Island* drew attention to me as a poet, the magazine gave me a position in the literary world, and many of the writers who appeared in its columns, such as George Orwell and Herbert Read, Alex Comfort and Roy Campbell, Mulk Raj Anand and Henry Miller and Kenneth Rexroth, became my friends.[1]

The first issue, dated Easter 1940 and published from his mother's house in Buckinghamshire, ran to twenty pages and was mimeographed. Contributors included Kathleen Raine, one of the Cambridge poets of the 1930s (though her first book did not appear until 1942), and her husband Charles Madge, as well as Lance Godwin, Woodcock's childhood friend, whose promise as a writer Woodcock always seemed to be promoting. Yet another was Roy Fuller, born the same year as Woodcock and also first published by R. A. Caton. Fuller was so classically handsome, Woodcock recalled, that he constantly attracted unwanted attention from homosexuals. A solicitor by training, he had joined the Woolwich Equitable Building Society in 1938 (the year before Caton published his *Poems*), becoming its managing director more than thirty years later. In contrast to Woodcock, Fuller supported his poetry with a business career and ended up with a CBE, a seat on the BBC board of governors and a term as Oxford Professor of Poetry, a most coveted elected position.

What set that first number of *NOW* apart, however, was the voice behind the editor's own unsigned contributions. "The intention of *NOW*", he began, "is to publish and perpetuate good writing and clear thought."[2] But he went on to lay out the magazine's political stance: "Art is antithetical to evil and violence. And evil and violence have their supreme avatar in war, when the common virtues are suspended and truth hibernates for the duration. It is no particular violence, e.g. Nazi violence, that we must oppose, but all violence, no matter what the cause that uses it. The man who tolerates war nurtures a beast that will destroy him, perhaps not physically, but certainly intellectually and morally."[3] Woodcock also noted likeminded publications at home and abroad, such as the American pacifist quarterly *Phoenix*, which printed Woodcock and many of the *NOW* stable (as well as Charlie Lahr's Kiwi friend, Count Potocki of Montalk); Derek Savage was British correspondent of *Phoenix*.

In tone, Woodcock was both self-critical and defiant:

> We are inclined, according to mood, to exaggerate or to minimise public feeling against the war, and are usually over-receptive of the impressions we desire, more rarely than of those we dislike. Our outlook always tended more to optimism or pessimism than to the middle grey of probability ...
>
> It is time literary scientists or scientific litterateurs with no knowledge of poetry ceased proclaiming what poets should do and what should be done with poets. We can very well look after ourselves and, in spite of the recent pontifications of an exuberant and ill-mannered anthropologist, this time there will be no war poets. Most of the younger poets are preparing to face the tribunals, and some have already done so. The soldier poet of 1914–1918 is replaced by the Conchy poet

of 1939–?, who in his neutrality of mind and opposition to *all* violence[,] perpetuates more faithfully the tradition of his calling.[4]

With the second number, *NOW* was printed letterpress. By the time
the seventh issue appeared in autumn 1941, the magazine had acquired
the subtitle "A Journal of Good Writing", grown to thirty-six pages
and climbed in price from 6*d.* to 9*d.*, a sum that still compared
favourably with that of other literary magazines, such as *Horizon* at
1/6 or *Poetry (London)* or *Life and Letters To-Day*, both at 1*s*. By that
time, *NOW*'s disparate yet somehow cohesive list of transatlantic radical contributors took in Julian Huxley, J. Middleton Murry, Frederic
Prokosch and Ruthven Todd, as well as the twelfth Duke of Bedford,
who collected parrots, supported the Oxford Movement's call for
moral re-armament and managed to espouse both pacifism and some
stand very close to fascism, views which, whether singly or together,
landed him in difficulty with the authorities as the war progressed.

Just as vegetarians like to trace their cause back to Pythagoras, the
Greek mathematician and astronomer in the fifth century B.C.E., perhaps pausing along the way at Leonardo and other famous herbivores,
so anarchists, seeking an unbroken chain of intellectual credibility,
sometimes see their roots in Taoism and Buddhism, in Coptic Christianity and in various still-unlighted corners of the Middle Ages. In
anarchism, this tendency takes on a special urgency at times, because
the anarchists' mandate of disavowing authority often comes down to
a matter of renouncing the accepted version of the past and rein-
venting the story in each generation. Anarchist history thus becomes
like a folk song that mutates from one singer to the next, for the
cumulative benefit of each new audience.

As the most widely read historian of anarchism, Woodcock generally eschewed this tendency to find proto-anarchists under every
ancient rock. Although he was certainly capable of spotting libertarian trace-elements where no one else had found them before (for
example, in Oscar Wilde), he stuck closely to the classical anarchists
of nineteenth-century Europe. These included William Godwin in
England, Pierre-Joseph Proudhon in France, Michael Bakunin in
Russia and, most vitally of all, Peter Kropotkin, another Russian, a

genuine Russian prince in fact. It was Kropotkin (1842–1921) whose intellectual heroics made anarchism an *ism*, a codified set of beliefs, to be trotted out for use in any political, economic or social circumstance. The life of Kropotkin that Woodcock wrote with Ivan Avakumovic would be perhaps the most significant of his biographies. The labour of which he would be proudest, however, was one that received virtually no attention outside the world of anarchist politics: his new introductions to the *Collected Works of Peter Kropotkin*, published between 1989 and 1995 in eleven volumes.

In the words of Colin Ward, one of Woodcock's British admirers, Kropotkin "was another of those extraordinary nineteenth-century Russians whose ideas seem on a global scale to fit the issues of the twenty-first century, as our own century has been wasted in an intoxication with profligate capitalist over-production on one hand, or authoritarian Marxist bureaucracy on the other."[5] Kropotkin was born in St Petersburg and as a youth served as a page at the court of Alexandr II. Then he chose a commission in the Amur Cossacks and was sent to Siberia and the territories in central Asia, only recently brought into the Russian empire by Bakunin's cousin, Muraviev-Amurski. Like many another army officer, Kropotkin was trained as a scientist, and in Siberia, whose vastness and lack of pity would play such a large role in his life and writings, he became known as a geographer. His theory of Asia's orography (the structure of its mountain ranges) became the basis of modern study of the continent. Later, he argued that much of Europe had once been covered, not by floating ice-fields as was then thought, but rather by glaciers, as is now accepted.

For Kropotkin, scientific discovery and political discovery seemed to go hand in hand. During his stay in Siberia, he came upon the works of Proudhon, and during research trips to western Europe and Britain made contact with anarchist groups. His political sensitivity thus heightened, he resigned his commission to protest the treatment of Polish exiles who had attempted to escape Siberia. Back in St Petersburg, he became a member of the Chaikovsky Circle, most important of the democratic movements of the 1870s, while also pursuing his researches. Woodcock's friend Paul Goodman, the American anarchist, once conjured up a scene in which, though "other agitators could get out of town and escape the police, [Kropotkin] had to stay and explain to the Geological Society his thesis on the Ice Cap."[6] For indeed, like

Bakunin before him, Kropotkin was thrown into that grim landmark on St Petersburg's riverfront, the Fortress of Saints Peter and Paul, where the Decembrists of 1825 had been executed. Conditions there broke his health. But after being transferred to hospital, he managed to escape to western Europe (for a time, to Switzerland, which expelled him) and finally to Britain, where he made a meagre living as a science journalist and author. In London, he showed the anarchist trait, so obvious in Woodcock later on, of involving himself in local conditions and local culture. For Kropotkin, this meant taking up the plight of the Eastern European Jews in Whitechapel and also founding, with the English anarchist Charlotte Wilson, an English-language paper called *Freedom*. This was in 1886. Over half a century later, when Woodcock arrived on the anarchist scene, Freedom Press was still publishing pamphlets and books and producing a fortnightly, *War Commentary*.

From the vantage-point of old age, Woodcock could see that by the time the war came, he "'was constantly searching'" for a father, perhaps a "'shaman-father [only to discover two figures who] became jointly the wise father as far as I was concerned, and I loved both of them, though with British reticence I never said anything about it.'"[7] He met them within a year of each other. They were George Orwell and Herbert Read.

Although still only in his late forties, Read already had invested more than a decade in championing art education and modernism in the visual arts, and had just relinquished the editorship of the *Burlington Magazine*. Such books as *The Meaning of Art* (1931) and *Art Now* (1933) coexisted uneasily with his works as a poet, literary critic and autobiographer. He had roots in rural Yorkshire and his northern accent always set him apart in the wealthy curatorial and gallery world in which he nonetheless wielded influence. Read carried the faint suggestion of being an outsider, even while being very much on the inside. To Woodcock, who would recall, for example, that "it was only in Read's company that I entered the somewhat gloomy portals of the Reform Club",[8] this was an attractive quality. The fact that Read was a member of the anarchist movement was appealing, as was his refusal, so typical of anarchist writers, to be confined within only one or two literary forms. They met in Cambridge during the summer of 1941, and Woodcock solicited an essay for his magazine. A little later, Read "suggested I contact [Freedom Press] to distribute the issue of

NOW in which I had published his 'The Paradox of Anarchism' ..."[9]
Neither Woodcock nor this anti-institutional institution would ever
be the same again.

Freedom Press was then located just off Theobalds Road ("with its
trams and its tornados of dust and torn paper"[10]) at the spot where it
was met by Red Lion Street, a thoroughfare destined to disappear,
leaving Red Lion Square landlocked midway between Theobalds and
Holborn. By tradition, this part of London was radical and literary
territory. Charles Lahr's Blue Moon Bookshop stood vacant at 69 Red
Lion Street, because Lahr had been imprisoned as an enemy alien and
sent to the Isle of Wight. At 25 Red Lion Square was Conway Hall,
home of the South Place Ethical Society (established 1797), which at
least as far back as the Anglo-Boer War had been well known as the
venue of last resort for political speakers whose extreme views denied
them a stage elsewhere. Nearby was the avant-garde bookshop run by
David Archer. In Red Lion Passage, a tiny lane connecting the street
and the square, Woodcock called at the Freedom Bookshop and introduced himself. Among those present was Marie Louise Berneri, then
twenty-two years old. As Inge Woodcock was to say, "Her beauty is
what animated the anarchist movement" at the time.[11] Indeed, from
the moment he met her in the bookshop George Woodcock's life was
changed forever.

Looking back at the end of this tumultuous decade, Woodcock
would note how the Spanish civil war had first piqued his interest in
anarchism, causing him to read works as far apart in time as those of
Kropotkin (whose *Mutual Aid* had reappeared in 1939, as a sixpenny
Penguin) and Read. He would remember how the war with Germany
that followed the so-called phoney war of 1939-40 "led me naturally
and logically to a full rejection of the state and its authority."[12] But
his anarchism was still a personal matter, almost private. He had not
been "aware of the existence of a group of people who were concerned
with the propagation of libertarian ideas."[13]

Berneri changed all that. She was the daughter of the Italian anarchist Camillo Berneri, who, to escape Mussolini, had fled to France
with his wife and two daughters (the second became a medical doctor). While they stayed in France, however, he went off to the
Spanish civil war, and was assassinated in Barcelona by the Spanish
communists in 1937. Thereafter the survivors withdrew to England,
where Marie Louise (she had taken this name over Maria Louise)

married Vero Recchioni, who changed his name to Vernon Richards but was known in the circle as Vero. Richards and Berneri had picked up the falling banner of Freedom Press and were moving it into the maelstrom of current events. They formed the Freedom Defence Committee to demand amnesty for deserters and other war resisters. Like *War Commentary* and their other ventures, the committee was funded partly by donations and partly by the revenue from the bookshop, which imported radical literature and also sold avant-garde books and other small-press publications. Woodcock met Marie Louise and fell in league with her. As an interviewer for an Italian newspaper put it simply more than forty years later, Woodcock "*convertito all'anarchismo dalla figlia di Berneri ...*" (was converted to anarchism by the daughter of Berneri).[14] Woodcock would remember that:

> Her beauty, seen for the first time, was almost startlingly impressive; later one found it so natural a part of her whole personality that one tended to take it for granted, though never to become unaware of it, for though her beauty became more mature as she grew older, it changed rather than diminished, and was always irradiated by the vitality of her character. Her manner on [our] first meeting was earnest, rather solemn, and a little shy, though she expressed her opinions with a very uncompromising candour. Her English at that time was still imperfect, and the strong and pleasant French accent was more pronounced than in later years. With her earnestness, there was evident also a certain youthfulness in her manner, which later became more manifest when one saw the light sides of her nature; it was a manifestation of simplicity rather than juvenility.[15]

As their friendship and comradeship developed, Woodcock and Berneri devised a plan to write each other a long series of autobiographical letters so that they could share the lives they had led before their first meeting. Berneri's sudden death, at thirty-one, prevented her from following through, but in 1982 Woodcock finally fulfilled his side of the bargain when he published the first volume of his memoirs, *Letter to the Past*, in which he writes of her even more vividly, if also less baldly, than in the quotation above. Reviewing the book at the time, a sensitive reader could only conclude that she must have been the great love of his early life, whether or not the love was requited. In drawing the obvious message I inadvertently embarrassed

Woodcock, who told me shortly afterwards, rather shyly, that whatever may have been the case at that time (he didn't elaborate), the relationship was superseded by his later one with his future wife and that that should be the end of the matter. Later I asked Vernon Richards what Woodcock's relationship with Berneri had been. He replied without hesitation, "Why, he was in love with her, of course!"[16] But then, as another of the Freedom Press group, the artist Philip Sansom, would recall, "We all were."[17] Saying so, Sansom then began sobbing at the memory. When I reported Sansom's reaction to Woodcock, he nodded with sad understanding. Woodcock had frequently written of Berneri in his later poetry, once telling her spirit: "Utopia has arrived. / You would not recognize / or like it ..."[18] He must have been recalling the report of Sansom's conversation when, in one of his last poems, he wrote:

> fifty years gone and
> men still weep for you;
> no day of mine
> goes without thought of you.
> Surely no startling beauty
> alone could keep
> such loyalty,
> such sad, persisting love
> for a mere dear absence![19]

Woodcock now had three addresses: his official one in the countryside, where he was supposedly performing his alternative service, and two widely separated rooms in London, where he carried on his literary and political activities. Any question of Berneri aside, there is evidence that growing disenchantment with agricultural work was an important factor in what followed. In February 1941 we find him writing from Langham to Lance Godwin, who was now in the army:

I've lived in this community now some nine weeks, and in another fortnight or less, I shall be moving on to Dry Drayton, near Cambridge, to satisfy the tribunal with a little market gardening, in partnership with D.S. Savage, the poet. Life here at Langham was, in many ways, not unpleasant. The people are, on the whole, more intelligent than the average. The work of farming is, to me, quite interesting and satisfying, and physically I feel fitter than ever before. But the lack of privacy is the one thing that has decided me to go away. It is quite impossible to write when one lives right on top of a great many people, when one even sleeps in a communal bedroom. And the fact of writing being impossible has forced me to realise more vividly than before how much it is my raison d'être. So I must get back to privacy, "a room of one's own".

But I daresay you must feel the lack of privacy as much as I do. I really can't think how an individual of your type, a fundamental anarchist, can accept army life. For me prison would be infinitely preferable. Still, short of prison, I think you're wise to go in for a commission. I know you'll enjoy the added privacy when you gain it.[20]

Woodcock mentions that he is still hoping to write a novel. He also alludes for the first time to the possibility of a biography of Aphra Behn.

As for the plan to grow vegetables with Derek Savage, Woodcock first found "life in Cambridge pleasant, my work on the land isn't really onerous, and I've certainly met the most charming people, and had some very curious experiences."[21] But after six months the allure of London life was proving irresistible. He wrote to Godwin:

Last evening, sitting over the beerpots with Roy Campbell, Dylan Thomas and Bill Empson, I thought nobly of you, and remembered that you'll be coming down this way some time soon. So I write to tell you where I am and what I'm doing of.

I've left Cambridge—not exactly for good and all—[Cambridge] is a place like Paris which you feel you cannot banish—but for the present hour. I got fed up with digging ditches, and asked for my cards in high dudgeon and came south again to hang parasitic on the great wen [the Great Wen was the not-so-affectionate name for London used by William Cobbett, the nineteenth-century radical].

At present I spend the best part of the week—Monday to Friday afternoon—gardening at a crank "progressive" school at Epsom, and the weekends in London, leading the vie de Bohème for all I'm worth. I've taken an enormous room in Hampstead [at 39 Primrose Hill] where I spend the odd hours when I'm not in pubs, night clubs, afternoon drinking clubs, the offices of *Horizon* or any odd dirty flat in Charlotte street ...

I'm going shortly to become partner in a nursery and orchard business near Richmond, beginning humbly my career as the anarchist capitalist.

To hell with this bloody war! To hell with everything! I feel a real lonely anarchist these days. But I suppose we've all got to lie on the beds we made. I for instance was fool enough to stay in England when I could have gone to the U.S.A. before the war and might well have been in Mexico or Brazil by now ...

This is a ballsy letter, but I've such a hangover! However, you should have seen Roy Campbell performing veronicas with his raincoat at the lassies in Regent Street last night![22]

The letter smacks of bravado for the benefit of his boyhood friend. In fact, London's appeal was far more than hedonistic. Woodcock was spending more and more time with Marie Louise Berneri putting out *War Commentary*, at 27 Belsize Road, NW6. Later, once police snooping discomfited the North London landlord, the publication returned to the old neighbourhood, to 27 Red Lion Street, though by then the area had been rendered almost unrecognizable by German bombing. At this point, Woodcock made the first of several decisions that would complicate his later life. He decided to quit agriculture altogether, to become, so to speak, a deserter from alternative service. So it was that in the autumn of 1942 he quit the countryside for London, where he gave up his rooms at Richmond and in Hampstead. There, without leaving a trace for the authorities, he hoped, he moved into the top floor of a Victorian house in Parliament Hill, the other side of Hampstead. The flat was rented to a fellow anarchist, Ken Hawks, and a young designer, Norman Potter. Woodcock didn't trust Potter, who soon departed; his spot taken by Louis Adeane, the poet. The place was furnished primitively; the carpeting was dusty felt.

Technically, Woodcock was on the run. But he was never more visible. Believing by now that he had intimate knowledge of agriculture and its problems, he published a Freedom Press sixpenny pamphlet, *New Life to the Land*, which argued that decentralized anarchist farming would amply feed the British people, ending the dangerous wartime dependence on America and the Dominions. By August 1942 the work was in its second printing. Herbert Read praised it and so did such people as the leader of the Polish Peasant Party, an anarchist now exiled in London, who reviewed it favourably and arranged through Read to meet its young author at Czardas Restaurant in Dean Street, Soho. This would lead to other Freedom Press pamphlets in succeeding years—*Railways and Society* in 1943 (for his long sentence at the GWR had given him some authority in the field), and *Homes or Hovels: The Housing Problem & Its Solution* and *Anarchy or Chaos*, both in 1944. The latter was a short book rather than a pamphlet (it was priced at 2/6). It was also more general and theoretical, as were *Anarchism and Morality* and *What Is Anarchism?* (both 1945). His last such work was *The Basis of Communal Living* (1947); the subject was one about which he then knew a great deal; it was also of intense concern to Berneri, who later wrote a book on utopias. These pamphlets were widely distributed in Britain and abroad, some being republished in *samizdat* editions as recently as the late 1970s. The English jazz singer George Melly recalls in his autobiography how he was cashiered from the postwar Royal Navy for, among other outrages, keeping "neat piles of pamphlets by Bakunin, Kropotkin, George Woodcock and Herbert Read" in his foot locker.[23] (When Woodcock, who wasn't familiar with Melly's name, was shown this passage, he first shrank with embarrassment but soon swelled with pride.) As late as 1954, a young man stood in the gallery of the House of Commons in Westminster to fling handfuls of Woodcock's *What Is Anarchism?* onto the MPs below; he had to be "hustled out, struggling."[24] *Anarchy or Chaos*, the most outspoken of the series, would come back to haunt its author.

4 GOING UNDERGROUND

JULIAN SYMONS, AMONG OTHERS, criticized the first seven issues of *NOW*, what came to be called the Old Series, 1940–41, for including all shades and types of anti-authoritarian opinion, even right-wing versions. In 1942, the magazine did not appear, owing mainly to the turmoil in Woodcock's personal and political lives, especially once he dropped out of the Agricultural War Committee and found it prudent to change addresses so regularly. By 1943, however, his prospects were brighter. *The Centre Cannot Hold*, his first poetry collection (indeed first book of any sort) to appear under a mainstream London imprint, was published by Routledge, where Herbert Read was a director. The two men would continue to have a close but awkward father–son relationship, characterized on both sides by the notorious male inability to express their feelings in conversation.

At a party in Bloomsbury early in 1943, Woodcock met a formidable and accomplished young woman, Ingeborg Hedwig Elisabeth Linzer Roskelly. The daughter of a German father and a Polish mother, she had been educated in Germany but had been living in Britain since fleeing European fascism in 1936. She spoke five or six languages and had trained as a potter under the famous Bernard Leach. She was married to a British journalist named Frederick Roskelly, and they had been living in Cornwall until their recent separation. She was intelligent, strong and independent—in general, the same type as Marie Louise Berneri. Like Berneri, she lacked the dependence on men that Woodcock had found so unattractive in his mother. She was intensely political (she soon became involved with *NOW* and to some extent with Freedom Press) but was also a bohemian spirit (having been part of a group of artistic rapscallions that included the husband and wife actors, Charles Laughton and Elsa Lanchester). Woodcock and Roskelly were taken with each other at once.

NOW was distributed to newsagents by Freedom Press, and quite successfully, too; the wartime publishing turbulence admitted all manner of odd reading matter into the railway bookstalls, and *NOW*, as thick as seventy-four pages, would sell about 3,000 copies at 1/6 apiece, making surprising inroads on the better established and better financed *Horizon*. Such being the case, Woodcock reasoned, why not have Freedom Press become the publisher as well, while he devoted himself completely to the editor's job and title? He made an arrangement to this effect with Vernon Richards and the others. Looking ahead to future issues, Woodcock stated in an editorial that "[s]o far as their social content is concerned, the volumes of *NOW* will be edited from an anarchist point of view [but where] their literary content is concerned, our criterion will be the quality of writing."[1] He went on to restate the policy that had drawn criticism: "Nor do we intend to exclude poets, essayists, story writers, because their political views do not coincide with our own. Indeed, we are grateful for their willing co-operation."[2] But for just this reason, the arrangement with Freedom Press lasted only one issue. "After that Tom Brown and Albert Meltzer objected to the inclusion of a variety of non-anarchist writers, and we reached the compromise, which continued for the next eight issues, by which I became the actual publisher, but Freedom Press distributed the journal for me and allowed me to use their address."[3]

Meltzer became Woodcock's most persistent enemy in the fractious little world of British anarchism. In his memoirs he charged that

the resources of Freedom Press were used by Woodcock to help advance his literary and academic career [in fact, he had no academic career until after leaving England]; in a movement expressly opposed to political careerism this inevitably appeared to many militants as something of a confidence trick and some of the bitterness that arose within the movement at that time must be accounted to this and in particular the publication of *NOW* ... The journal was not a Freedom Press publication and had nothing whatever to do with it apart from having its mail sent "c/o" Freedom Press and being printed at the press.[4]

Down through the years, Meltzer passed up no opportunity to take a swipe at Woodcock. "One of the minor amusing effects" of Woodcock's rising literary renown, he would recall, "is how the *New Statesman* praised the 'usual brilliancy' of a very humdrum essay by the other George Woodcock—the TU bureaucrat—in an anthology, obviously confusing him with the author George Woodcock who belonged to the fraternity of reviewers and was hence entitled to his little laurel."[5] Being confused from time to time with George Woodcock, the long-serving general secretary of the Trades Union Council, would amuse the writer Woodcock as much as it did Meltzer, as did being confused with a *third* George Woodcock, another Vancouver resident of the same name. "Your letter reached me only today," Woodcock once wrote to the critic Peter Buitenhuis, "having been sent to the wrong George Woodcock by the unfortunate method of consulting the telephone book instead of *Who's Who.*"[6] In any case, Woodcock would always be hard pressed to explain Meltzer's spitefulness except by attributing it to jealousy. That explanation may well be correct, especially if one includes sexual jealousy, which must have hung heavily in the air around Freedom Press. This in addition to the anarchist movement's tendency to splinter itself into ever tinier factions, almost to the point at which each person becomes a separate faction.

In fairness, though, Woodcock, despite what Derek Stanford called his "quiet gentle manners",[7] often gave inadvertent offence simply by his deep-rooted habit of preventing his various circles from overlapping, or by letting drop one group after he had passed through their lives—as many British friends would conclude he did after emigrating to Canada.

But then again, Woodcock's precarious political situation during the war was cause for caginess. He recalled, for example, how he let drop his decade's worth of connections with his old fellow workers at the GWR,

and indeed met few of them again, and mostly as an unwelcome presence—for had I not left in order to take my stand as a conscientious objector? I remember going with Vero, still a respectable civil engineer, to a construction site where I had worked a few months before and where his firm was fulfilling a contract. All the people I had known as good old pals shunned me; the exception was one elderly engineer who had once worked in Bolivia and had a sense of the real world, and he welcomed me as an obvious reproach to his colleagues. Another strange ghost appeared one night at a Prom Concert I had gone to with Marie Louise. A little man in [a] snappy lieutenant's uniform appeared at my side. I thought he was attracted by ML, but he was targetted on me like a wasp. "What are you doing in the war?" he whispered venomously as Sir Henry Wood whipped up the trumpets. "Don't you feel you have a duty, you rat?" as the trombones broke in. As the drums rolled Marie Louise whispered to me, "Who on earth is that ridiculous little man?" I introduced him as "Lieutenant Harris, who is winning the war for us", and she directed at him such a glance of fine Tuscan scorn that he uneasily melted into the crowd.[8]

His personal life was happier. Sometime in 1943

Inge and I moved over to Highgate West Hill, where we occupied a floor in a somewhat bomb-damaged early Victorian house. First we had the second floor (counting the English way). One night we decided through some strange common intuition to sleep on the big convertible couch in the living room. In the middle of the night we heard a crash, and found the ceiling in the bedroom, weakened by a bomb blast, had fallen on our bed. We always had odd feelings about that room, because the architect husband of the sprightly landlady, Joy Baines, had died there. Later we moved upstairs to the big top room, all sloping ceilings but with a fine view of the Heath. Here Orwell used to visit us, wheezing up the three flights of stairs.[9]

Here they would live for almost five years, far and away the most stable domestic arrangement Woodcock had known since quitting his mother's house in Marlow.

The friendship that developed between Orwell and Woodcock is by now a storied one, made familiar by Woodcock's critical memoir *The Crystal Spirit* and by most of the many important books on Orwell that have appeared subsequently. During the war and for the remainder of the decade, the editors of literary magazines and small publishing houses in Britain and the United States made much more serious attempts to communicate with one another than they did later on. Even an American as naturally anglophobic as the San Francisco anarchist poet Kenneth Rexroth was interested enough in England to edit a significant anthology for New Directions, *The New British Poets*. It included names already known in America, such as George Barker, Lawrence Durrell, Hugh MacDiarmid, Kathleen Raine and Dylan Thomas, as well as a few curiosities, such as Paul Potts, a Canadian poetaster who had become a familiar figure in the streets of London by selling copies of his work to random passersby. Rexroth also included virtually all the important poets of *NOW*, among them, Louis Adeane, Alex Comfort, Derek Savage, Julian Symons and of course Woodcock. Rexroth was familiar with them because he was the American correspondent of *NOW*, for which he wrote splendidly rich and incomprehensible jeremiads about U.S. politics.

The traffic flowed in both directions, and George Orwell used one of his London Letters to the *Partisan Review* in New York to excoriate Woodcock for his pacifism. He charged that the newly revived *NOW* was including the fascist viewpoint beneath its fully unfurled umbrella of opinion. The attack appeared in 1942. Woodcock, who by coincidence was writing an essay about Orwell for *NOW*, responded with a counter-attack that called into question Orwell's credentials as a commentator, pointing out that he was an old Etonian who had served in the colonial civil service in Burma under his original name, Eric Blair. Orwell sued for peace, inviting Woodcock to come to the BBC, where Orwell was producing programmes for broadcast to India, and to take part in a panel. An often reproduced photograph of the occasion shows Orwell and Woodcock with Herbert Read, Mulk Raj Anand, William Empson and Edmund Blunden: a remarkable diversity of poets. His hair already turning white (a family trait), Woodcock, with hands thrust into the pockets of his unpressed tweed coat, smiles a boyish smile. Their friendship lasted through the war to Orwell's early death in 1950, following the success of *Animal Farm* but just prior to the even greater triumph of *Nineteen Eighty-Four*.

When Orwell left the BBC to serve as literary editor of *Tribune*, the left-wing weekly broadsheet, Woodcock sometimes called at the office in the Strand, where Orwell occupied a desk piled high with books and manuscripts. Woodcock remembered that on several of these occasions they heard the V2s in the distance as they chatted. The impression Woodcock leaves of Orwell and the environment is one of all-pervasive greyness and decrepitude. Often they would lunch, sometimes alone or with Read or Symons. In an often-quoted passage of *The Crystal Spirit*, Woodcock tells of the spartan delight with which Orwell tucked into boiled cod and bitter turnip tops, the only food available at a particular restaurant that day. Orwell was stuck between social classes, as one might become stuck between floors in a lift. This was a situation he had chosen, it was central to his view of himself, and it provided him with grim amusement. Woodcock remembered:

> He always poured tea into his saucer and blew on it, particularly in front of people whom we didn't know: he wanted to see how they'd take it. And then you go off to a pub and you go of course into the public bar, where all the workers were. But of course old George, he could never get on with them because he ... spoke in a tired Eton accent that was very flat because of his throat wound [from the Spanish civil war]. He never mixed with them. He always looked the tired English sahib in his shabby old sportscoat ...[10]

As he was too upper class for the workers, he was too déclassé for the upper class. When *Animal Farm* was adopted by the Book of the Month Club in the U.S. and Orwell received his first sizable windfall, he invited Woodcock to an expensive restaurant, where "he stood up and very ceremoniously took off his jacket and hung it over the back of the seat, looking at me meanwhile with his challenging eye so that I had to do the same."[11] In an effort to repay Orwell's generosity, Woodcock then suggested that they top off the meal with a visit to a pub he knew near Covent Garden where one could still purchase genuine absinthe. The plan was ruined when the pub regulars, seeing through Orwell's socio-economic disguise, referred to the two outsiders as toffs.

Even though Orwell was never an anarchist, the two writers discovered a rich fund of shared political ideas. Indeed, when, after the war, Woodcock turned away from most anarchist activity in order to concentrate on literary work, he found himself in a political position much closer to Orwell's. Orwell became, even more than Read, the wise father—significantly, a wise dead father. For the rest of his life, Woodcock referred to Orwell's works and ideas more than to those of any other writer, including even Kropotkin. Orwell set a standard

of intellectual honesty against which Woodcock would measure his
own unfolding performance.

≈

By 1944, Woodcock was spending less time on politics and more on
his life as a writer. This extended beyond editing *NOW* and supporting himself with unsigned reviews in the *Times Literary Supplement*
and signed but poorly paid ones in a kaleidoscopic array of other
papers and journals. Although he kept his hand in at *War Commentary*, he was determined to begin producing full-length works of prose.
He had found his first topic, the life of William Godwin, the author
of works as different as *Enquiry Concerning Political Justice* (1793) and
the novel *Adventures of Caleb Williams* (1794). These classics were well
and truly forgotten by the 1940s, and so was their author, except as
a footnote in the story of Percy Bysshe Shelley, his son-in-law. Woodcock, however, saw Godwin (no relation to his own childhood friend)
as a pioneering anarchist philosopher, and he set about the simulta-
neous and equally difficult tasks of constructing a biography and finding someone who would publish it. So it was, then, that Woodcock
was absent from the Freedom Press offices when, on 12 December
1944, a Tuesday, the establishment was raided by the Special Branch
of Scotland Yard.

The raid was in response to publication, two months earlier, of a
War Commentary "manifesto to the armed forces that the other editors intended to circulate in military camps where they had contacts.
It advocated mass disobedience as soon as peacetime came, if not
before ..."[12] The police seized a large quantity of papers and files.
They searched, without success, for the typewriter that had been used
to cut the mimeograph stencils of the manifesto.

The first Woodcock knew of the raid was a telephone call that
evening from Marie Louise, asking him to meet her and Vero at the
Camden Town tube station. A fog—one of the last of the so-called
pea-soupers, with which, in the age before environmental awareness,
London was practically synonymous—had greatly reduced visibility as
the three anarchists met on the platform. Richards and Berneri told
Woodcock what had happened, and how they expected to be arrested
soon, perhaps along with others. They warned him to return to Highgate West Hill and dispose of his typewriter. Someone would be

needed—now more than ever—to keep *War Commentary* alive, they told him. It was best that he disappear for a while.

For once the secretive strain in Woodcock's personality could be put to proper use. Changing buses frequently, using the back doors of certain pubs, he made his way to Highgate, gathered up the type-writer and his personal papers, and then, by means equally circuitous, went to Euston Station and caught a night train to Carnarvon. He knew a pacifist farmhouse in the wooded mountains near Snowden where he could stash his effects until matters in London had been resolved. In a couple of days, he returned to the capital and made contact with Herbert Read (who had taken some anarchist literature the police had overlooked and hidden it in his own house) and Alex Comfort to hold a strategy session. By this time, the police had arrested Richards and Berneri and two other editors: Dr John Hewetson, a casualty officer at Paddington Hospital, and Philip Sansom, a painter, designer and practised anarchist speaker and a CO, who did the lay-outs for *War Commentary* (and also the covers for *NOW*). All four were charged with violation of the Incitement to Disaffection Act. What sounded like some ancient and dusty statute in truth dated only to 1934, when it replaced the Incitement to Mutiny Act of 1797, which had been used against agitators effectively before, during and after the Great War, but under which convictions against civilians, it was feared, were too difficult.

In 1939–45, curiously, the authorities were quite tolerant of anti-war opinion so long as the war was going badly for Britain and her allies. Perhaps they were too distracted to persecute dissenters. But now, when the invasion of Normandy had clearly turned the tide against Germany, prosecutions increased. Albert Meltzer's friend Tom Brown had been sent up for fifteen months in September 1944 after publishing a pamphlet that the military interpreted as a call to sabo-teurs. Two months later, John Olday, a deserter who was *War Com-mentary's* cartoonist, was arrested for possessing a false identity card; he went away for a year. In January 1945, Philip Sansom began serv-ing two months in HM Prison Brixton for failing to keep the military informed of his address and for possessing an army coat.

At their plenary meeting, Woodcock, Read and Comfort agreed that the police were attempting to shut down the publication by removing its staff and that they might have worse harassment planned. Before the police could strike a second time, the three men decided, a public counter-attack should be mounted on civil-libertarian grounds. They petitioned a wide variety of prominent writers, artists, musicians and public personalities to sign a letter protesting the police raid, an action that laid the foundation for the Freedom Defence Committee. The committee soon acquired other functions as well, such as defending the rights of deserters and freedom of speech in general. It outlasted the war.

As customary in these situations, some unexpected loyalties were revealed. For example, T. S. Eliot, who seemed to Woodcock a rusty old reactionary, lent his name with alacrity, while Stephen Spender, whom one might have expected to be more sympathetic given his writings during the Spanish civil war, was harder to convince. Spender, now a civil servant in the Foreign Office, did in fact put his name to the document, but he backed off civil liberties issues after the foreign secretary upbraided him. Figures as different as Dylan Thomas and E. M. Forster signed. Membership of the committee itself included Aneurin Bevan (he was co-chair), Cyril Connolly, C. E. M. Joad, Augustus John, Harold Laski, Kingsley Martin, Henry Moore, Bertrand Russell and Osbert Sitwell. Many were attracted because they knew that the Civil Liberties Association had been effectively taken over by Stalinists. Orwell was another member; Woodcock would remember him making one of his rare platform appearances on the committee's behalf, speaking to a crowd in Red Lion Square. In a clever strategic move designed to thicken its veneer of respectability, the FDC rented an office in the heart of Mayfair, "and through its doors passed an extraordinary mixture of volunteers—workmen, and writers, old anarchist veterans and young conscientious objectors, gay society photographers and debutantes in rebellion."[13]

Meanwhile the legal machinery ground forward. If the criminal case was a rallying cry for the left, it was also an excuse for outrage from the more hormonally driven of the Fleet Street papers, such as the *Daily Express* and the *Daily Mail.* An article in one of their now-forgotten rivals, the *News Chronicle*, conveys the feeling perfectly. Under the heading 'FIGHT, FOR WHAT?' POEM READ AT OLD BAILEY the paper reported as follows during April 1945:

Extracts from a paper which was said to have advocated anarchy, and verses of a poem which asked that landlords should do the fighting, were read at the Old Bailey yesterday.

Three men and a woman pleaded not guilty to having conspired to cause disaffection. They are:

Vernon Richards (29), civil engineer, and Marie Louise Richards (26), secretary, both of Eton Place, Hampstead; John Christopher Hewetson (32), medical practitioner, Willow Road, Hampstead; and Philip Richard Sansom (28), commercial artist, Camden Street, N.W.

They also pleaded not guilty to endeavouring to cause disaffection by disseminating copies of a paper called *War Commentary*.

The two Richards[es] were further charged with having a leaflet headed: "Fight! What for?"

The Attorney General (Sir Donald Somervell) said that *War Commentary* was a paper which was headed "For anarchism."

Among the objects of the anarchists' movement was opposition to "normal means of maintaining a class-divided society—Parliament, the legal system, the police, armed Forces and the Church."

"The principle these people advocated," said Sir Donald, "is an armed revolution."

"'Hold on to your arms' is an expression repeated in two successive numbers of the paper."

Sir Donald read a circular letter, which was headed Freedom Press, 27, Belsize Road, October 25, 1944, and began "Dear Comrades." One extract read:

"These discussions bring sympathy and unity of feeling to barrack rooms which authority is always trying to split. Solidarity frightens authority. You should, therefore, do everything possible to establish closer contacts ...

"One of the most important questions, in our opinion, is that of the action of soldiers' councils in a revolutionary situation."

When Mr. Justice Birkett asked the meaning of "C.P." in the letter and Sir Donald replied "Communist Party" there was a burst of laughter from the public benches.

The charge against Richards and his wife related to a poem in the leaflet "Fight! What for?" Two verses read:

> Your country, who says you're a country?
> You live in another man's flat.
> You haven't even a backyard.
> So why should you murder for that?

> You haven't a hut or a building.
> No flower, no garden, it's true;
> The landlords have grabbed all the country;
> Let them do the fighting—not you.

A number of soldiers in whose possession copies of *War Commentary*, or the circular letter, have been found[,] gave evidence, and said they had not been disaffected.

The Attorney General said he would not press against Sansom the charge referring to the dissemination of *War Commentary*.

Mr. John Maude, K.C., for the defence, maintained that none of the accused had had the slightest intention of disaffecting any single man in the Army.

The hearing was adjourned until today, and the accused were released on bail.[14]

Then came a remarkable turn of events. As Woodcock would recall, "In court each day Marie Louise Berneri looked so much the part of a tragedy queen that the Crown sought and found a technicality on which to release her."[15] In effect, the prosecutors became enamoured of her, as men seemed always to be doing, and they pointed out that, as husband and wife were legally as one, a wife could not be accused of conspiracy with her husband since, by definition, conspiracy, like the tango, requires two. The charges against her were dropped. She was understandably furious. Like her sister and mother, she was a feminist (the three of them spent their free time smuggling birth control devices into Ireland), and she found this sexual discrimination reprehensible—if also, in this case, useful.

Woodcock sat in the visitors' gallery, covering the trial for John Middleton Murry's *Peace News* and chuckling at some of the Crown's low comedy, as when a police officer became confused about the difference between anarchists and surrealists. Now Berneri was free to help Woodcock in putting out *War Commentary*, which mocked the police cruelly. He would recall how the two of them

wrote much of the paper ourselves in joint day-long sessions fuelled by strong Italian coffee. We took the copy to the typesetter who operated at the top of an old warehouse in Covent Garden; we read the proofs; we did the layout of each issue; and then we looked after its production in the antiquated printing house in the East End that the Freedom group had bought for a song in a bankruptcy sale. Sometimes when volunteers were scarce we helped to mail out the subscription copies. And in mid-career, the week the war ended, we changed the paper's name from *War Commentary* to *Freedom*,[16]

thus reviving the title that Kropotkin and his confederates had used in 1886. Woodcock would never forget the

crowded, urgent days, with all the satisfaction of working to the edge of one's strength in a common cause with a beautiful and intelligent woman whose mind and mine seemed in almost perfect timing and who into the bargain was the most intriguing of companions ... I have not in all the forty years since then written better journalism than I did for that obscure paper with its four or five thousand readers. In every way it was one of those times of heightened living when one's perceptions and one's mental responses to them are tuned to their highest level and one has a strange sense of being outside and above oneself.[17]

The Crown's case seemed to wax and wane; a number of prosecution witnesses, once in the witness box, turned out to be of more value to the defence. One was Colin Ward, the future architect and anarchist writer, then a young soldier on duty in Orkney.

Owing to some absolutely trivial military offence, I was actually in detention so they had to fetch me over from the island of South Ronaldsay to Stromness, which is one of two towns in Orkney, for my kit to be in order for [my] copies of *War Commentary* and so on to be found. And I was called as a witness for the prosecution in magistrate's court and then in the Old Bailey [where] the judge asked me if I was influenced by the material. "Did you agree with everything you read in this paper?"

I, no doubt shivering, said, "I wouldn't say that categorically, My Lord." So when I went back [to camp] after this, they used to be call me Not Categorically Ward ...

It was curious, the soldiers—I think we were all soldiers, rather than sailors—who were called for that trial. There were six of us, not known to one another. I was in the Royal Engineers and the others were in,

I think, something called the Non-Combatants' Corps or the Pioneer Corps: some non-military bit of the Army. We obviously had agreed [among ourselves] to stress that we hadn't been seduced from our duties to King and Country by reading Freedom Press literature. Except for one that is. Suddenly, deep in his heart, he felt that he *had* been seduced. Not at all useful to the defence ...

It's sort of a great joke that I was a witness for the prosecution against them, for when I finally got out of the army, they asked me to join the editorial group.[18]

The defendants, found guilty, served eighteen months in Wormwood Scrubs (the maximum penalty was fourteen years). During this time, Woodcock worked with Berneri and lived with Mrs Roskelly, who, by the seventh number of the new series of *NOW*, was using the name Inge Woodcock and was listed on the magazine's masthead as business manager.

Colin Ward would always maintain that the persons convicted "were not the authors of the alleged subversion".[19] Who was? The text, when compared with their other writings, might have been by Woodcock or Berneri or both. Those closest to the case always remained coy on this question, none more so than Woodcock.

As a great proponent of the loosely organized cantonal form of government in Switzerland, he became a booster of Swiss culture generally, and in his last years in Vancouver sometimes took guests to a small and not very satisfactory Swiss restaurant on 41st Avenue. There, in a way that called to mind his anecdote about Orwell, he would attend to the menu with an exuberance that was undeserved. During one of my lunches with him there, I finally got up the courage to ask about the authorship of the manifesto. He was fully co-operative yet magisterially unhelpful, as he could be when faced with a direct query that threatened to contradict his recollections. Finally, after a certain amount of circumlocution, he lowered his voice and said, with genuine self-mockery at the person he had once been, "I was foolish to let her talk me into that!"

5 STARTING OVER IN THE NEW WORLD

THE WAR TURNED everything topsy-turvy. Young men of twenty-one were suddenly officers, responsible for the lives of others even younger than themselves. Women found, at least temporarily, new opportunities that would have been unthinkable in peacetime. The old patterns of literary reputation were disrupted as well, and the geography of literature shifted. Soho, for example, was displaced as the centre of bohemia.

The name, it is said, comes from an old Anglo-French hunting cry: "So hoe! The hare ys founde!" This evolved into So Ho (or Soho) Fields, an area west of the old City that was kept open for a hunting ground but also because its natural springs made building difficult. Yet a village of sorts sprang up on the periphery. So Ho was also the name of what later (in honour of Sir Edmund Wardour, who had run a hospital during the Plague) was called Wardour Street; in the early nineteenth century, Wardour Street was synonymous with the second-hand book trade, and later with antique dealers, but by Woodcock's time it had become a shorthand reference for the British film industry.

In fact, high life and low life seem to have coexisted in Soho almost from the beginning. In the seventeenth century a barber ran a notorious gaming club frequented by such people as the Royalist poet Sir John Suckling, and Sir Christopher Wren complained of "the divers small and mean habitations" in Windmill Field, so called because there was indeed a windmill, on the site of which rose the Windmill Theatre, a risqué establishment where Woodcock's scapegrace uncle worked as stage manager. The final part of the original meadow to be covered over was a patch just east of Carnaby Street; it was left till last (in the 1730s) because it had been used as a mass grave for plague victims. Soho's first note of cosmopolitanism came in the 1680s, when Huguenot refugees poured in. By 1711 Soho already had 8,133 people, a large concentration for those days (it now has two million). One modern historian of Soho points out reassuringly that as long ago as 1895 there was a spirited Clean Up Soho campaign in recognition of the fact that, in its organizer's words, "our respected workers are in many cases being literally driven out of house and home to make room for the traders in vice who can afford to pay exorbitant rents."[1] The arts were as important to Soho as the sin trades.

Handel once lived in Frith Street, Mozart in Brook Street and Wagner in Old Compton Street. Truer to the preconceived image, perhaps, is Dean Street, where, in the eighteenth century, lodged a scandalous actress with the wonderful name Peg Woofington, who was one side of a ménage à trois with David Garrick and a fellow actor, Charles Macklim. In the nineteenth century, Dean Street was likewise the home of Marx; his flat was above what is now the Quo Vadis, one of the celebrated restaurants to have survived from previous generations. Shelley lived in Portland Street and Hazlitt in Frith Street, whereas Josiah Wedgwood had his shop in Greek Street. So many artists, writers and other unstable types crowded Soho in the nineteenth century that St Anne's, the local parish church, was described matter-of-factly as "a prolific place for suicides."[2]

The bohemianism that everyone associates with Soho flourished there through the 1930s, feeding on its reputation, rather like Greenwich Village in New York, with which Soho could be profitably compared. Just as escalating costs would drive New York's bohemian element to annex the East Village, to the ultimate impoverishment of the original homeland to the west, so too did Soho's centre of gravity move to Fitzrovia, north of what De Quincey once called "the great Mediterranean of Oxford Street."[3] As the historian Andrew Sinclair points out, the name Fitzrovia

> was first coined in the Thirties to distinguish the bohemian nature of the artists and writers who gathered at the Fitzroy Tavern ... The Wheatsheaf and the Marquis of Granby, the Swiss and the French pubs saw the encounters of most of the leading writers, painters, actors and

musicians of the day. These were the Fitzrovians, brought together in a transient bohemia, blooming under the Blitz and the black-out, conscription and rationing.[4]

Certainly the war was the turning-point. For one thing, Soho, the original Soho, was devastated when Italian immigrants, perhaps the most important foreign group after the French, were rounded up as enemy aliens, some of them for transportation to Canada. And of course the German bombardment had a horrifying effect. In one incident still remembered, though it was only one of many, a band-leader called Snakehips Johnson and thirty-three others were killed when a bomb struck the Café de Paris in Coventry Street. This fact also gives some hint of the way that entertainment and nightlife had changed, reflecting the tastes of soldiers, sailors and airmen out to have a good time while they could. In some complicated way, Fitzrovia was part of the same process.

Another commentator on the matter, Hugh David, argues that "Fitzrovia had none of the neat coherence with which it has been imbued in many later accounts and memoirs".[5] Fitzrovia was the bohemia of Dylan Thomas and the notoriously difficult Julian Maclaren-Ross rather than of elderly dandies and aspiring flappers. Maclaren-Ross, like the self-publicizing Paul Potts, was free to roam Fitzrovia for most of the war because he had been disqualified for military service on psychiatric grounds. The Fitzrovian crowd included that fine painter Nina Hamnett. She played the same role in London —drunken old fool, cadging drinks—as Maxwell Bodenheim did on the other side of the Atlantic. She jumped out of a window onto a spiked railing, whereas Bodenheim managed to have himself murdered by a psychopath. Woodcock used to see Hamnett trying to barter pencil sketches done on kraft paper for drinks. He once encountered her with Aleister Crowley. The two must have made the most striking contrast while also looking pathetically similar against the unflattering Fitzrovian backdrop.

We can sometimes learn about a writer's career by looking past his or her own books to observe how quickly, and by whom, the subject's work was accepted in journals and republished in anthologies. In the wartime literary economy, with its bomb-damaged publishers and paper rationing, poetry anthologies took on a greater importance than before or perhaps since, and Woodcock was included on equal terms in many of the most significant. He appeared (along with a number of his circle, such as Comfort, Savage and Symons) in the early gathering *Poetry in War Time*, edited by Tambimuttu and published by T. S. Eliot at Faber and Faber. In 1944 Woodcock was still considered sufficiently Welsh to merit inclusion in *Modern Welsh Poetry*, also a Faber title, edited by Keidrych Rhys, another writer declared unfit for the army after psychiatric evaluation. In 1945, Woodcock appeared in the *Little Reviews Anthology*, whose editor, Denys Val Baker, had been skimming the cream of the small literary magazines each year since 1914; in the first volume of *Focus*, an annual "symposium" anthology edited by B. Rajan and Andrew Pearse; and in the new *Poetry Folio*, a series of chapbooks edited by Comfort and Peter Wells. In the last three cases, these were not his sole appearances in those publications, but are given here simply to suggest the frequency with which his name was appearing, and in whose company, as the war came to its end.

Woodcock was a busy young man indeed. He had stepped up his literary production, using much of the energy formerly given to the Freedom Press group, about whose role in peacetime he, like Herbert Read, was anxious if not sceptical. He was struggling to find an opening in the curtain that separated him from the wider audience. Read tried to be helpful, as he usually was not only for Woodcock but the rest of his group (such as the perpetually insolvent Savage, whom he shoe-horned into reviewing for the *Listener*). His best bet for making literary hay of his specialized knowledge of anarchism seemed to lie in his plan for a biography of William Godwin, an idea with which Read, as a director of the publishing house Routledge Kegan Paul, tried to help.

When Woodcock set to work on the subject during the hectic last part of the war, the fame of Godwin (1756–1836) as a slightly risible philosopher, crank and pamphleteer had come and gone. The best-known facts about him—that he was the husband of Mary Wollstonecraft, who wrote *Vindication of the Rights of Woman*, and hence the father of the other Mary Wollstonecraft, the author of *Frankenstein*, who married Shelley—showed a certain biographical potential. But Woodcock knew he must find a way of conveying to readers the story of how Godwin's thought evolved, within a framework that was rather curious yet, in a way, altogether typical. Typical, that is, for a radical leveller from the provinces who became a figure in London. Typical for a social climber who was often on his uppers, driven to incredible feats of scribbling by the way money slipped through the same fingers that so nimbly held the pen.

When he was a boy in Norfolk, Godwin had the opportunity to sit in a chair once occupied by Cromwell (whom he afterwards always called "Cromwel"—eliminating double consonants in names being part of his programme for spelling reform). The association is symbolically appropriate. Godwin was the offspring of dissenting ministers and himself preached for a while. One of his schoolmates was so overcome by Godwin's rhetoric that he kissed him, giving him what a later biographer than Woodcock would call "an early taste of the subtle pleasures of the priesthood."[6] In the end, like so many others then and now, Godwin became a reformer. There had never been a social evangelist quite like him.

Godwin's breakthrough came in 1793 with the book *Enquiry Concerning Political Justice*, political justice being "Godwin's term for the duty of every individual to treat every other individual justly in every individual transaction."[7] All that prevented the spread of such golden-rulism, Godwin believed, was the evil of monopoly, the man-made usurpation of power over fellow humans. Thus government was of course a monopoly and so was the monarchy. So too was marriage. "So long as I feel to engross one woman to myself," he wrote, "and to prohibit my neighbour from proving his superior dessert and reaping the fruits of it, I am guilty of the most odious of all monopolies." One can easily imagine how that opinion was received in normal society at the time.

The literary romantics such as Coleridge, Wordsworth and Southey chirped Godwin's praises. Radicals such as Tom Paine, Joseph Priestley and Thomas Holcroft (whom he later satirized in his novel *Caleb Williams*) welcomed him. Everyone else attacked him. In any event, he was famous overnight. For a while, in fact, he was England's best known philosopher. He was certainly one of the people an angry mob had in mind when it burned Priestley's house with cries of "No philosophers!" His public support for the French Revolution kept the opprobrium from fading.

At about this time, when he was forty and still a virgin, Godwin wed Mary Wollstonecraft, the Anglo-Irish feminist who had published her *Vindication* four years earlier. The union put his principles to the test, to say nothing of hers, but it was short-lived, for she died soon after giving birth to their daughter. The hooting of his enemies increased in volume when he promptly married Mary Jane Clairmont. Their children included Claire Clairmont, who had a child, Allegra, by Byron—by which time Godwin had long since run through his celebrated relationship with Shelley.

One imagines young Shelley with an invisible wind constantly tousling his fine blond hair. He turned up one day in 1814, declaring himself Godwin's disciple. Godwin did not discourage him from such worship but reserved the right to condemn him in return, for the twenty-two-year-old poet, then married to Harriet Westbrook, had fairly obvious intentions towards young Mary, aged seventeen. Godwin spoke of how susceptible she was to his charismatic personality. Shelley's defence was to explain that, like many other Godwinites, he had extended the boundaries of the New Philosophy to embrace Nairism, a type of feminist polygamy. The term had been made popular by James Lawrence, another follower, who wrote that he was modelling the idea on the Nair tribe of India, among whom—in Lawrence's words—he was another spelling reformer—"it is the privilege of Nair ladies tu hav menny lovers."[8]

Godwin was torn between rationalism and parental responsibility. While deciding, he began borrowing money from Shelley, for his overheads had grown enormous by this time, while his politics in other areas remained undiminished (he condemned the victory at Waterloo), which made him as unpopular as ever. Shelley was fighting for custody of his children by Harriet Westbrook (which he won, but then abandoned them), and in the end he and Mary were forced to elope. That was in 1816. She wrote *Frankenstein or The Modern Prometheus* two years later, directed by what monsters of her own we can only imagine, and it was in 1822 that the poet drowned. She survived him by nearly thirty years.

Godwin wrote an enormous amount of prose, most of it less than electric in its power and simplicity. He was so prolific that Woodcock and other early biographers were never much troubled by the fact that no copies of Godwin's first published novel were known to exist, for there was so much else to read (a copy finally came to light in a Scottish castle in 1978). His journals, letters and notebooks are almost as extensive as his public writing. In the circumstances, given how prolific he was, Godwin needed a certain gall to litter his writings with gibes against mere hackney writers (so called because they plied for trade like the drivers of hackney carriages).

For years Godwin kept a bookshop in Skinner Street, near Fleet Market. Thus he was both bookseller (when the term also meant *publisher*) and writer, both exploiter and one of the exploited. He was a familiar figure in the now lost world around St Paul's Churchyard, the centre of English printing and publishing from the fifteenth century to the time it was blown away by the Nazis. Godwin limped along until, as happens to radicals with good genes, he finally came to be seen as a grand old man. Towards the end, the pioneer anarchist went so far as to accept a post from the government, as yeoman-usher of the Exchequer, a job unencumbered by any duties to speak of.

In 1945, even more than now, Godwin seemed an acquired taste, not necessarily because his ideas were uncongenial to the British public (though they were) but also because his prose is so arduous. Hazlitt was a great champion of *Caleb Williams*, but such defenders, though conspicuous at irregular intervals, were reasonably few. A few books on Godwin had appeared in the 1920s and 1930s and had not impressed large numbers of readers favourably. Aside from these, the last full-length look at the subject was *William Godwin: His Friends and Contemporaries*, a two-volume life-and-letters published in 1876. Its compiler and nominal author had been Charles Kegan Paul, the poet, vegetarian, positivist and spiritual hypochondriac who had done well publishing Tennyson, Meredith, Hardy, Stevenson and others and whose memory was still enshrined in the name of Routledge Kegan Paul, the house where Read exercised some power.

Woodcock began his research on the Godwin book in 1942. By the time he began composition, in 1944, his anarchist views had hardened and clarified under Berneri's tutelage, and so he devoted what must have seemed a disproportionately large part of the manuscript to the ideas in *Political Justice*. Read, who was naturally sympathetic to the philosophy involved, was nonetheless disappointed in the partial manuscript Woodcock showed him in late 1944. Yet Read felt that with direction the book might be made publishable. Accordingly, Woodcock submitted the full text shortly after completing it in May 1945. The evaluation process was painfully slow. October came before Read wrote a frank and detailed rejection letter, explaining how he could not overcome his colleagues' views about the many weaknesses of the subject and its treatment, all of which he enumerated. The blow must have been crushing. Rejections from two other important houses soon followed. (In the end, though, Read wrote a preface for the revised work.)

With publishing returning to normal once the war ended, new small houses were again starting to sprout, including one, the Porcupine Press, with a declared interest in prickly politics. *William Godwin: A Biographical Study* appeared under its imprint late in 1946. In the first days of 1947 it was reviewed enthusiastically in the *Daily Telegraph* by Harold Nicolson, who praised it in unambiguous terms as "balanced in tone, sympathetic in treatment, and comprehensive in scope. From this direct and sincere study there is much to learn."[9] The other reviewers, including the anonymous one in the *Times Literary Supplement*, seemed to take their cue from Nicolson. The book was a succès d'estime as well as a commercial boost for the author and the fledgling publishing house. Woodcock would write years later that from that point forward he never had difficulty finding publishers or living by his pen. But the main boost must have been to his confidence. In the bargain, it also made Godwin respectable as a free-standing subject, apart from his relationship with Shelley and the others, to the extent that academic writing about Godwin was stimulated for the next two decades. The huge reference *Godwin Criticism: A Synoptic Bibliography* by Burton R. Pollin (University of Toronto, 1967) is ample testimony to just how much more work had been done by that time. Woodcock's biography, like many biographies of forgotten figures, was eventually seen to contain the seed of its own replacement by later, fuller works.

During the war Woodcock had contributed to *The Illiterati*, an arts journal published in California by a group of conscientious objectors including William Everson, the "Brother Antonius" of U.S. poetry. Now the same group had evolved into a small press in Pasadena, the Untide Press, which brought out Woodcock's first substantial collection of poetry, *Imagine the South*. For Woodcock the literary life was trending favourably now. Characteristically, he was quick to become involved intimately with Porcupine Press, editing and writing introductory material to the Porcupine Pamphlets, short classic texts such as Wilde's *The Soul of Man under Socialism* and Shelley's *A Defence of Poetry*, and he made plans with the firm for two further books of his own. The first was *A Hundred Years of Revolution: 1848 and After*, which he edited to mark the centenary of the workers' uprisings across Europe. The other was *The Writer and Politics*, his first collection of essays and articles, a genre of book crucial to the tradition of the independent man or woman of letters, though one often looked down on by others. Woodcock's collection lacked the breadth of Read's *A Coat of Many Colours: Occasional Essays*, which had appeared in 1945, reprinting material from *NOW* and numerous other sources, but it was also more a unified suite of essays and less a scrapbook like Read's.

Woodcock had been interested in the Victorian botanist Henry Bates since age twelve when his father made a Christmas gift of Bates's 1863 work *Naturalist on the Amazons*. Here was his opportunity to share the fruit of his long enthusiasm in an essay. In 1947, a small press actually announced in *NOW* a book it hoped to commission from Woodcock about the works of the American Henry Miller, who had a cult following among anarchists and others; the press never found the money to fulfil the commission, but *The Writer and Politics* includes an essay on Miller, "The Peroxide Saint", that doubtless owes its origin to this unrealized project. Conversely, one sees, in essays on Proudhon and Kropotkin and Orwell (and indeed the one on Bates) the embryos of future Woodcock books, not to mention essays that became Woodcock's standard anthology pieces, including an unusual (for him) exercise in music appreciation, "The English Hymn". The old hymn-writers, he contended, were a sort of spiritual vanguard for "the great missionaries of the nineteenth century who acted as emissaries of the British Empire, the forerunners of trade gin and syphilis, the rifle and the whip."[10]

Perhaps the most remarkable and uncharacteristic quality of the collection is the way it treats high political discourse and discussion of popular culture with the same seriousness, though perhaps it was what connected the two that interested him most. *The Writer and Politics* included the first serious discussion of Graham Greene between hard covers: an essay that had first appeared in *NOW*; Orwell had sent Greene a copy, evoking a letter from Greene to Woodcock, on the letterhead of Eyre & Spottiswoode Publishers, expressing admiration for Woodcock's insight and wisdom. *The Writer and Politics* was also the first book to discuss Orwell seriously at length. Woodcock inscribed a copy "To George Orwell, from George Woodcock, 8th May, 1948", and posted it to Scotland, where Orwell was in a sanitarium being treated for tuberculosis.

That same year, following a dispute with their landlady, the Woodcocks moved to another large room in yet another Victorian merchant's house, this one in Kensal Green. As Woodcock recalled, "It belonged to a painter named Peter Rudland, a small truculent man who suffered from Gargantuan constipation—often four days without

a crap—and behaved intolerably because of this."[11] Later in the year
they moved to a one-room studio in Kensington Church Street—"a
dolls' house studio at the end of a little cobbled yard close to a famous
Church Street *pâtisserie*",[12] in the words of the anarchist writer Derek
Stanford, a former fellow conchy who had worked the land in Cambridge and now lived near the Woodcocks with Muriel Spark. Of the
Woodcocks, according to Stanford, Spark "used to say that he and his
wife must be very much in love for him to be able to write so much
in the cramped quarters of their tiny abode without their strangling
each other."[13] Although not herself a poet, Spark was then the editor
of the *Poetry Review*. The previous year she had given Woodcock "a
pile of books—by people then unknown to me who have since become
my friends and literary familiars—and said, 'You're a Canadian, aren't
you, George? Don't you think it's time you wrote about Canadian
poetry?'"[14] This assignment, he would recall, "was one of the bells that
started me moving homeward."[15]

In 1945–46, just after the end of the war, the Woodcocks had a rare
period apart when Inge accepted an assignment from *Peace News* to
go to Germany as its correspondent. The coming of the peace signalled many changes in their world. In 1947, *NOW* died of natural
causes. A magazine's mere availability was no longer a virtual guaran-
tee of access to the W. H. Smith railway stalls; *NOW*'s circulation
figures began to recede, to a point where they could no longer recoup
the production costs. As for other possible sources of revenue, the
periodical carried only exchange advertising, possibly on principle, certainly because it did not appear with such regularity to merit paid
adverts from publishers.

Woodcock first thought *NOW* might be saved if he could raise a
large endowment and use interest on the capital in perpetuity.
Response to the scheme was weak, though Orwell, after first begging
off, saying that he had only ten pounds on hand, later sent five pounds
anyway. With that contribution came something more valuable: advice. Orwell believed that *NOW*'s time had passed, since it was still
dealing with ideological and literary echoes of the 1930s; these had
continued to pass current during the war, which was in a sense the
outcome of the thirties and their cure; but an entirely new set of

circumstances now obtained. Herbert Read was more or less in agreement. In a way, Woodcock's situation was analogous to that faced
earlier by his friend Dwight Macdonald in New York, when, at a similar turning-point in the history of public discourse, he had *started* a
partly anarchist journal, "breaking away from *Partisan Review* to found
his own journal, *Politics*, [thereby doing] something altogether splendid and moving, in getting to clear new moral ground, away from
Leninism, Trotskyism, the usual hates and polemics of the left."[16]

Another reason for letting *NOW* die a dignified death was that
Woodcock, with the success of the Godwin book behind him, was
attempting to complete the transformation from poet-pamphleteer to
serious literary historian, biographer and critic. His next project, a life
of the Restoration playwright Aphra Behn, was completed in the
summer of 1947, at the same time as he was getting out the final (and
seventy-two-page) issue of *NOW*, which is dated July-August of that
year. At the time, Behn (1640–1689) must have been as marginal as
Godwin, though Virginia Woolf's praise of her in *A Room of One's
Own* in 1929 (two years after a monograph on the subject by Woolf's
friend Vita Sackville-West) was still ringing in the public's ears. The
women had asserted that Behn was to be revered partly because she
was the first Englishwoman to make a profession of writing. Modern
feminist scholarship has torn apart this claim without diminishing—
indeed, while elevating even higher—Behn's status as an early female
author. In any event, Woodcock considered himself a feminist, as the
term was then used, as a noun without gender; in his private writings
more than in his public ones, and in his personal relationships, he
remained faithful to this brand of pre-war feminism, writing in his
last years, "We all, I like to believe, become in feeling and thought
more androgyne, approaching the condition of the angels."[17] Simply
in the light of such coeducational feminism, still less in his subject's
sheer obscurity, he was "regarded as highly eccentric to spend my time
on Aphra Behn."[18] The value of *The Incomparable Aphra* (a real 1940s
title, that; for the 1990 reprint, he changed it to *The English Sappho*)
is not only that it broke a lot of ground but that by doing so it helped
to chart some of the changes that Behn's reputation has undergone.

Curiously enough, the best documented part of Behn's career are
the days when she was an English spy in the Low Countries. Governments and politicians keep records. Friends don't always feel the same
compulsion. So while there are many mentions of her at the height

of her theatrical fame, and tributes from such people as Dryden, there is precious little hard information. The carefully extracted pith is that she was born Aphra Johnson near Canterbury and grew up in a middle-class Royalist household during the Civil Wars and the Commonwealth. In 1663, her foster parents took her with them on a journey to Surinam. When she returned in 1658, "the Cromwellian dictatorship was still unchallenged, and the iron rule of the Saints and Major-generals was absolute",[19] in Woodcock's unminced words. Her secret mission to the Netherlands coincided with the Great Fire of 1666. She returned "poor and in debt, to a London where ... great acres of ruins greeted her with sights more strange than the jungles of Surinam".[20] She spent time in prison for debt, as later she would do for libel. Then, by now a widow (her husband having died in the Plague) and still pressed for money, she turned to writing, as one might turn to crime. She wrote in every conceivable form and was admired mainly for her verses, but most of her energy, and it was remarkable, went into the stage (though her novel *Oroonoko* is her best-known work among modern readers).

With Charles II back on the throne, the theatres were reopened, and females were allowed to perform; Nell Gwynn herself appeared in some of Behn's plays. She was true to her upbringing in that she wrote as a Tory, but ultimately that fact only exaggerated the distortions about her, though these were motivated by other passions. "No one who reads Aphra Behn's poems and plays can fail to be impressed by her continual preoccupation with love," Woodcock wrote, adding rather quaintly: "And, indeed, it was as an erotic writer and as a reputed adept in the art of love, that she was celebrated in her own age and has been judged by posterity, finding on these grounds approval or rejection according to the tastes of the critics."[21] That is to say, male Whigs were quick to condemn her as a bawd, in her life and in her writings alike. In truth, there was just barely enough erotic content in her works to let the Victorians, for instance, damn her even more, but never enough to satisfy the curiosity of those who sought her out in more liberal times.

On close examination, Woodcock would conclude, "there is a sense of dignity and proportion in all Aphra Behn's work, and a hatred of extremes of behaviour, that make it unlikely that she was ever addicted to immoderation in her style of life."[22] The romantic side of her existence seems fairly tragic in fact. Her closest male friend was John

Hoyle, a lawyer who was homosexual; they appeared to have hurt each other deeply.

The book was published by Boardman, where Woodcock's poet friend Louis Adeane was a reader. Although a small firm, Boardman was at least commercially minded, and its books were automatically co-published in the United States, at least in token fashion. Both Boardman and Woodcock were buoyed by the relative success of the book, and they decided that their next project together should be rather more ambitious—a full-scale biography of Kropotkin, about whom little was available in the English language. One reason for this was that most of the research material was in Russian. Such was Woodcock's dilemma when, at the Freedom Press bookshop, he chanced to met Ivan Avaku-movic, a Serbian refugee from Yugoslavia who had been educated at Oxford and whose father was a former diplomat. Avakumovic's knowl-edge of Russian was excellent. Woodcock quickly persuaded him to collaborate on Kropotkin, and they perfected a system of collaboration that would serve them again in the future, when both ended up teaching at the University of British Columbia: Avakumovic doing the translations into English and Woodcock drafting the chapters for Avakumovic to comment on. *The Anarchist Prince: A Biographical Study of Peter Kropotkin* was the last book Woodcock wrote in England. By the time it was published, in 1950, the Woodcocks had immigrated to Canada, to the amusement, scepticism, faint good wishes and, most of all, the bewilderment of their friends and colleagues.

Why the Woodcocks decided to go to Canada is in some ways the most important question to be raised in this book, yet it is also the one whose answer is the most complicated and elusive. Woodcock had gradually withdrawn from the anarchist movement, yet the break-through into the first rank of literary London had eluded him. Per-haps he wanted to put physical distance between himself and Marie Louise Berneri. Perhaps others wished that as well. Certainly he was tired of the urban life that seemed so alluring when it was new to him, as a young clerk. Also, he hoped—indeed, in conversations with Vernon Richards, and no doubt others as well, had said flatly—that in Canada he could tap into a new vein of his own creativity and devote himself to fiction and poetry exclusively. Certainly it's significant that he chose as his destination the westernmost shore of Canada, much farther in-country than Arthur Woodcock had penetrated, either symbolically or literally. And, then, too, there is a sense in which the decision to homestead in Canada was trading in the theoretical study of anarchism for an experiment in actual anarchist living. He had a little taste of agriculture as a CO, had sampled communal life and had written on both these subjects, as well as on the constant themes of collective decentralization and individual Tolstoyean simplicity. Now, in Canada, perhaps, he would be acting on these abstract principles, putting his body where previously only his intellect had been. In any case, it is clear from his correspondence that the die was cast as early as 1947 and that by the turn of 1948 the formalities were under way.

As for *how* the idea came to them, that is a more straightforward matter. During the last days of *NOW*, in 1947, George met, through Freedom Press, a young veteran, Doug Worthington, who had become a pacifist-anarchist. Canadian-born, Worthington was teaching at a London free school named Burgess Hill, and became one of the people who would see the Woodcocks for evenings of pub-crawling. He was planning to return home and, knowing of how displaced and rootless the Woodcocks felt, suggested that they join him there when he returned. As Worthington recalled in 1994: "They wanted to move out of England. I said, 'Why not come to Canada and come to the best part, which is Victoria?'"[23]

Woodcock told me that he had first claimed his birthright to a Canadian passport in 1939, at the start of the war. To people seeking out negative interpretations, this could suggest that he had it in mind to emigrate sooner—to bolt for the duration, and beyond, as Auden did, to his eternal discredit. Woodcock may have misremembered the date and the circumstances, or it may be that in 1947 he had only to renew a passport that had expired. In any event, he seems to have availed himself of the no doubt gratis assistance of his friend Roy Fuller, the poet-solicitor, as guarantor, for Fuller reports in a letter in the first few days of 1947 that he has returned the completed forms as asked, joking that the unattractiveness of the passport photograph was the only thing that could keep the Canadians from admitting him. In a subsequent letter, a little more than a week later, Fuller is reassured to hear that Woodcock's passport has arrived.

With his penchant for secrecy, born of his need to distance himself emotionally from his mother and encouraged by his wartime brushes with authority, Woodcock was again leading a kind of double life, carrying on his literary and journalistic work as though nothing was out of the ordinary, all the while preparing himself and Inge for the wrenching change that would be the central dividing-line of their lives.

Much else remained to be done. In the eyes of the law, Inge was still Mrs Roskelly. This was resolved at the end of November 1948 when she received her decree absolute from the High Court, indicating the marriage "be dissolved by reason that the Respondent had been guilty of adultery with George Woodcock, the Co-Respondent".[24] Now the Woodcocks could marry and Mrs Woodcock could accompany her husband as the spouse of a returning native-born Canadian.

If this was a period of intensive work for Woodcock, as his files indicate, it must also have been a time of intense melancholy. Other people were leaving England, too, for their own, different reasons. The young poet Denise Levertov, who had been taken up by Woodcock, Read and others, departed for America in 1947, when she was still only twenty-three. George took Inge on what he hoped would be a nostalgic trip to Marlow and other boyhood sites, but time had changed the physical surroundings and his relatives were still unforgiving of his pacifism. The couple also returned more than once to France and other parts of Europe, staying for a time in Paris with Marie Louise's younger sister, Giliane, but they found the atmosphere oppressive. There was no past now, only a future—though, as events developed, they were entering a more peripatetic style of living than any they had known in England.

The Furness Line, with offices in the City, was one of a number of steamship companies operating freighters between Britain and Canada that also carried a limited number of passengers. Early in 1949, Woodcock purchased passage for himself and Inge on a vessel departing Liverpool for St John's and Halifax in April. He also purchased railway tickets to take them across Canada to Victoria. The Woodcocks packed only a few books and some clothing, using two old steamer trunks that Arthur Woodcock had carried on his quixotic journey to Canada half a century earlier. Most of the other books went to second-hand dealers; those remaining were given to friends such as Derek Savage. Fuller took the furniture. There were soulful goodbyes exchanged with Spark, Tambimuttu, Symons and many others, perhaps especially Marie Louise. To their everlasting sorrow, they were unable to travel to the tip of Scotland to see Orwell one more time.

With their possessions now reduced to the minimum, the Woodcocks spent their last night in the Kensington Church Street studio.
The next evening they stayed over with Louis Adeane before catching
the boat train to Liverpool. After settling their debts and purchasing
their fares, the Woodcocks had $750 in cash, but Dwight Macdonald
in New York had offered to lend them a thousand, which he would
have waiting for them in Victoria. Special Branch were waiting at the
quay in Liverpool to scrutinize every object and piece of printed matter they were taking with them, though logic would suggest that relief
and not anxiety should have been the police attitude towards Woodcock's departure. The North Atlantic was still rough at that time of
year, and all the passengers except Woodcock became ill to one extent
or another. He ate heartily, took in the sea air, and relaxed by reading
Henry Mayhew's *London Labour and the London Poor*, a going-away
gift from a friend. In time, the vessel put in at St John's, Newfoundland, a place then in the news. In Elizabethan times, the island had
become Britain's first colony. But only a fortnight before the Woodcocks landed, the Newfoundlanders, in their second referendum on the
subject, had voted by a narrow margin (52 to 48 per cent) to enter
Confederation rather than become a dominion in their own right. His
freelance survival instincts still sharp, Woodcock collected information
for an article on Newfoundland that appeared later that year in the
New Statesman and Nation. The ship then put in at Halifax and lay at
quarantine in the harbour over the night of 13 April.

That night Woodcock had a dream. He was lying alone in an empty
room when an unidentified male voice informed him that Marie
Louise was dead. Not, at the time, one to put much faith in dreams,
he dismissed it. The Woodcocks boarded the transcontinental train
for the five-day journey across Canada, including the parts that Arthur
Woodcock had trod and those he had only dreamed of treading. At
Vancouver, they caught the ferry for Victoria. There a cablegramme
awaited them, with the news that Marie Louise had died unexpect-
edly of heart failure.

Even when he began to feel at home in Canada and would distract
himself with forty years of projects both literary and charitable,
conducted in an atmosphere of self-sufficient marital harmony and
partnership, Woodcock would never cease to feel the pang of grief.
All the more reason, therefore, not to look back.

6 BLACKLISTED

THROUGH THE WINDOWS of the Canadian Pacific Railway, the Wood-cocks found that "the east of Canada [was] a bit dreary, the Prairies nearly, though not quite so monotonous as people had warned us, but the Rockies were magnificent, and British Columbia is a green and restful land."[1]

True to his word, their London acquaintance Doug Worthington had paved the couple's way in Victoria, finding them temporary accommodation at his brother's flat on Oscar Street. After about a week, they moved to a twenty-acre parcel Worthington owned in Sooke, a village twenty-three miles southeast of the city. The local city directory for 1950 lists Sooke as having 399 residents, most of them loggers and fishermen, a few farmers. When the enumerator for the directory called on the Woodcocks, George straight-facedly gave his occupation "sign wrtr",[2] feeling perhaps that lettering was the only type of writing considered legitimate by his neighbours.

Worthington's property "was just brown land"[3] but it fronted Church Road and was close to such amenities as existed, including the post office presided over by A. F. Brownsey, next door to Doug Brownsey's general store. Worthington would recall:

> George and Inge came out and looked it over out there, and they made a deal with the fellow next door, Ronny France, who had originally bought the acreage from the Helgesens, the original pioneers there. And they rented an old trailer from Ronny. I cut off a half-acre of my place and we arranged a deal with them that they could have that. I gave

them a hand and they built a cottage [now 2271 Church Road] on the half-acre. They set up ... a wood stove and all the country-living stuff ... At the time George had no income at all. They were very much church-mouse poor, and he did the digging out of the foundation and all that by hand ... They got an old bricklayer to build the brick chimney for them, and the rest of it we built between us with a little bit of my help and most of their labour. They set in fairly comfortably.[4]

In a letter to friends written a month after getting off the ship, Woodcock described himself and Inge

sweating our guts out under the summer sun, trying to clear [the land] and lick it into a state for cultivation ... At times there seeps through rusticating consciousness the feeling that we are not made to be farmers, and I have a feeling that the time of the summer will see us stealing down to the fleshpots of California. Not that the fleshpots here are so very bad, with plenty of food, and salmon in the village at 35 cents a pound, beef, if you buy it in bulk from the farmers at 25 cents ...

But, he went on,

Apart from our digging and ploughing, we have been very idle. I've written a few journalistic articles, Inge has so far done no painting at all. But soon I hope to get down really thoroughly to my book of essays on English writers.[5]

In fact, Woodcock was never idle. The essay collection of which he wrote became instead a series of talks for CBC Radio in Vancouver. They were written at about the same time that he was coming to the end of the Kropotkin biography with Avakumovic. Woodcock suggested, and Avakumovic agreed, that it would be "a nice gesture at this time for us to dedicate the book to Marie Louise, as a disciple of Kropotkin."[6] As Woodcock finished off old obligations, he began discovering a place for himself as a writer within the Canadian context. When he had been in the country only six weeks—many months before Boardman published both the Kropotkin biography and *The Paradox of Oscar Wilde* and Grey Walls Press brought out Woodcock's edition of *The Letters of Charles Lamb*—he was writing to a distinguished Canadian poet, Earle Birney of the University of British

Columbia, using a tone of begging adulation that he would come to know so well in future years from letters he himself received from young writers.

Dear Mr Birney,

You may not know me by name, but, if not, I introduce myself as a friend of [the English poet] Howard Sergeant, and a Canadian-born English poet and biographer. You may possibly have seen my articles and poems in English and American periodicals, and notices of some of my books, such as my biographical studies of William Godwin and Aphra Behn.

I have just returned to Canada, and intend to live for some time in British Columbia. I am very anxious to get some idea of the "literary scene" in Canada, and, as you are the Canadian author whose work and name are most familiar to me, I am writing to ask whether you could give me some idea of what is going on in writing and the other arts at the present time, and also recommend to me any periodicals which would give me an idea of the situation of Canadian writing, both in the West and in French Canada. I should also be very pleased to make your acquaintance at some time which might be mutually convenient to us.[7]

Even though he was busily finishing his novel *Turvey*, Birney took time to reply at length. He told Woodcock of various writers living in the province, such as Roderick Haig-Brown, Dorothy Livesay and Malcolm Lowry, and he apprised him of the existence of the country's few literary magazines, *Contemporary Verse* in Vancouver, *Here & Now* in Toronto and *Northern Review* in Montreal. (Woodcock moved so quickly that he had a review, of the American poet Allen Tate, in *Northern Review*'s October–November issue.) Birney also warned the newcomer away from the Canadian Authors' Association unless he was interested in passing an evening with persons who had difficulty accepting Browning and certainly hadn't yet come to terms with Swinburne. And he proposed a meeting as soon as time allowed. When Birney visited shortly afterwards he found Woodcock "living off wild berries and ... turnips and advances on radio scripts ... full of bushed exuberance, spilling over with other writers' talk. I was able to suggest further CBC contacts for him ..."[8] A long friendship was born.

Woodcock soon threw himself into local politics, though he found the process rough going. In June he wrote to Avakumovic:

> Most of this letter has been taken up with the Old Man [Kropotkin], and I have therefore little room to reply to your exhortations and suggestions. Indeed, I am not lost to the revolution, though the workers here, being mostly small farmers who do casual wage work to eke out, are as impermeable as most prosperous peasants. We tried to do some anti-voting propaganda among them in connection with the present elections, but it did not get very far. However, they at least know what mutual aid is, and are very helpful to each other and even to strangers in all kinds of practical ways. There may be a hope in that.[9]

Worthington would recall that "George objected to paying the hospital insurance at that time. He said it was an imposition, and he was taken to court and they had a foofaraw in Victoria about it. I don't know if he ever paid it or not. He'd stood up for his rights and got some publicity for it."[10]

By August, the Woodcocks were making plans to begin exploring the province methodically, beginning with visits to the Doukhobor community at Hilliers and to a number of Native reserves. They thought they might like to visit the Pacific U.S. as well, even though "reports of the witch hunts which have been brought by one or two visiting Californians are truly hair-raising, and we wonder whether we shall escape the stake and faggots."[11] Most of all, they longed for an extended period in Paris, and "have already decided to try to return to live in France in less than three years."[12] This revelation comes in a letter to Avakumovic, which is full of other important nuggets, too. It reveals Woodcock working on what would be yet another discarded novel, for example. It also shows him "turning over in my mind"[13] a history of the libertarian tradition that Avakumovic had suggested to him back in London, a project that would finally surface more than a dozen years later as *Anarchism: A History of Libertarian Ideas and Movements*, which he proposes to dedicate to Avakumovic (but never did). In this same letter, Woodcock responds to Avakumovic's report that Vernon Richards of Freedom Press had received the Kropotkin biography negatively:

> So he thought we were secretive about the Kropotkin book? I don't really know what he means, since everybody knew we were writing it,

and writers don't usually run about reading their half-written chapters to all their long-suffering friends. I hope this remark did not spring from some theory that "the comrades" should have a chance of looking over books which may affect the "movement", though I fear it probably did. Such remarks at times make me despair of anarchism ever growing out of its short pants and becoming, in England at least, a *real* movement and not just a sect.[14]

Earle Birney bought one of the squatters' shacks on the beach at Dollarton near Vancouver, a community of about forty such places, including the one occupied by Malcolm Lowry. He did so with the intention of getting the Woodcocks to move there rent-free in exchange for minor repairs. (Woodcock was able to earn some cash by hiring himself out for small jobs of carpentry, supplementing his take from the sale of beans and other vegetables. During the holiday season, he went door to door hawking Christmas trees he had harvested himself.) But though they decided that they wanted to live on the water, the Woodcocks chose to remain on Vancouver Island instead of accepting Birney's offer.

At UBC meanwhile, Birney was "sounding out the English Department, which was looking far and wide for new staff, to discover if Woodcock could get a part-time teaching position."[15] Before he could hire Woodcock, however, the department head, Garnett Sedgewick, died suddenly; he was succeeded by Roy Daniells, who, Birney would contend, "had little experience to help him understand a self-made biographer and philosophical anarchist like Woodcock and, in any case, he wouldn't hire anybody who did not have a B.A."[16] But Birney was able to arrange for Woodcock to deliver some guest lectures. The university issued these as a booklet entitled *British Poetry Today*: the first Canadian imprint on what would be Woodcock's long shelf of books, booklets and pamphlets.

The Kropotkin biography was going well. Reviews were long and friendly, sales were surprisingly brisk and there were many inquiries from translators and foreign publishers. The *Times Literary Supplement* praised it in a front-page review that spilled over onto a second page. Like all *TLS* reviews in that era, it was unsigned, but Woodcock later learned the writer's identity: Isaiah Berlin, the Russian-born liberal historian. "I'm sure this is a review which really will bring the sales up with a real rush", Woodcock wrote to his co-author. "But why do you give all the credit and congratulations to me? Congratulations to you, without whose energy, Russian scholarship, ideas on construction and chapter divisions, sense of proportion and perpetual criticisms of my excesses in verbiage and thought we should certainly have never got more than an inch in that venerable paper's columns!"[17] Perhaps Woodcock saw a problem looming. They would again work together, notably in the 1960s on their study of *The Doukhobors*, and Avakumovic would make an important contribution to Woodcock's *Festschrift* in the late 1970s. After that, however, the relationship cooled. Woodcock believed that Avakumovic became jealous of his larger readership and greater recognition; Avakumovic declined to be interviewed for this biography.

In any case, Woodcock had reason to be optimistic. He was still attempting to write fiction while Inge was seriously painting for the first time in years. He thought, wisely, that he would capitalize on his rapidly solidifying reputation as a biographer. At the same time, he would move into another genre entirely, the travel narrative, a form that could be moulded to fit his and Inge's ambitious travelling plans and one for which a substantial audience existed back in Britain. Accordingly, in October 1950 he applied to the John Simon Guggenheim Memorial Foundation in the U.S. with a proposal for a biography of the nineteenth-century French anarchist Pierre-Joseph Proudhon. If awarded the grant, he would go to France in the spring to conduct research. Earle Birney, Herbert Read and Dwight Macdonald wrote letters of reference, and Woodcock sat back and waited —though not idly, of course. For by then he had already conceived of his first book *about* Canada, the one that would be published as *Ravens and Prophets: An Account of Journeys in British Columbia, Alberta and Southern Alaska*. He had been accumulating material for some time, perfecting the method he would use in later travel books: writing up rough notes day by day and later reworking them into a coherent whole.

David Koven was a San Francisco anarchist, an electrician by trade, who had become a self-taught writer and painter. He was married to a fellow anarchist with the splendid name Audrey Goodfriend. The two of them drove up to Sooke to visit during the Woodcocks' first Canadian summer, and immediately formed a bond with them based on "our shared *Weltanschauung*."[18] The Woodcocks did not possess an automobile (and only Mrs Woodcock was a licensed driver). So the following year Koven and Goodfriend returned and accompanied the Woodcocks on a complicated trip around the northernmost part of the province. One of their stops was at Kitsiookla, where a short-lived intentional community had been established recently by Fred Brown, a direct descendant of John Brown, the martyred American abolitionist. Brown "took us to visit some of the Native American villages where the old buildings and totem poles were still intact",[19] Koven would recall. "The joy of the trip was enhanced by the fact that George and Inge were so knowledgeable, good humoured, and comradely."[20] In fact, *Ravens and Prophets* drew scattered protests after its publication in 1952. The journeys Woodcock described were ones of discovery, undertaken for the purpose of getting to know his own country. He was new to the process, and to the geography, and although he did an ambitious amount of reading and research beforehand, as would be his custom, he did, in his inexperience and naïvety, make some errors of fact and judgement in this first instance.

As he travelled in the north, Woodcock was seized with the idea of also writing a book on Native art of the West Coast. Like so many of his projects, this one would have a long gestation period, finally appearing in print in 1977 as *Peoples of the Coast: The Indians of the Pacific Northwest.*

Always a prodigious correspondent, Woodcock left a sort of shadow commentary on these expeditions in his letters, particularly those to Herbert Read, which were published in 1982 as a limited edition entitled *Letters from Sooke.* In the preface, Woodcock writes:

> Looking back over my part of this correspondence, I am partly amused and partly embarrassed by the mingled cockiness and naivety that characterized many of my statements. I was eager to learn, yet overwilling to make judgments. To me now, the views I expressed on Sooke and its people in the last of my letters seem facile. Yet then I willingly went to live in Sooke, and now, with greater knowledge of myself and British Columbia, I would not think of doing so. Perhaps the foolhardiness or courage that took me there and the willingness to make quick judgments were part of the same adventurousness which later spent itself in the long travels that result in my books on Latin America, on Asia, on Oceania.
>
> Certainly by the time I came to write those books I had learnt enough—and learnt it largely in those years at Sooke—not to be hasty

with opinions, and not to make rash remarks like those contained in the postscript to my first letter, in which I tell Read that I have encountered the Kwakiutl Indians, and then go on to give what purports to be a description of their way of life. By that time we had been a bare three months in Canada, and though we had indeed got as far as Campbell River, any contact we may have made with the Kwakiutl people must have been slight, and almost certainly I was confusing them with the Cowichan, whom we had encountered. Even in talking of the Cowichan, I was making the kind of judgment by first impression which I later learnt to distrust; indeed, I saw everything I mentioned in the letters, but what I did not see—I later came to realize—was perhaps more important than the deceptive appearance of a people in disintegration. I hope that in my more recent writings on the Coast Indians, and particularly in *Peoples of the Coast*, I have made up for the hasty assumptions ...[21]

When, in 1993, *Ravens and Prophets* was reissued by a B.C. firm, the author, for the only time in his career, acquiesced to expurgation; following suggestions made by Charles Lillard, the editor of the new edition, and Dick Morriss, its publisher, he agreed to drop several references to Natives and their cultures.

Returning from the journeys described in *Ravens and Prophets*, the Woodcocks sold their cabin at Sooke in order to help finance extended travels into the forty-eight States. In the meantime, they accepted the loan of a primitive cottage at Saseenos, on Sooke Basin. After living there approximately a month, they received the surprising news that Woodcock's application for a Guggenheim grant had been approved. He would receive $3,000 to support twelve months' work on the biography of Proudhon. The bulk of the research lay in France, but now they could afford to proceed there at leisure. They penetrated the American border without incident and crossed the United States by bus. In New York, they stayed with Dwight and Nancy Macdonald before taking ship to France. For a month they lived in a small street in the Latin Quarter, at the Hotel du Lys, which offered, Woodcock would remember with Orwellian delight in the austerity, "minimal comfort, washing at one's basin and sharing the can on the landing."[22]

Then they went to Austria and spent two months in a green wooden farmhouse in the mountain village of Brand, above Blundenz. From there it was back to Paris and various other cheap hotels. The research was exhausting but extraordinarily productive.

Proudhon (1809–1865) was a pamphleteer and rabble-rouser and the first person to call himself an anarchist in the philosophical sense. Writing his life in the early 1950s, when interest in radical thinking appeared to be at its lowest point, proved an unrewarding task materially, though Woodcock had the pleasure of working with primary documents, which had not been possible in the case of either Godwin or Kropotkin. Still, the manuscript when completed was rejected several times, and the book finally appeared only in 1956 and then through the good offices of Herbert Read at Routledge Kegan Paul.

Woodcock knew that his quarry had kept a diary, because an extract had appeared in an obscure magazine about 1910, and at length he discovered its whereabouts. Along with a few relics, such as Proudhon's ink-pot and spectacles, the diary was in the possession of the only surviving grandchild, who also owned the famous portrait by Courbet. Woodcock recalled how "on a table underneath it our hostess lay out the twelve worn thick black notebooks we had come to see, and every day we worked there Proudhon's face glowed with ironic benignity."[23]

Once published with such difficulty, the biography quickly passed out of print and wasn't revived except for a transient paperback in 1972. Insofar as the general audience is concerned, the reissue of 1988 was virtually a new work, particularly since it contained a great deal of fresh material, for it came at a time when much more work had been done on Proudhon by others. By that stage, for example, the diaries had been published in toto, and even the portrait had been hung for public inspection in the Musée du Petit Palais in Paris. Yet in another sense Proudhon had gone out of vogue once more, this time because he seemed an old-fashioned agrarian radical, out of step with the problems imposed by internationalism and technology. It is largely his place in the agrarian tradition, however, that concerned Woodcock.

Proudhon grew up in Besançon, where he knew the famous utopian Charles Fourier. He was of near-peasant stock and always remembered the humiliation of wearing *sabots* to school when others wore boots or shoes. He was intended for one of the trades. In an era when the

back shops of newspapers were schools for autodidacts, he became
first a printer's devil and then a compositor and taught himself Latin,
Greek and Hebrew—and became a radical, "an anti-utopian socialist", in Woodcock's words, "who shares at least equally with Marx the
distinction of having realised the significance of the working class as
an independent social force."[24] For the rest of his life he was an ink-
stained wretch, writing for, or running, one struggling publication
after another, in the manner of William Cobbett and so many others.
His view that the state was an evil intrusion blocking the individual's
path to fulfilment was built up from the ideas of Shelley and Godwin. It found expression in Proudhon's famous 1840 book *What Is
Property?*, which made "Property is theft" a catch-phrase. What he
meant was that exploitative rents and such were a form of theft; he
had nothing against small freeholders, who were in fact basic to the
paradisal community he envisioned.

He was a personage with more influence on his successors than on
his contemporaries. Bakunin and Kropotkin both hailed him as a trail-
blazer, for example. As Woodcock painted him, he seems a sympathetic figure to modern eyes, idealistic in a practical hard-working way
and genuinely concerned with the betterment of his fellow humans.
A streak of anti-feminism (but not misogyny) is the only disagreeable
trait and even that did not prevent his friendship with the pioneer
feminist Flora Tristan. It speaks well of him that he also knew and
liked George Sand, received a courtesy call from Tolstoy and couldn't
get along with Marx.

Some of the biography, like some of the subject's life, is involved
with matters once revolutionary but now accepted as commonplace.
For example, he was concerned with the sort of mutualism whose
direct descendant is nothing more dangerous than the nearest credit
union or building society. Yet he retains a wider interest because he
witnessed some of the larger events of the day, including the Paris
revolution of 1848 and the coup that resulted in the Second Empire
in 1851. It was by criticizing Napoleon III that he contracted two
occupational diseases: imprisonment (he wrote some of his important
work in a cell) and exile (he later fled to Belgium). The way his
opinions isolated him, as Woodcock suggests, tended to make him
appear less distinct than he might have otherwise, even to those
who share his general outlook. The fact that Proudhon wrote a variety of convoluted French political prose that is not easily translated is

perhaps an even bigger factor in his comparative lack of fame, though his obscurity seems to come and go. Woodcock's book remains probably the only non-technical one on the subject; Woodcock himself always considered it to be intrinsically the most successful of his lives of the great anarchists.

In autumn 1951, research completed, the Woodcocks took a freighter to Quebec City and travelled to California, again by bus, crossing the border once more without difficulties. In San Francisco, they called on Kenneth Rexroth, the autodidact man of letters and outrageous mythomane ("George, when I was a young man in Chicago, selling dogs for sexual purposes").[25] They also visited David Koven and Audrey Goodfriend, who

> took them to one of the frequent fund-raising *festas* that our Italian anarchist comrades had during the year. I can still hear George comment how different this jolly, musical, personal, friendly, dancing, drinking fund-raiser was from the formal, subdued anarchist parties he had attended in England.[26]

One of the Italian-American comrades, Joe Rainer, invited the couple to use a house he owned in the redwood country of the Russian River, near Camp Meeker, the former place of internment for COs. In six months there, Woodcock turned the Proudhon research into a manuscript. Another anarchist couple, John and Elvira Vattuone, who raised chickens nearby, would stop round and give the Woodcocks a week's worth of free fowl. With the literary labour done and autumn weather approaching, the Woodcocks returned to B.C. and the borrowed cabin at Saseenos to determine what their next move would be. "We surprised even ourselves by deciding there was nowhere else than Canada for settlement."[27]

Specifically, they decided that they wanted to live on the water's edge. Doug Worthington would recall that "an old Swiss guy, a real character, offered them a cheap lot on the waterfront down by Whiffen Spit"[28] on a cliff overlooking Sooke Harbour above the Juan de Fuca Strait. Woodcock negotiated a deal involving a little cash plus a great deal of labour in kind. This time they put up a more ambitious structure, in the Swiss chalet style. But as Worthington recalled: "With the fog and all, it's miserable there, and they didn't stay too long."[29] Deciding that in any event it was impossible for them to survive financially on Vancouver Island, they soon sold the chalet to a closeted lesbian couple and accepted an invitation from Jack Shadbolt, the painter, and his wife Doris Shadbolt, the art historian, to use a cabin located on their property on what was then the thinly settled side of Burnaby Mountain.

The Woodcocks met the Shadbolts at a party one snowy night at Earle Birney's (possibly the same occasion on which Woodcock learned of Orwell's death). They had been brought along by Bill McConnell, a young lawyer and writer, the linchpin of a local writers' group that included Dorothy Livesay. The two couples had travelled together on some of the trips described in *Ravens and Prophets*, particularly the one that took in Barkerville and Wells, two as-yet-unrediscovered gold-rush towns, the first from the 1860s, the second from the 1930s. Now the Woodcocks "were talking about a place to live ...," Jack Shadbolt recalled, and "we mentioned this cabin, and somehow or another they thought this might be just the thing."[30] The cabin, or shack, barely visible through the trees from the Shadbolts' window, measured only about eight by ten feet and had neither electricity nor running water, but the Shadbolts (they can't be called the landlords, as no rent was involved) allowed them to run a power line and a water hose from their place. Woodcock built bunk-beds. Each couple had privacy but could still intermingle socially. Sometimes the Woodcocks would invite the Shadbolts to dinner, a few yards from home. Once, during a particularly severe cold snap, when the cabin's smelly little kerosene stove proved unequal to the task, the Woodcocks had to move into the big house, sleeping on the floor in their clothes. They appeared to thrive on such inconveniences. "They seemed very happy", Doris Shadbolt recalled. "It was a great time all around".[31]

The Woodcocks, however, seemed never content for long in one of their miniature homemade utopias. What they wished, in fact, was a paradise to use as a base camp, from which to venture out on strenuous journeys, and retreat back to when they needed to recuperate and turn their travelling to good account. So in the autumn of 1954 they set off on a three-month trip through Mexico, spending more than half that time in San Miguel de Allende, which was then still relatively untouched by tourism, and penetrating as far south as Oaxaca. They returned to the Shadbolts' cabin to winter.

Woodcock, who seemed able to write anywhere he could find a little quiet, was tireless in proposing ideas to editors, compliant with their wishes when they accepted and never bitter when they did not. The trip to Mexico had been preceded by—was, to some extent perhaps, the urgent result of—Woodcock's immersive study in Mexican history and culture. Its ultimate by-product was his next book, *To the City of the Dead: An Account of Travels in Mexico*, which Faber and Faber published in 1957. This was the beginning of a long, productive relationship with that firm, which encouraged him to build renown as a writer of travel narratives. Now he was busy mining his reading and his note-taking for articles. Swallowing his distaste, he queried Kingsley Martin at the *New Statesman and Nation* about a so-called letter from Mexico and other Latin destinations; Woodcock would continue to query him for the next couple of years, though Martin was always more discouraging than not. Woodcock's relations with what, in his time, had been the English literary establishment were never warm. John Lehmann, the Bloomsberry who was editor of the new *London Magazine*, turned down a suggestion on Dylan Thomas and another on André Gide as a novelist. Yet Woodcock's brand of writing found a congenial home in *History Today*, the slick magazine published by the *Financial Times* of London under the editorship of Peter Quennell and Alan Hodge, both Lehmann-like figures. He sold them pieces on Maximilian (about whom he also attempted to write a play) and on the British Columbia gold rushes. The editors also suggested ideas of their own: a piece on Vancouver, for example, or one on the Oregon Boundary Dispute between the U.S. and Britain in the 1840s. In 1957, Woodcock wrote for *History Today* on the self-righteous American politician William Jennings Bryan. As a rule, Woodcock was not comfortable with Americana even at its most radical; he held a low opinion of Emma Goldman's importance in the anarchist movement, for example, and dismissed the Wobblies as more Marxist than anarchist. Yet one had to support oneself, and Woodcock was already becoming an old pro who would carry off any assignment with aplomb. His many early talks for CBC Radio, for example, included a series on the lives of American First Ladies: a less Woodcockian topic could hardly be imagined.

His increasingly cordial relations with Quennell and Hodge were also atypical. More representative was that between Woodcock and Stephen Spender, who was then editing *Encounter*, supposedly unaware that the journal was being covertly funded by the American CIA. Spender had bought a Woodcock piece about Mexico. On the basis of this recent revival of their acquaintanceship, Woodcock wrote to ask him whether he would be a reference for an application to the Nuffield Research Fellowships. Spender replied that he couldn't recall meeting Woodcock. The applicant replied with the novel face-saving suggestion that Roy Fuller, whom both respected and were respected by, draft a recommendation for Spender to sign, which he did. Woodcock's other references were G. D. H. Cole (who had praised the Godwin and Kropotkin books) and the English writer H. N. Brailsford. (Woodcock received the grant, which financed further travels.) Thanks largely no doubt to Woodcock's strong conciliatory tendencies, all these rough edges were smoothed over eventually. In years to come, for example, Woodcock would contribute to a *Festschrift* for Lehmann, and Spender would appear in *Canadian Literature*.

≈

Woodcock had been sending out feelers in the hope of more work, and friends had been doing the same on his behalf. In August 1954, just after settling comfortably into the idea that Canada would be his future, Woodcock received an offer to teach for the 1954–55 academic year at the University of Washington in Seattle. His title would be assistant professor of English and he would live in the U.S. under what was called an exchange-of-professional-personnel visa. Both parties hoped the experiment would lead to Woodcock becoming a permanent part of the faculty.

Still essentially footloose and unburdened by possessions, the Woodcocks closed the Shadbolts' cabin and set off across the border. Until May 1955, when the term was coming to a close, they lived in the basement of a jerry-built house at 4742 21st N.E., within sight of Lake Washington and walking distance of the campus; the apartment upstairs was occupied by Margaret Duckett, one of Woodcock's colleagues in the English department. Woodcock's most vivid memory of the place was "that the grass around was infested by fleas which got into our heavy piled carpets and into the fur of our then cat Tim, and took a great deal of trouble to expel."[32]

Woodcock's most complex friendship at Washington was with the university's poet-in-residence, Theodore Roethke, an important voice in American poetry in the 1950s, always struggling to expand form and contain madness, and an important influence on writers such as

James Dickey, Seamus Heaney, Ted Hughes, Sylvia Plath and James Wright. Looking back across the years, Woodcock would remember him as

> in general a man of great humanity, yet I have seen him being verbally cruel for little reason, and he loved pricking academic pomposities; his favourite term for pedants was "horse's asses", and in my early days at Washington he introduced one of them to me as "the armpit of the department". I was Ted's kind of man, because I went to the University of Washington as a poet and critic who had never attended a university or taught a class in my life, and in that traumatic situation (I was 41) Ted was a great and understanding support. Dignity? In a way, though he always looked unkempt, rather like a car salesman who has let himself go. But I have also seen him abjectly drunk. He did indeed need emotional reinforcement, and he did feel a great personal inadequacy, which made him somewhat aggressive towards his colleagues, though very gentle with his students.[33]

Woodcock's truest ally was the chair, Robert B. Heilman, the person responsible for bringing him into the fold. Heilman was well satisfied, in that probationary first semester, with his new teacher's performance —and with his contacts. Woodcock not only brought Birney to Seattle to read "David", he also persuaded Herbert Read, who had a lecture engagement at UBC, to make the side-trip there as well. To the outrage of almost everyone in the anarchist movement except Woodcock, who defended him on the grounds of personal liberty, Read had accepted a knighthood from the new monarch, Elizabeth. Woodcock was careful to discreetly remind his American superior of protocol when writing Read to finalize arrangements: "You should direct the letter to 'Sir Herbert Read' and begin with 'Dear Sir Herbert'."[34]

Heilman offered Woodcock a renewable three-year contract beginning September 1955 and the appointment was confirmed by the university. Procedures required that Woodcock then recross the border and apply in writing for an immigration visa. This involved submitting copies of his and Inge's birth certificates (along with a certified translation of hers), copies of documents showing her divorce from Roskelly and her marriage to Woodcock, statements from banks in both countries, and background checks by the Seattle police and the RCMP; the last of these necessitated their being fingerprinted.

The Woodcocks returned to the Shadbolts', where the painter cleared a work-place for Woodcock in a corner of his studio. "George was just as regular as clockwork", Doris Shadbolt would recall. "He'd come down in the morning and you'd hear him typing away."[35] Doris and Inge alternated cooking for the combined household on a weekly basis. They would also, under Inge's leadership, undertake various strenuous projects, such as building a stone retaining wall. According to Jack Shadbolt: "She really worked Doris's butt off, because she'd never stop, she's a demon for work, just can't stop working."[36] While in Seattle, Mrs Woodcock had become interested in Tibetan language and culture, and each afternoon she would break off from whatever else she was doing in order to study.

The American officials in Vancouver asked Woodcock for a copy of his 1944 book *Anarchy or Chaos*, the most ambitious of his Freedom Press publications but also perhaps the one least representative of his actual beliefs over time—it was written, like the notorious *War Commentary* manifesto, at the height of Berneri's influence on him. Woodcock complied, no doubt in the belief that it would further his case to be co-operative. As caprice would have it, though, pointing at random to a page in *Anarchy or Chaos* is almost enough to allow one to visualize the near-apoplectic effect it must have had on the U.S. consulate at the Marine Building on Burrard Street in 1955:

> There remains, then, only one way to a free society. That is by a struggle which will aim not at a political revolution, but at an entire revolution in social and economic relationships in which the state, class and property will be abolished at one and the same time. Thus the anarchist conception of the class struggle differs from the Leninist conception in that it does not envisage or in practice involve the stewardship of any class during a period of transition, but stands for the immediate ending of the social and economic system which involves the division of society into exploiters and exploited and in its place advocates a society where there will be no kind of exploitation and where, therefore, class divisions will be abolished. The only true class struggle is the struggle, not for the replacement of one class of rulers by another, but for the elimination of class itself.[37]

Woodcock sent Heilman a copy of the book, too, suggesting that it be compared to the title essay of *The Writer and Politics*, and "The

Folly of Revolutionary Violence", which had appeared in the *Adelphi* in January 1947 and illustrated that his "change of attitude shown over the years ... is considerable."[38]

Week after week went by without word from the U.S. government. When his own inquiries were ignored, he asked Heilman to write to C. H. Stephan, the U.S. consul at Vancouver. When this brought no satisfaction, Heilman got Henry Schmitz, the president of the university, to write to the consul, pointing out that, as lectures were set to begin on 28 September, a decision was needed soon. Finally, on 12 September, Woodcock received word by telephone that his application had been denied even though it had been concluded that he was not a social revolutionary but an intellectual or philosophical one. The same day Stephan sent him a letter confirming "that you have been found to be inadmissible to the United States and ineligible to receive a visa under the provisions of Section 212 (a) (28) A/B of the Immigration and Nationality Act ..."[39] Woodcock was another victim of cold war politics.

Joseph McCarthy had been censured by his U.S. Senate colleagues in 1954, signalling the beginning of the end of his career as an anti-communist witch-hunter. The so-called red scare, however, was still very much in session. Many communists were sent to prison or driven into hiding, and anyone who held, or once had held, radical views was suspect. Civil servants, teachers, figures in the labour movement and (in the Chinese sense of the word) intellectuals were all harried and harassed, a great many to the point of unemployment, some to the point of suicide or other early death. Insofar as foreigners were concerned, the main instrument of this policy was the Immigration and Nationality Act of 1952, popularly called the McCarran Act; passed at the midway point in the Korean War hysteria, it contained a provision barring those who advocated, whether by writing, publishing or teaching, the economic and political doctrines of what the act called "world Communism". Yet Woodcock's case was far more complicated than the norm. He was being charged not with generalized radical sympathies but with being an anarchist in particular. Section 212 (a), subsection (28) barred "Aliens who are, *or at any time have been* [emphasis added], members of any of the following classes: (A) Aliens who are anarchists; (B) Aliens who advocate or teach or who are members of or are affiliated with any organization that advocates or teaches, opposition to all organized government." This section of the act, incorporated from previous pieces of legislation, harked back to the original red scare, immediately after the First World War, when the young J. Edgar Hoover ensured his future career by deporting Emma Goldman and Alexander Berkman to their native Russia though they were American citizens. From that point forward, anarchists were specifically prohibited from entering the United States. As the anarchists had no friends in power and were misunderstood by the public, the rule had remained in effect, though by 1955 it cannot have been invoked very frequently: its unstated additional purpose, of keeping out European Jews with leftward leanings, had long since been subsumed into other legislation.

Until just a couple of years before his death, Woodcock suspected that he had been betrayed by an American military officer stationed in London during the war who had infiltrated the anarchist movement, probably on behalf of U.S. Army Intelligence, and had befriended Marie Louise Berneri; after the war, this American, who was of Russian ancestry, went back to the States, turning up in New York anarchist circles. Later, however, Woodcock came to a simpler view: that when it became known that he was removing himself to Canada, Scotland Yard (which, after all, had noted his emigration carefully) routinely passed on to the Royal Canadian Mounted Police the file it had built up on him during the time surrounding the anarchist trial of 1945, and that the Mounties in turn had shared the information with the FBI.

Throughout this ordeal, Heilman was a master of diplomacy in dealing with officials and bureaucracy, a master of the art of supportive friendship in his letters to Woodcock. He researched a recent instance in which a candidate being hired by the history department was denied a visa on the grounds of communist affiliations—a matter that was resolved only when the university put pressure on a United States senator to intervene. Woodcock, for his part, responded by one of the most intriguing pieces of writing in his long career: an eleven-page letter addressed to John Foster Dulles, President Eisenhower's secretary of state. In a sense, Woodcock's reaction demonstrated his unfamiliarity with American ways. In Britain, a literary figure of some repute might write to the Home Secretary and expect the letter to find its way into one of the dispatch boxes. The minister, doubtless a public school old boy with an Oxbridge education, might actually read it and respond. In America, however, such a letter probably would not reach the addressee and was likely to fall on deaf ears in any case (as Woodcock would soon learn). Moreover, Woodcock had sent the letter to the wrong arm of the bureaucracy, it being one of the oddities of the U.S. government that final decisions on the admissibility of aliens lies not with the secretary of state but rather with the attorney general. Still, it was a masterful defence.

> The grounds for my appeal against the rejection of my application are as follows:
>
> 1. That I am not and have never been an anarchist in the sense contemplated by United States laws;
> 2. That Consul Stephan's decision was based largely on a book, *Anarchy or Chaos*, which I wrote fourteen years ago and published almost twelve years ago, and whose contentions I have largely abandoned during the past decade;
> 3. That the contention that I "advocate and teach opposition to organised government" is substantially unjustified;
> 4. That I have a clear record, not merely of non-involvement in Communist or Communist-infiltrated movements, but also of direct and emphatic opposition to Communism.[40]

He discoursed on the etymology and subtle changes in the meaning of the word *anarchism*. After discussing his past as a co and his life as a writer, he split hairs with a surgeon's precision, writing,

> I have, it is true, implicitly *rejected* coercive and direct government as a form of political organisation that has failed to produce social harmony; I have also *criticised* governmental institutions and the theories that support them. But I would submit to you that the intellectual rejection or criticism of an institution does not constitute *advocating or teaching opposition* to it, particularly since it is clear that in this context what is meant by the law is *physical* rather than *intellectual* opposition. I would further submit that the right to criticise any person, idea or institution is assured to citizens and aliens alike under the Constitution of the United States.
>
> Today, indeed, it is as a critical *point d'appui* for the consideration of literary and social values, rather than as a possible blue print for action, that I consider the ideas of absolute freedom that lies at the

core of anarchist beliefs, an idea which I believe must be preserved as an ultimate criterion if we are to remain aware of freedom at all. I have long abandoned the idea of influencing other people; the most I hope is that the statement of my views may contribute fruitfully to the flux of thought within society as a whole. As for any attempts to make converts, I am confident that the most rigorous investigation of my record as a teacher would reveal that in the classroom I have done no more than duty to make the minds of my students as receptive as possible to ideas in general; any attempt to implant my own personal theories in their minds I would have considered an unpardonable breach of trust.[41]

As for views that might be found in his published writings,

It is true, indeed, that I have contributed articles and reviews to periodicals edited by anarchists. I have also contributed a far greater quantity of work to periodicals edited by liberals, socialists, Catholics, Democrats, and Republicans[42]

from the *New Republic* to the *New Yorker*, from *Saturday Review* to the *New York Times Book Review*.

The summation was brilliant but much of it must have been over the juries' heads. For good measure, Woodcock also wrote to Lester Pearson, the external affairs minister in Ottawa, whose assistant raised the question with the American embassy but to no avail.

Heilman, who was clearly ashamed of his country's policy in such matters and wrote of his feelings with bitter irony and embarrassment, followed up with his own letter to Dulles's office, while President Schmitz, for his part, met on his own initiative with the Canadian consul in Seattle for a strategy session. As time went on, the cause became more general. Dwight Macdonald, now at the *New Yorker*, and Nancy Macdonald, executive secretary of the Spanish Refugee Aid Inc., became involved themselves and brought in others. There was a considerable infrastructure in place to help accused leftists, and groups with names such as the Workers' Defense Committee (a civil liberties arm of the labour movement) and the American Committee for Cultural Freedom soon became involved, as did the American Civil Liberties Union. At one point, Arthur Schlesinger, the liberal historian at Harvard, and George F. Kennan, America's former ambassador to the Soviet Union, both tried to assist Woodcock. So did Norman Thomas, head of the Socialist Party, who had run for the U.S. presidency in 1928, 1932, 1936, 1940, 1944 and 1948. In a letter to Woodcock, Sidney Hook, the fiercely combative anti-communist yet Marxist philosopher, suggested that the grounds on which Woodcock was being silenced could have been used against Thoreau, Tolstoy and even Jefferson. Much of this activity, not to mention a petition addressed to Dulles, was the work of Woodcock himself, whose organizational skills tended to increase when he was threatened.

Ultimately, the effort failed. The letter to Dulles was referred to Stephan in Vancouver for disposition, and in the first week of October Stephan again wrote Woodcock, this time to express "regrets that a careful review of your letter ... does not warrant a change or reversal of [the] decision that you are ineligible to receive a visa."[43] Woodcock met this body-blow with another flurry of strategy, putting his case in the hands of the ACLU's legal branch. Heilman still thought the best course might be getting the university's regents to put pressure on one of the state's U.S. senators to introduce a special bill that would override the rejection. Until that became necessary, though, Heilman was anxious lest too much publicity frighten the university's president. Thus Woodcock and Heilman, while still allies, came to different views on how to proceed. In the end, the effect of Woodcock's self-defence campaign, with a little help from Birney and others, was to crack the resistance of UBC, which offered him a job—a far lesser job than the one at Washington but a job nonetheless. As Woodcock's appointment at Seattle had already been confirmed, it was necessary for him to request an unpaid leave of absence from the position he was forbidden to take up in order to extricate himself, and his supporters in Seattle, from the dilemma. Eventually, the controversy petered out.

After returning from Seattle for what they thought would be just a short wait for the visa, the Woodcocks had moved even more often than was usual, staying at the Shadbolts for a while, then for a month or two at Earle Birney's on West Third, and finally at an apartment found for them by the painter Molly Lamb Bobak on Lonsdale Avenue in North Vancouver; the last included "a study where the air quickly became dense and I would doze over my typewriter. Here quite a number of people came to see us, including Herbert Read, the then still unfamed Allen Ginsberg, and Norman Levine, then writing *Canada Made Me* in which he mentions Inge's 'Polish' meat balls."[44]

The Seattle debacle, for all its drawn-out agony, would finally bring some stability to the Woodcocks' lives, perhaps even the fulfilment of their destiny. Astute observers such as Jack Shadbolt knew instinctively that Woodcock would never renounce his views, past or present, to gain entry to the U.S. and the equally stubborn American government wouldn't accept a renunciation in any event. Woodcock would recall how "the night we were refused Jack went down into his studio and produced [a] painting to celebrate the fact, saying, 'Now you belong to us.'"[45] The painting included representations of the bottles the four of them emptied that night. When the Woodcocks finally settled into a house of their own in 1959, the painting was given pride of place, and hung there as a reminder for the rest of Woodcock's life.

7 CANADIAN LITERATURE

THROUGHOUT THE LONG embarrassment over his immigration status, Woodcock was characteristically busy. His talks on literary subjects for CBC Radio, a genre that still flourished in imitation of the Third Programme in Britain, and had a strong regional base in Vancouver, were a steady source of revenue. He also appeared occasionally on *Critically Speaking*, a network radio magazine originating in Toronto. In his talks, Woodcock was learning how to extend the useful life of his research and turn to good account certain fields with which he was already familiar. In 1955, for example, his subjects included Aphra Behn as a novelist, Graham Greene, Bernard Shaw as a political thinker, British poets of the Second World War, William Godwin's novel *Caleb Williams*, the poetry of Dylan Thomas and George Barker, Sir Herbert Read's novel *The Green Child*, and the works of Ford Maddox Ford, as well as "Defoe and the Eighteenth-Century Novel's Debt to the Restoration". Talks such as "Earle Birney—The Poet as Wanderer" showed Woodcock's growing understanding of Canadian literature, which he sometimes sought to explain for the British audience, as with an article in *Tribune* as early as 1953.

The year 1956 turned out to be pivotal for Woodcock. In September, the Shadbolts were leaving for Europe on an Overseas Fellowship, a government scheme, administered by the Royal Society of Canada, to use, in this instance, funds blocked in France. The Woodcocks arranged to move back into the mountainside house in Burnaby with its magnificent view. Woodcock thought that his next travel narrative, an outgrowth of *To the City of the Dead*, should deal with the Andes.

When finally published by Faber in 1959 as *Incas and Other Men: Travels in the Andes*, the book owed much to the financial skills he was learning quickly, ones so necessary if the independent scholar is to support his or her own research and work; in 1956, Canadian Pacific Air Lines agreed to pay Woodcock $1,810 for a series of articles about Peru that would publicize the fact that CP flew there. This was only $62.70 less than the Woodcocks spent that same year for their first motor vehicle, a four-cylinder Volkswagen Deluxe Coach. George was never discovered to be automotively gifted; for the duration of their marriage, Inge would do all the driving. Cars were always registered in her name, not his, and thus could pass unmolested over the U.S. border.

Most important of all, in 1956 Woodcock finally broke into the faculty of the University of British Columbia. His first appointment, as a lecturer in the English department, was to run from 1 July 1956 to 30 June 1957 (and later he would teach in Asian studies as well). Thus began a long, tangled and not altogether happy relationship with an institution with which, nevertheless, he became so identified that he would be asked to write its centenary memorial volume.

Characteristically, Woodcock had no sooner entered the gates of UBC than he was plotting to bring in his friend Avakumovic, then at Aberdeen University, newly married, and searching for a position in North America.

> I will let our Slavonics people here know about [you], and hint that you are willing to come as soon as something opens up with them. Let me know when you make your own application to them, which I should certainly do as soon as you have your D. Phil. A first appointment here would probably be at the Instructor level, or possibly as a Lecturer, and might not, to begin, bring much more than $3,500 a year—but it is only a 6 months' teaching year and you can usually earn more by teaching Summer School if you wish. I get $5,000, but I had to pull all the weight of my books and my repute as a critic to get that much.[1]

This makes it sound as though Woodcock saw himself as having settled into the comfort of a sinecure. In fact, memories of the Great Western being what they were, Woodcock, though now forty-five, was still restless, still too young, he thought, to be tethered to any damnable institution. Wanting to research a book about the contemporary French novel, he followed Shadbolt's example and applied for an Overseas Fellowship, marshalling "a formidable battery of recommendations from Canadian and American scholars and writers,"[2] including Northrop Frye. The announcements were made in June 1957. Three B.C. residents had won: Woodcock, the painter Bruno Bobak, and a young poet, "Miss Phyllis J. Webb, 30, of Victoria" ...[3] As it happened, the news coincided with a strenuous upsurge of work from the CBC, for Woodcock had also broken into the marketplace for radio drama, contributing to *Summer Stage, CBC Wednesday Night* and *CBC Sunday Night* as well as to *Vancouver Theatre*, produced by a literary friend, Robert Harlow. The work consisted mostly of adapting classics, and before the Woodcocks could leave the city George had to complete seventeen instalments of *Don Quixote* at $175 each, for a net, after deductions, of $2,231.35. "I succeeded," he reported to Avakumovic, "but only by working myself to the edge of a nervous collapse, so that it took about three weeks for me to get back to normal humanity after it was over. However, the production was very successful, and seems to have placed me more securely than ever as an odd but interesting radio writer."[4]

Eager to become better acquainted with the rest of Canada, Woodcock had proposed a travel book about the country to Sir Herbert Read at Routledge. The offer was declined (and Woodcock would not return to the task until *Canada and the Canadians*, published in 1970). The rejection, however, did not alter the couple's plans. At the end of August, they left Vancouver by car, headed east, "stopped in Toronto to attend a few parties and appear on TV, and then sailed from Montreal on the 8th September, reaching France on the 14th."[5] Leaving George in Paris, Inge made a trip to Germany to see her parents: this would be one of the currents of their travel as the years rolled on. By the end of the month she met up with her husband in Paris and they removed to Menton in the south, cheap in the off-season and close enough to Aix-en-Provence to permit occasional visits to the university library.

They basked in the warmth while Woodcock read deeply in Proust and Gide, all the while working on his manuscript about Peru. Spring 1958 found them back in Paris, "in various crummy hotels, belatedly gathering books for my fellowship task"[6] at the stalls along the quais, with interludes in Italy and the French Alps.

They sailed back to North America at the end of the summer. They arrived well in time for the start of studies at UBC, where (he informed

Avakumovic) "after a long wrangle with them, I gained all my points—appointment to the regular faculty as Assistant Professor, a raise of $1,000 a year, and the courses I demanded. As my appointment is for two years, it looks as though I shall be there until 1960, and, since I intend to cut down very severely on journalistic and radio work, I should have plenty of time to work on the critical opus."[7] As it happened, though, the study of the French novel would be one of the surprisingly large number of projects that Woodcock never completed—in fact, astoundingly large in view of the enormous total he did produce in his career. Like the journeyman he was, however, Woodcock used the material in another form, as lectures.

Back in Vancouver, the Woodcocks rented an apartment on West 10th, at the corner of Discovery, overlooking a gas station. They complained of the high rent—$120 a month—but they would be near the university, and the university, as it developed, was about to suck Woodcock into its orbit.

Scores of individuals later prominent in Canadian literature and other fields passed through Woodcock's classes over the years. The poet George Bowering and the critic Frank Davey were both Woodcock students, for example. Another was Wayson Choy, who emerged a generation later as the author of the much-acclaimed novel *The Jade Peony*. He took Woodcock's comparative literature course in 1959–60 and would remember being "impressed by his reputation"[8] and by his unusual classroom style. Woodcock was "articulate and clean, [teaching] from a brilliant set of notes, which he deviated from rarely. I felt even then that he inclined towards the political sense of literature, not its spiritual development but the structure of books and of the communities they came from."[9] If Choy had a criticism, it was that Woodcock "perhaps didn't realize that some of us were from backgrounds where we had no literature except what was taught us in high school."[10] Sometimes, he remembered, Woodcock "would break into Latin. I'd write it down phonetically so I could later ask someone else"[11] what it meant. Woodcock was serious and "more than fair".[12] Unlike Roy Daniells, he was one of those "teachers who paid you the compliment of not being entertaining."[13]

A few years later, Judy Stoffman, later the books editor of the Toronto *Star*, took Woodcock's European-literature-in-translation course, which began with *The Odyssey* and ran through *Don Quixote* and Goethe to Dostoevsky, Kafka and Malraux. She recalled him as he was then, in a classroom in the north wing of the Buchanan building:

> He was the only one of our teachers whom we had to address as Mister [because he didn't have a degree], and it felt somehow disrespectful, awkward. He was very serious—definitely not one of the jovial profs who made jokes or ironic remarks to keep students' attention. His voice was soft and gentle and his manner almost diffident before the class; we had to move up a few rows from our place in the back to hear him. [He] was a scholar who loved literature ...[14]

The classes were large. In 1959, Woodcock had more than 130 students.

In 1958, the university began to entertain the idea of a quarterly journal to be called *Canadian Literature*, which would be the first one devoted to the study of the subject, French as well as English. Woodcock of course had a lingering reputation as an editor of journals—particularly of *NOW*, which was already, a dozen years after its closure, the subject of some readers' nostalgia—and also as one of the founders of *Dissent*. He was thus in an excellent position to bolster his role in "the little zoo of Canadian letters".[15] In a memoir, the teacher and editor Carl F. Klinck would suggest that Woodcock had not been the university's first choice. Klinck wrote that the position would have gone to Reginald Watters, the folk bibliographer, "but for an accident of timing—he was invited to Australia at the time an editor was required—".[16] Certainly Watters seemed a pioneer just then; the first edition of his monumental *Check List of Canadian Literature* was set to appear in 1959. Woodcock, however, remembered the university's decision-making process differently, and the UBC archives would seem not to settle the matter. In any event, by January 1959 Woodcock wrote to potential contributors such as Earle Birney (then living in England), outlining the editorial philosophy that would give *Canadian Literature: A Quarterly of Criticism and Review* an important role in the coming maturation of Canadian writing and publishing.

> One of the tasks which I want to carry out in the quarterly is to cultivate a kind of evolving history of writing in Canada, involving

re-assessments of established writers—dead and living—and studies of
new writers worth consideration at length, as well as more general considerations of literary periods and environments ...

Secondly, I want to publish articles by writers about the problems
of their own craft[17]

in addition to, as a handbill promised, reviews of all current books of
Canadian literary interest and an annual bibliography of Canadian
literature. Frequent looks at Canadian writing by people in other literary cultures would be another feature favoured by Woodcock. "One
thing I want to avoid like the plague is orthodox academic writing",
he confided to Avakumovic.[18] Less than two weeks later, he ended
another letter to Avakumovic: "PS. *We have bought a house.*"[19]

A decade after leaving Britain, Woodcock still supported himself
with a complex patchwork of writing jobs big and small. In 1959, the
year they moved to their new home in the Kerrisdale section of
Vancouver, he was basking in the good reviews of *Incas and Other
Men*, including a long one by V. S. Pritchett, while freelancing furi-
ously on any scale offered. Asssignments ranged from a $100 article
on "Revolutions" for *Collier's Encyclopedia* (he had been suggested by
Irving Howe) to a $400 adaptation of *The Island of Demons* for Bob
Harlow's CBC drama series, *Vancouver Theatre*. (In that same year, the
always astounding Inge turned out *two* plays, adapting Kurt Goetz's
Lohengrin, also for Harlow, and translating as well as adapting *The
Enterprise of the Spaceship Wega* by Friedrich Dürrenmatt—space travel
being one of her abiding interests.) Yet 1959, clearly, was also a financial turning-point for them, with what promised to be a permanent
career at the university stretching to the distant horizon of retirement.
In anthropological terms, the Woodcocks were making the transition
from hunter-gatherer to farmer. For the first and only time in his life,
Woodcock ventured into the world of stocks and equities, when he
purchased shares of a new private venture called the Readers' Club of
Canada, a book-club for Canadian works exclusively. In 1965, he sub-
scribed for ten more shares in the same company, bringing his total
to thirty shares, even though he had never received a dividend and
never would. Within a year of purchasing their little house for $15,000,
the Woodcocks retired the mortgage, and they would spend the
coming decades renovating and decorating, filling the place with books
and paintings from Canada as well as with artworks and artefacts from

their travels. Perhaps for the first time since leaving Marlow, Woodcock felt settled. "I know that there are opportunities in the East—
'but somehow I think that the climate here is worth quite a bit", he
confided to Avakumovic. "I can't see myself living in either Calgary
or London, Ontario; I need at least as much of a metropolitan atmosphere as Vancouver gives, and I find it hard, now, to live far away
from the mountains."[20]

What constrained him was not Vancouver but rather the idea of
institutional life. Returning from an academic conference in Saska-
toon, he "found the jollyboy atmosphere rather annoying and, in any
case, [I] am allergic to mass gatherings since the anarchist days. Professors, barbers, libertarians, they're all the same in the mass."[21]

The small two-storey frame house at 6429 McCleery Street, near
the golf course of the same name, was set far back from the street on
a large lot. In time, it would be hidden from McCleery (formerly
called Cherry Street) by a hedgerow, just as it was protected on the
other side by the edge of the escarpment overlooking the north branch
of the Fraser River. Eventually it would take on the feel of a fine old
cottage on somewhat larger-than-cottage scale, as though it had been
transported piece by piece from a quiet English village. At first,
though, it was rather less comfortable-looking. Woodcock would say:

> It's not architect-designed but just a piece of carpenter's gothic. The
> earliest accounts I have of it are from 1920. Old Kerrisdale people still
> talk of this as being a little house they remember standing in the field
> [in what] is actually one of the earliest settled areas of Vancouver if not
> the earliest. A man named Fitzgerald McCleery came here in 1862, a
> full quarter-century before the city was founded. The story is that this
> house was one of his hired man's cottages, or one of his son's hired
> man's cottages . . .[22]

For Woodcock, the selling point was the large ground-floor room at
the back, overlooking the garden, where he could write. He put up
bookshelves all round and made a table using iron legs cast off by the
Shadbolts. He built his own desk and painted it red. "The drawers
still stick", he confessed in the 1990s. "I'm not a very skilled carpenter."[23] Perhaps this was the lesson he learned by building first the one
cabin at Sooke and then the other. When the Woodcocks took possession of McCleery Street in April 1959 the top storey was a maze of

tiny rooms, and Woodcock "hired a rough carpenter for two-dollars-fifty per hour and worked with him all through the summer, knocking down walls and generally reconstituting it."[24] The phrase *two-dollars-fifty* is interesting, suggesting that in some deep posterior section of the brain he still thought in sterling rather than in Canadian dollars, even more than forty years after quitting England.

The first issue of *Canadian Literature* appeared in September. It was of impressive heft, at one hundred pages, and of striking appearance as well, reflecting the design talent of Robert R. Reid and the typographic style characteristic of Charles Morriss of the influential Morriss Printing Company of Victoria. The premiere number was also a vivid map of Woodcock's editorial approach. Among Woodcock's friends was Roderick Haig-Brown, an Englishman who, when the expiration of his U.S. visa forced his retreat from Washington State in 1926, had settled on Vancouver Island. There he was appointed a lay magistrate and built a fine reputation for his essays and fiction about fishing in particular and the environment, and aboriginal attitudes towards it, in general. He was Woodcock's kind of man: an autodidact, a humanist, a radical of sorts, a person forever trying to find and maintain the proper balance between the intellectual and the natural worlds. Haig-Brown lived at Campbell River, and Woodcock snagged an essay by him, "The Writer in Isolation", for the first issue. CL No. 1 also contained an article by A. J. M. Smith on Duncan Campbell Scott, another by Hugo McPherson on Gabrielle Roy, and one by a francophone colleague, Gérard Tougas, on "Bilan d'une Littérature naissante". As he would continue to do from time to time, Woodcock imposed on his friendships with well-known foreign writers to contribute; in this instance, Roy Fuller surveyed three recent collections by Canadian poets (Irving Layton, John Glassco and Ronald Bates) while Dwight Macdonald examined five magazines (*Canadian Forum, Tamarack Review, University of Toronto Quarterly, Queen's Quarterly* and the *Fiddlehead*). The sudden appearance of *Canadian Literature* was like a call to which the growing number of writers seeking a voice responded. Among other contributors to the first ten issues were novelists ranging in age from Jack Ludwig to Ethel Wilson, poets as different as James Reaney and Wilfred Watson, and Quebec literary figures such as Jean-Guy Pilon and Gilles Marcotte. But Woodcock was especially sympathetic to, and thus *Canadian Literature* especially rich in, all manner of critics. There was space for the likes of Desmond

Pacey, Milton Wilson and Warren Tallman, representing three generations (and three distinct flavours) of academic life. Woodcock also had room for the antiquaries, such as Klinck and Watters, and, more importantly, for the younger commentators and broadcasters, such as Robert Fulford and Robert Weaver. Woodcock even managed to secure from the flashy journalist Pierre Berton the one piece he could undertake that would be practically made-to-measure for *Canadian Literature*: an essay on the guidebooks and narratives of the Klondike gold rush. Eyes from outside Canada during the same period ranged from Peter Quennell to Conrad Aiken. The latter appeared as part of a special issue (No. 8) devoted to Malcolm Lowry.

Woodcock was commencing not only at the right time but at exactly the right place as well. Even after considerable decentralization in the 1970s and 1980s, Toronto would always remain the publishing hub of Canada, but by 1959 Vancouver was well on its way to being the imaginative centre of the country's creative writing. Elsewhere at UBC, for example, Earle Birney was introducing the very concept of creative writing as a field of study, though the discipline became a full-fledged department only after Birney retired in 1964 to go to the University of Toronto as Canada's first writer-in-residence. Such events as the Vancouver Poetry conference of 1963 cemented the notion of Vancouver as a hub of vital activity, in touch somehow with both East Asian cultures across the Pacific and with the ferment taking place in San Francisco—a link forged by people such as Ronald Bladen, a Vancouver visual artist and saxophonist living in the Bay area since the 1950s, or indeed Woodcock himself, whose involvement with American anarchists such as Kenneth Rexroth had set up another kind of connection between the two cultural city-states (as they tended to see themselves).

Dealing with Woodcock in his role at *Canadian Literature* would always be a pleasure, so quick, helpful and generous were his responses. The editorial face he presented to the public was that of an unflappable and infinitely patient helper. He was not the sort of editor, a kind he himself must have encountered on scores of occasions, who dismissed outside ideas out of hand, believing that only those generated in-house could contribute to the realization of some secret overall design, which only the editor was in a position to see and understand. On the contrary, a rejection by Woodcock almost always carried with it an assignment to do something else instead, while an acceptance was an implicit solicitation for further ideas. Privately, however, he sometimes allowed close friends to see the frustrations that came with editing such a journal. He once expressed delight with Avakumovic for writing *fewer* words than assigned, not more. In Woodcock's experience with his contributors, "most of them—the Canadians at least—write at least 50 per cent more than I ask for and involve me in either aggravating correspondence about cuts or in hopeless efforts to fit twelve pages of material into the eight I have at my disposal. Blessings of the White Jesus upon you!"[25]

At other times it was difficult to wring anything out of them at all. In the first year of his editorship Woodcock began attempting to get a contribution from Sir Herbert Read, and once thought he at last had found, in Edmund Carpenter's *Eskimo*, a book for him to review. When at length, during a pause in his world travels as an art-explainer, Read had time to look it over, he had to decline. His grounds were that it was an arbitrary and eccentric production, too full of reproductions of work by Frederick Varley and of a text by Carpenter, an old associate of Marshall McLuhan, that Read thought incoherent and uninformative. Also in the Woodcock Archive is the record of Woodcock's painfully persistent attempts, lasting a decade, to solicit a substantial contribution from F. R. Scott, the Montreal poet and legal scholar. Woodcock keeps suggesting ideas and Scott keeps begging off with one excuse or another. For example, Scott can't write an article on the victory over censorship in the *Lady Chatterley's Lover* case as he had acted for the defence, but neither can he write a more general article on the new censorship laws because he cannot quite distil the essence of their meaning into words. Nor can he review books by people with whom he is acquainted (and of course he is acquainted with most everyone). For a time it seemed that Woodcock might be allowed to print Scott's exchange of letters with Anne Hébert, but at the last moment Scott gave the material to a French journal instead. Woodcock made do with a translation by Scott of a 1606 poem by Marc Lescarbot, the French writer and traveller. When Woodcock planned to devote part of an issue to Scott and A. J. M. Smith, who were both publishing volumes of *Selected Poems*, Scott first agreed to write an essay about his poetics but then pulled back, forcing Woodcock to accept four of Scott's found poems instead.

Woodcock, never nagging, never pleading, was the model of gentle persistence, just as, at other times, he was the master of strategic contrition. He wrote to one reviewer:

The role of the editor, as I am uncomfortably aware, all too easily takes on the look of the villain's role. There's no question of willingly delaying your piece. It is just that I am in the position of having a quarterly when—given the amount of good material that is coming in these days—I need a monthly. I try to restrain my acceptances, and do turn back some excellent pieces which I would love to publish, but still I find there is always more material than I have space for, and I am straining my promises and raising doubts in the minds of my contributors. Rest assured, your piece is still liked, and is even now with the printer, definitely due to appear in our next issue. With the burden that rests on me at present—since there are no funds to pay a secretary and I have to do all my letters (our one office worker is fully occupied with subscriptions and sales) I cannot possibly, with the best will in the world, inform every contributor when there is a delay.[26]

During the more than seventeen years he edited *Canadian Literature*, Woodcock wrote a number of reports and assessments of the journal, its growth and comparative influence, and his own role in its history. Some of these were public documents whipped up for anniversaries and other turning-points, while others were for purely internal purposes. In 1960, in a memorandum apparently intended for the dean or the president or both, Woodcock quickly fell into the botanical metaphor that came to him so easily, stating that

the new review is like a young plant. It is a new strain ... and everyone is interested in its possible novelty. After the first issue, however, novelty is not enough. The plant must show its endurance, its power to proliferate, the vigour and variety of its blooms, and if it does this it will be able to carry on into those years of useful life which every good magazine enjoys before its purpose is finally fulfilled.[27]

In fact, the early issues of CL were met with repeated attacks in scholarly circles and even in the local newspaper press.
Woodcock went on:

I should say that no thought of literary nationalism entered my editorial thoughts at this or any other stage; from the beginning I have held that any attempt to see literature in political terms would be doing it no service—in fact that it would be doing it a positive disservice.

So, from the beginning we have been concerned with literature as the expression of a certain social environment and of a people who by now have recognised the fact that they differ collectively in some important though not always easily definable ways from French and British and Americans ... For, in fact, the problems that face the writer in Canada are just as complex as those that face his counterpart anywhere else, and the number of people who are writing their way through these problems towards literary creativity is increasing with every year.[28]

For indeed what made *Canadian Literature* distinct was its critical tone of voice. The essays and reviews were serious but not academic, popular but not journalistic, contextual more often than textual: a diction Woodcock developed for others largely by his own example, writing a great deal for the journal himself. CL occupied the high middle-ground, a position Woodcock was forever having to defend against one argument or another. One especially revealing letter dates to the early 1970s, during the great explosion in Canadian writing and publishing (which *Canadian Literature*, for all its wariness of literary nationalism, had done its part to ignite). In response to a complaint that the journal paid too little attention to the literary aspects of non-imaginative writers, such as philosophers and narrative historians, Woodcock pleaded that his avoidance of the academic had to be matched by

what is *practical*. If I am to give space to the literary qualities of a writer without literary intent, like [George] Grant, where am I to end? Why should I not give space to essays on the literary qualities of [Donald] Creighton or, for that matter, Goldwin Smith, both of whom I find much better *writers* than Grant? Ideally, I would rather like this. I would have to have enough money to turn *Canadian Literature* into a monthly of writing *and* the humanities in general. But I don't, and, though the journal has almost doubled in size since I started it, there is still not enough space to consider everything that is happening in the novel, drama, poetry, criticism, etc. I have just compiled a checklist of poets working during the past decade. No less than 482 of them published volumes of some kind, and yet we have dealt with less than half these poets in *Canadian Literature*. We are just now trying to expand our coverage to give some idea of what is happening in Quebec; that will soon take up a quarter of our already heavily taxed space ...[29]

As it was, in another of his interim statements, in 1963, Woodcock noted the fact that the journal had achieved a circulation of 1,500 copies (1,200 by subscription, 300 through bookstores and newsstands) putting it

> *second* among Canadian literary magazines; in this field *Tamarack Review* alone has a larger circulation. Among Canadian University quarterlies it is second only to *Queen's Quarterly*, and in its three and a half years of existence has attained a circulation greater than that of such long-established journals as the *University of Toronto Quarterly* and *Dalhousie Review*. The circulation is rising slowly, but the experience of other magazines shows that, like *Tamarack Review* (whose subscription [base] is 1,400), *Canadian Literature* has reached nearly the maximum circulation for a Canadian literary periodical given the nation's present reading habits.[30]

Sad but true. But its influence was out of all proportion to its numbers: a cliché of course but in this case a true one.

8 ANARCHISM

IN THE 1840S, a time of mass credulity not unlike our own, William Miller, an American farmer turned self-ordained divine, convinced his flock that Judgement Day would fall on 23 April 1843. The cult members forgathered expectantly. Nothing happened. Consulting the Scriptures again, Miller recalibrated and announced that the End would come on a specific day in October 1844. Once again he was disappointed. In fact, Miller would see his prophecy fulfilled only to the small extent that he himself dropped dead in 1849. By that time, most of the Millerites had moved to Canada. This risible episode in the history of utopia comes to mind only because it was exactly a hundred years after Miller's death that Woodcock resettled in the land of his birth, another victim of dashed millennialism—not of the Christian sort but rather of the anarchist variety. As Donald Rooum, one of his least generous British critics, would write in *Freedom* years later, when Woodcock

> migrated to Canada, he still thought of anarchism as millenarian, but stopped believing in the doctrine himself. He insisted that Freedom Press withdraw his *Anarchy or Chaos*, and as a professional writer became an expert on anarchism from outside. During this period he wrote the article on 'Anarchism' in *Encyclopaedia Britannica* and the first edition of the Penguin book *Anarchism*.[1]

Indeed, Woodcock would confess that when he wrote his 1962 classic study *Anarchism*, he did so in the certainty that anarchism as an attainable social mechanism had had its day. But when the book turned out to be, in a quiet manner uncharacteristic of the period, one of the signal works of the 1960s, he watched interest in the topic revived by successive waves of younger people. Demand has since kept the work in print almost continuously. Later in the decade, according to the accepted chronology of Woodcock's thinking, he began calling himself first a philosophical anarchist and, later, once again answered to the simple title of anarchist, without qualification or modifiers. In this, he was influenced by the sense of regional identity he felt as a British Columbian first and a Canadian second, especially at the time of the province's and the country's great cultural flowering, in both of which he was a central figure. His thinking was also no doubt shaped by *Anarchy in Action* (1973) by Colin Ward, who during the 1960s edited *Anarchy*, probably the most cogent and exciting libertarian periodical ever published in English. One also sees throughout this period—a period, not coincidentally, of rising nationalism in Canada—his abiding (indeed, growing) sympathy for Kropotkin over the other old anarchist thinkers. Dimitri Roussopoulos, the Montreal anarchist who would publish Woodcock's edition of Kropotkin's works, pointed out that "Woodcock's anarchism was the anarcho-communism of Kropotkin, not the anarcho-individualism of Max Stirner, or the anarcho-syndicalism of Michael Bakunin."[2]

One sees the essential change in Woodcock's beliefs by comparing two statements separated by a generation. To the writer of *Anarchy or Chaos* in 1944, the anarchists, into whose way of life he had been inducted by Berneri,

> envisage no static blueprint for a future world. For, when men have been freed from social and economic repressions, the evolution of human institutions will undoubtedly attain forms we cannot conceive. Proposals for future organisations must not therefore be regarded as permanent and hence dead, but as the bases of future social evolution.[3]

As Rooum pointed out, this was the *when* not *if* viewpoint of someone who had made his way to anarchism from socialism via the classic pre-Kropotkin texts. By 1990, however, Woodcock wrote rather the opposite, that anarchism is not a revolutionary doctrine in the millenarian sense of offering, like Christianity, a New Heaven and a New Earth. It is rather a restorative doctrine, telling us that the means by which we can create a free society are already there in the manifestations of mutual aid existing in the world around us[,][4]

a statement that represents Kropotkinism boiled down to its basic broth.

Between these two poles, at the fertile middle stage of Woodcock's career as a writer on anarchism, came the book both less pessimistic and less optimistic, at once both anti-doctrinal and tribal: *Anarchism: A History of Libertarian Ideas and Movements*, to give it its full title. This was the work that established him in the minds of a large international audience as an anarchist while giving focus to the disdain of his former colleagues in Britain. It is a simple matter to take the book for granted, because it seems always to have been there. Certainly, it has its weaknesses and frailties. Woodcock had little patience for American strains of anarchism, for instance, and he said nothing at all of China, where anarchists had played an important role in radical politics in the early days of Sun Yat-sen's first republic, nor of Japan, where anarchists were once important enough to be assassinated. Yet the work was genuinely organic. The original edition stopped at 1939, as seemed logical to someone who saw the high-water mark as the Spanish civil war, and fittingly modest to one whose own involvement came later. But as successive editions were called for, he kept updating the material, adding sections and correcting misstatements. During this process of growth, the author seemed obliged, in fleshing out the subsequent story of anarchism in Britain (always a minor part of the book), to enlarge the mention of himself, until finally he would make the following comment: "The 1950s were a period of somnolence for anarchism in Britain. The movement had lost two of its leading figures in 1949 when Marie Louise Berneri died and George Woodcock departed to start a new kind of life in Canada."[5] This innocent statement provoked the further ire of British colleagues, who, like those in the British literary world, misunderstood or mistrusted his motives for leaving. Beginning in 1959, Woodcock was periodically back in Britain for short stays, either on publishing business or making travel connections to other places, particularly to India, the Middle East and East Asia. Although he maintained cordial epistolary relations with many of his old friends there, such as Roy Fuller and Julian Symons, he was always reluctant to look up his long-ago colleagues, fearing perhaps they would pummel him with questions— questions about why he went to Canada, for example—for which he could not supply simple conversational answers. More than one acquaintance or friend thought himself singled out for harsh treatment when Woodcock, known to be in Britain, failed to stop round or ring. In fact, Woodcock stayed in the U.K. each time only as long as was necessary to complete his transactions. London was almost unrecognizable to him now, and too full of ghosts; for years to come it would remain the cornerstone of his publishing life, but the city belonged to a younger generation, the one that would take up *Anarchism* as a basic instrument of their education.

Like *The Crystal Spirit*, the other most important of Woodcock's many books, *Anarchism* had been growing inside him for years. The story of anarchism was important to him and to many of his contemporaries because they were of the generation whose dreams and nightmares had been shaped by events in Spain between 1936 and 1938, just as an earlier generation had found the First World War the great informing event of their lives or as a much later one would have the same relationship with Vietnam. A significant fact about the Spanish civil war was the anarchists' support of the Loyalists. Never had the anarchists been so prominent; paradoxically, never had they seemed such a cohesive movement as when they stood together engaged in retaliatory violence against Franco. Or, put another way, never had misunderstanding about them and what they stood for been so widespread. In the intense heat of the moment, it was perhaps not always clear to what extent the anarcho-syndicalists had been a factor in Spanish politics since the middle of the nineteenth century. The contextual void must have been all the more obvious in view of the way the world's attention was concentrated on Spain. At this great distance one can be forgiven for guessing that it was this situation that set the young Woodcock to work on the anarchist tradition, a labour that would engage him until the end of his life. (*Fields, Factories and Workshops*, the penultimate volume in his edition of Kropotkin's *Collected Works*, appeared about six weeks after Woodcock's death, while the eleventh and final volume, *Evolution and Environment*, the last such undertaking Woodcock completed, followed a few months later, in June 1995.)

But there was more to the anarchists' craving for knowledge about their own history than the Spanish war. History in general was especially important because it is in the nature of anarchism, as the denial of rigid ideology, bureaucracy and hierarchy, that it must lack the artificial memory built into formal political institutions. Ironically, this weakness has helped keep anarchism vital by giving it so much of the plasticity that it requires of itself and promises to others. Anarchism continues—*still flourishes* would be too strong a phrase—in reaction to both authoritarian socialism and slash-and-burn capitalism, yet without having much in common with liberalism, save optimism about the future of the human spirit. Godwin, Proudhon, Tolstoy and those other nineteenth-century figures to whom Woodcock returns us again and again were the ultimate idealists, with their dream of a free association of equally free individuals acting in their own collective best interests, without the yoke of government or other man-made institutions. Their faith in the essential goodness of human nature has never been surpassed; it can hardly be equalled without lapsing into organized (indeed corporate) religion—a superfluous progression, given the vernacular religious impulse that often underlay those classic anarchists of old. The Taoists' complaint about the Confucians was that the Confucians, in giving definition to the concept of morality, had therefore made immorality inevitable. So, too, did centralized administration make anarchism inevitable when it eclipsed the idea of the tribe and other small self-governing units. This basic notion of counterpoise is what gives anarchism its flexibility and therefore its resilience. Woodcock's fellow critic Northrop Frye reminded his readers how the Bible was promulgated in order to supplant the ancient mother-goddess religions, which were based on the idea of an all-powerful matriarchal figure at the centre of Nature, with the Christian concept of a patriarchal God who urges reliance on human institutions rather than on objects and forces found in the natural order: an essential theme of Judaism and Islam as well. Anarchism is a tiny voice of corrective protest, urging that old harmonious arrangements be re-evaluated at the expense of artificial grids. This is why it has been so easy for anarcho-feminism and eco-anarchism to become the most important new forms of anti-authoritarian thought in recent years, important to anarchism itself and to the larger movements of which they are a part. Constant renewal of the premise gives anarchism its ability to adapt to present realities. That might almost be

Woodcock's underlying message in a single sentence, though it was scarcely his only key point.

In surveying the ground, he was careful not to inflate the importance of anarchism. Such restraint must have been difficult given the low-grade melancholy of the past tense in which he wrote. Nor did he try to make his topic any more respectable a historical phenomenon than it was or is; he himself had always been a pacifist, and had written his denunciation of revolutionary violence in the *Adelphi* in 1947, but he could not deny the existence of those extremists in the past who themselves had been unable to reject violence. What he sought was a better understanding of the subject, particularly the way it developed differently in various countries but following the same basic pattern as the novel, with the Russian and French strains being the most complex and self-confident, the English the most artful and evocative, and the American the most energetic but ultimately the least substantial.

The book began to seep through his skin in 1959, after he had been in Canada a decade. The initiative was undoubtedly his own. But his literary agent (Woodcock was always fortunate in having skilled agents in London—during this period, Christy & Moore, and, later, Anthony Sheil) broached the prospect to World Publishing of Cleveland, which wished to publish a cloth edition and then bring out the book in its Meridian line of original trade paperbacks. In the matter of a British co-publisher, Woodcock himself seems to have approached Sir Herbert Read at Routledge. Sir Herbert replied enthusiastically at the idea of a 90,000-word manuscript that would survey and summarize the field with a combination of firsthand knowledge and objective distance. The deal soon fell into place, and Woodcock spent much of 1960 and the first part of 1961 working away with his customary diligence, but only after begging from Routledge, not an extension of time, but a commitment to a longer work, about 120,000 words. Woodcock had the "History of Anarchism", as the manuscript was titled provisionally, completed by the summer of 1961, and Routledge were pleased, with Sir Herbert suggesting only minor changes of emphasis—more about Tolstoy, for example. He also warned Woodcock, no doubt superfluously, that some of their old comrades would be upset.

The year 1961 was particularly busy for Woodcock. Faber and Faber commissioned him to produce a book-length travel narrative on

India, a subject in which the Woodcocks had immersed themselves increasingly since the start of the Chinese communists' campaign to destroy Tibetan culture. In 1959, the Central Intelligence Agency in the U.S., in what was perhaps its last display of humanitarian usefulness, had spirited the Dalai Lama out of his mountain kingdom into exile at Dharmsala in northern India, where he was joined by a large colony of his followers; such matters were still very much in the news.

In August the Woodcocks left Vancouver for Britain and Europe. True to his pattern, Woodcock stayed only three days in London, avoiding his old friends, but seeing V. S. Pritchett, the novelist and essayist, and Hugh Thomas, the historian of the Spanish civil war (for the twenty-fifth anniversary of whose outbreak Woodcock was doing a documentary for the CBC). Then, after a stay in their beloved France, the Woodcocks travelled to India and met with people as different as the socialist leader Ashoka Mehta and the Maharajah of Jaipur, as well as with the Dalai Lama. This first visit quite overwhelmed their senses. Woodcock wrote to Avakumovic that "the book that comes out of it *should* be my best, but the material is so vast—and India itself is so fascinatingly complex, that I am not even sure where I can possibly begin. However, that will be my task till the 1961–62 session begins."[6] Typically for someone who for the rest of his life would posit schemes out loud about retiring to some more remote corner of the world (once to Sri Lanka, like Arthur C. Clarke), Woodcock added that "we are at the moment trying to devise some plan that will enable us to go there and live—preferably in the North near the Himalayas— for at least two years, so that we can really get a proper feeling of the country."[7]

Then they were off to West Germany to visit Inge's family, who were living at Offenbach on the Main River east of Frankfurt. It was during this trip that Woodcock was reading the galley proofs of *Anarchism*, a book that soon ran into trouble. In what they claimed was an innocent error, World Publishing brought out its Meridian paperback before the planned hardcover, which was thus of course cancelled, and this situation caused Routledge to back away from publishing its own cloth edition. The situation was saved—rather magically in fact—when Woodcock's agent engineered the sale of British and Commonwealth paperback rights to Penguin. It was first as a Pelican (Penguin's non-fiction line) and then as an actual Penguin that *Anarchism* penetrated into every bookstall, and into every bibliography on the subject of anarchism, becoming a small annuity of sorts for Woodcock and doing so much to keep the embers of anarchism alive. Along with his later study of Orwell, it would also become Woodcock's most widely translated book, appearing in Stockholm as *Anarkismen*, for example, and in Milan as *L'Anarchia: Storia delle idee e dei movimenti libertari*. In time there would even be a Japanese edition.

Woodcock seemed to have taken on Kropotkin's personality. The manner he showed to the public and all but a very few friends was polite, generous, gentle and concerned. There were few hints of the unhappiness he felt, except when the unhappiness manifested itself as wanderlust and in the middle of letters he would suddenly confide his latest plans for escape—at this time, the hope of a temporary teaching appointment in either India or Japan. He still faced a long haul on writing what became *Faces of India: A Travel Narrative*, but now commissions were coming to him steadily: as a follow-up, Faber suggested the narrative that appeared in 1966, two years after *Faces*, as *Asia, Gods and Cities: Aden to Tokyo*. And during this period, his broadcast work began taking new directions, with more ambitious plays and adaptations. In England he had dreamed of achieving the proper balance of manual labour and intellectual labour, but the ideal had always proved elusive, more of an either-or situation than a matter of contented coexistence. So, too, on Vancouver Island, except that there the physical drudgery had overwhelmed his intellectual life. In moving to Vancouver, he had simply replaced actual carpentry and market gardening with the metaphorical tool-box and hoe of classroom teaching (an activity that Woodcock did not disparage but simply thought himself unsuited to). *Canadian Literature* had been a godsend, because it reduced the amount of time he had to teach while preserving his modest university salary; being a quarterly, it may also have given a cycle to his movements that would have appealed instinctively to the agriculturalist locked inside him somewhere ("George is very *country*, isn't he?" the English-reared poet P. K. Page would ask rhetorically).[8] Yet to satisfy his appetite for work (his own classroom, in which he was both professor and pupil) he found that he had to binge, taking leaves from the faculty to go abroad for his travel books and other commissions, only to bring the diaries and research materials home to his cave on McCleery Street, where he fell into nocturnal writing habits, retiring to the study after a pitcher of martinis with Inge and guests to write through the night, consuming small malodorous cigars at a rate of up to twenty a day. He got virtually no exercise, and soon his weight shot up to levels that his slight frame could not accommodate without danger.

In that era, Canadian passports were valid for ten years, and before disposing of the cancelled one that had been issued to Inge in 1961 George made a list of all the entry and exit stamps it contained (of those which were legible). This document now provides a vivid insight into their life together during the early 1960s, showing visits to, to give a purely alphabetical and highly selective list, Alexandria, Athens, Bangkok, Basel, Bombay, Calcutta, Chiasso in Switzerland, Decca, Dhanukhkodi, Hong Kong, Karachi, Kuala Lumpur, Lahore, Lisbon, Macao, Naples, Palam, Phnom Penh, Port Said, Portabou in Spain, Rotterdam, Singapore, Talaimanner, Teheran and Yokohama. No wonder that he sought some revised accommodation with UBC that would permit him more freedom and allow him to transfer more classroom hours to the writing desk.

Woodcock (who continued to work on his never-to-be-completed study of the French novel) confided to Avakumovic in January 1963:

> The Indian book creeps with difficulty towards its conclusion. I am still leaning strongly towards a return to the freelance life; in fact, I owe almost all that I earn in writing to my past books, not my academic position, and with the CBC to the fact that I established contacts there long before I went on the staff at UBC. I have been careful not to use my academic rank as an inducement to editors and publishers, always with the idea in my mind that one day I would once again stand as myself. I agree that it would be a pity to abandon *Canadian Literature*, and there I hope some means of retaining a connection may be worked out. As for teaching, there are many teachers as good and better than I am, and I have never thought of teaching as something that particularly commands my dedication. I do enjoy it, but not where it begins to interfere with deeper wishes. I still love the West Coast, and shall retain Vancouver as a base; I may even teach an occasional summer; but the permanent career—the indefinite prospect of it—fills me with despair when I realise that I have a perfectly viable alternative.[9]

By May he was reporting:

> There have been interminable negotiations, Departmental Head reluctant to see me go, President reluctant to make special terms for my staying, representations by other Departmental Heads, a petition by English Professors on the loss to the nation if CL were left headless, and finally, this morning, the news that the Pres. has agreed to recommend my change of status to a part-time Special Lecturer whose duties will be understood to extend not beyond the editing of CL. If this goes through, I shall accept it as a fair compromise.[10]

In fact, the compromise had to collapse before it could be reinflated and made workable. In a memorandum of 26 June, the president "accepted, with regret,"[11] Woodcock's resignation as an associate professor in the Asian Studies department effective the end of that month. This was a necessary prelude to Woodcock's appointment, effective Dominion Day 1963, to a one-year lectureship at $4,000, or 20 per cent less than he earned in his first year, 1956. Then came a gap, followed by another $4,000 contract as "an honorarium lecturer" in English. Finally, on 1 July 1966, he began lecturing in both departments for a combined payment of $13,000. Not until July 1967 was the compromise achieved by which he would at last give up all teaching to edit *Canadian Literature*, a position that paid him $7,500 in the first year but whose compensation rose by annual increments until 1977. When, at that time, he retired from the journal and passed the editorship to William H. New of the English department, his stipend was $16,937, hardly a grand figure, especially considering twenty years of inflation.

With his academic obligations lessened and specified by contract, Woodcock was thus better able to arrange his travels in the most advantageous way. In a letter typical of his adventures during this period, Woodcock thanked Avakumovic for his letter,

> which was awaiting us—having been forwarded from Delhi, when we arrived late in Singapore—after a month incommunicado in East Pakistan, Thailand and Cambodia and a leisurely journey down through Malaya—three days ago. I was glad to hear from you and felt very guilty that I had not written before. But our life has been v. busy, what with finishing plays, lecturing on Orwell in India and turning my lecture into an article for a Karachi magazine, collecting material for

three radio programmes, and going through the other chores of keeping copious diaries and the monstrous labour of travel itself, with all
its manifold arrangements and frustrations . . . but on our trip from
Singapore to Hong Kong [to Tokyo]—we sail in two days' time—
I hope to make up by writing at least three . . .

Singapore, alas, is all too like Vancouver, though we are told that the
almost continuous rain that has fallen since we arrived is exceptional
and that it marks the last kick of the rainy season. But if you can
imagine Vancouver rains combined with an equatorial heat and humid-
ity, that is Singapore at this moment. We are looking forward with
desperate eagerness to setting out over the China Seas for what we are
told is the much better climate of Hong Kong and Macao. We shall
eventually find our way to Japan somewhere about the 17th of March.[12]

Woodcock's reputation in Canadian letters was growing stronger as
he became busier and busier on the international front. Ryerson Press
in Toronto, the hearthstone of Can lit, offered to publish a volume
of his poems if he could find a British house to co-publish it (he
couldn't, and so his life as a poet went into a long hibernation). He
did undertake, however, a school anthology for Ryerson. *Variations on
a Human Theme*, one of his least memorable productions, was nonetheless one whose availability, perhaps to his minor embarrassment,
dragged on until 1982, when McGraw-Hill Ryerson, successor to the
original company, reported that sales had "declined to the point where
it is no longer possible to keep it in stock."[13] At about the same time
as the commission from Ryerson came one from Oxford University
Press in Toronto. Oxford was a house with which Woodcock would
develop a stronger relationship through time (he dedicated one of his
last books to its editorial director, William Toye). Now it asked for
an anthology of the first four years of *Canadian Literature*, to be called
A Choice of Critics, the first of numerous books he would cobble
together from the pages of the journal.

In 1965, Woodcock served as one of the judges on the Governor
General's Award panel, convened by the Canada Council to select the
best books published during the 1964 calendar year, and during the
past three years he himself had received $6,100 in travel grants from
the Council in aid of his books about India—for Faber had followed
Faces of India (quickly translated into Italian and Japanese) with
contracts for what became *The Greeks in India* (1966) and *Kerala:*

Above: George Woodcock and his mother, Margaret Gertrude Lewis Woodcock ("a very, very strict woman"), outside the family home at Marlow in Buckinghamshire. From 1928 until his mother's death in 1940, Woodcock commuted from there to a lowly job at Paddington Station in London, headquarters of the Great Western Railway. *Ingeborg Woodcock.*

Inset: George Woodcock's father, Arthur Woodcock, whom George "always idolized and perhaps idealized", left England for Canada to make his fortune early in the century, but returned home in failure. *Ingeborg Woodcock.*

Above: George Woodcock as a boy in the 1920s, playing along the Thames with his younger cousin, Lewis Cooke (foreground). Whereas Woodcock grew up to be a famous anarchist, Cooke would become an international banker. *Ingeborg Woodcock.*

Right: The scene in one of the BBC studios at Broadcasting House in London on 8 September 1942 as six authors prepare to make a joint broadcast to listeners in India. Standing (left to right) are Woodcock, the Indian novelist Mulk Raj Anand, Woodcock's friend and mentor, George Orwell, and William Empson, the poet-critic. Seated are the art critic and anarchist Herbert Read (left), another of Woodcock's father figures, and the poet Edmund Blunden. *BBC.*

Above: Woodcock exploring British Columbia history in the early 1950s. *Queen's University Archives.*

Facing page (top): The Woodcocks outside the second of two cabins they built for themselves on Vancouver Island. *Queen's University Archives.*

Left: Marie Louise Berneri (who converted Woodcock to the anarchist cause—and aroused his passions) clowning with him in Cambridgeshire in 1946. With them, her face turned from the camera, is Ingeborg Linzer Roskelly. Woodcock and Roskelly would marry in 1949, when they were preparing to leave together for Canada. *Ingeborg Woodcock.*

Above: Inge and George near Hope, B.C., in 1950, during one of the trips described in George's first book about Canada, *Ravens and Prophets* (1952). *Queen's University Archives.*

Facing page (top): The Woodcocks with the Dalai Lama during their first visit to Dharmsala, his place of exile in India. The Woodcocks became friends of the exiled Tibetan spiritual leader, who would visit them in Vancouver. *Queen's University Archives.*

Right: The Woodcocks founded three charities—one to aid Tibetan refugees, a second to improve sanitation and medical care in parts of northern India and a third to assist Canadian writers in financial distress. In all, they helped to raise millions of dollars for these causes. Here, Woodcock distributes clothing to needy Tibetan exiles in the Punjab. *Queen's University Archives.*

Above: One of the last photographs of George Woodcock, taken in 1994, the
year before his death, in Dunbar Park, near his home in the Point Grey area of
Vancouver. "I like the picture", says Alan Twigg, who took it, "because it shows
(I think) George's vulnerability and venerability." Inge Woodcock kept this
photo on her late husband's writing desk as she completed his last project,
a new translation of Proust. *Alan Twigg, B.C. BookWorld.*

A Portrait of the Malabar Coast (1967). In time he would become a private and public critic of the Council, which he saw as an expression of the trend towards the centralization of power, with all the attendant bureaucratization. Eventually he would write to one of the younger writers he admired:

> I've ceased to wonder at anything that happens in that bureaucratic haven ... my standing at the Council has declined recently; I am regarded as a misanthrope who—cardinal sin—never goes near Ottawa.[14]

Later he expanded his views:

> There is something wrong not only with the juries that are selected but with the method used to select them; and I am saying this in my book [*Strange Bedfellows: The State of the Arts in Canada*, 1985]—or rather, have said it already. I look back in sadness to the good days of Peter Dwyer [the former Council director—and wartime British intelligence officer], who may have been an old spy, but was also a generous human being to whom one could appeal and who would do his best to understand one's appeal and find some way of doing justice. The first time I smelt something wrong was several years ago, when, having served on juries, done various other donkey work for the council, and being well-known as a writer born in Canada, I was suddenly asked for my birth certificate in connection with some small application.[15]

In 1965, Faber commissioned Woodcock as general editor of a series of short books to be called The Great Travellers. Ten volumes appeared between 1969 and 1975, including two of Woodcock's own, *Henry Walter Bates: Naturalist of the Amazons* (a kind of closure on a writer to whom his father introduced him) and *Into Tibet: The Early British Explorers* (by contrast, a proof of his growing interest in the problems of that besieged culture). In the same vein, he contributed to a friend's series, writing the volume *The British in the Far East* for Peter Quennell's Social History of the British Overseas.

One document in particular attests to Woodcock's fecundity at this point. In November 1965 he prepared for his superiors at UBC a sort of supplement to his c.v. covering the period since his last such report, in 1962. He listed many of the more mainstream publications for which he was writing (passing by such others as *Limbo*, a local neo-surrealist magazine). He enumerated the original and adapted dramas he had done for the CBC as well as the growing number of his own works translated into other languages. In addition to the Penguin edition of *Anarchism,* he could lay claim to *Faces of India,* a new paperback of *Incas and Other Men,* two books in the press (*The Greeks in India* and *Asia, Gods and Cities*), and one commissioned and just completed (*The Crystal Spirit,* his long-aborning book about Orwell). In addition, he had just begun some research on a commission from Oxford for a study, *The Doukhobors.* That would be his last collaboration with Avakumovic, to whom he wrote a month later (from the wonderfully named Mascot Hotel at Trivandrum in Kerala):

> Here is a very hasty note to tell you where we are. Actually we arrived almost a week ago, after a week in Germany and almost another week in Delhi. I have spent a great deal of that time trying to crawl out from under the burdens that followed me from the Vancouver life. In Germany I was overtaken by the proofs for the book on Asia, and had to correct these and prepare an index (which had its own uses as it did release me from too much involvement in in-law affairs). When we arrived in Delhi the greater part of the proofs of the *Canadian Literature* anthology were awaiting me there, and I had to struggle with them in the midst of a quite hectic Delhi social round, not to mention having to advise my host on a book which he had half finished writing. And since researching here we have been meeting at least two people a day, as well as making tours, keeping up diaries and running along with basic research. However, I don't think there is much doubt that we shall come out in the end with a vast mass of material, and that the main problem will be selection and shaping.
>
> We plan to stay here in Trivandrum until early January. There will be enough involved in meeting people and in basic research until that time. Then we shall go on a big oval trip north along the coast as far as Cannanore, and then south through the inland routes so that we can touch all of the important nodal centres and stay in each of them a few days, reaching Trivandrum again at the end of the month ... But I hope that during all this travel the above address will serve as an efficient forwarding post for mail.
>
> I am afraid I feel too much under the burden of facts and impressions to say much about Kerala at the moment, except that the weather is warm and wonderful and the people most helpful and hospitable.

But my head is not too full of Kerala to have forgotten the
Doukhobors. I am sorry to be leaving the main burden so much to
you at present, but I am thinking about it, and we are now considering whether we shouldn't return to Canada via Ottawa, and do whatever needs to be done [in the Public Archives] there before we get back
to Vancouver.[16]

Freed from his mother's household at Marlow, freed from the life of
a clerk in the railway, freed from the class, political and romantic
constraints of Britain itself, freed of the drudgery of a faded utopia
on Vancouver Island and now in a state of virtual manumission from
UBC as well, Woodcock was a writer gagging on fresh air, gulping it
down faster than he could swallow, and working in a mad and exhil-
arating rush of adrenalin.

Not many months after they were back in Vancouver, Woodcock
suffered a major heart attack one night at 3 A.M.

I felt a hard pain searing up my arm and into my jaw and gripping
my chest in a relentless vise. I knew what was happening, and I felt
detached as I told Inge and she went to call our doctor. I then lay there
wondering, for I had always thought myself as a coward and had
imagined that faced with a threat of death, I would be paralyzed with
fear. Instead, I felt an equanimity, somewhat troubled by the thought
of the difficulties for others my death might cause, and an immense
curiosity.[17]

That night in hospital he had a morphine-induced dream, rich in
folkloric and religious associations, about being the only passenger on
a train that was running parallel the Mekong in southeast Asia. The
train pulled up at a wharf where a steam ferry waited to take him
across to a city of pagodas on the opposite shore. He attempted to
disembark, but as he stepped down onto the platform, the ferry hooted
and left without him—and he woke up in Vancouver alive, facing a
long convalescence under the direction of Inge. Years later, travelling
in Burma, he stumbled on the village that he had seen in his dream.

Woodcock had come to Canada looking for a simple life. Now he
would have to make good on the promises he had made to himself.
Significantly for Woodcock, though, this involved not writing less but
writing more—and more happily, focusing even more intensively on

Canadian literature and its problems while slowly, one by one, completing most of the other British or foreign projects he had set for himself, but doing so at a pace that, while rapid, was totally his own, not hastened by outside engagements or the pursuit of what other people thought of as a career.

9 FROM ORWELL TO THE DOUKHOBORS

VIEWING HIS WORK as a whole from this distance in time one sees clearly that a few of Woodcock's books were mere pieces of journeyman joinery, some were topical efforts designed for the moment and others (continuing up the evolutionary scale) were glosses on subjects he had written about in the past and would write about again. Those in this last category, however, can often exert a powerful hold on the reader. A perfect example is the narrative to which Woodcock first gave the working title "India's Stepchild: A Portrait of Kerala" but was finally published, by Faber in 1967, as *Kerala: A Portrait of the Malabar Coast*.

The southern Indian state of Kerala was bound to fascinate Woodcock. That matriarchal society had India's highest literacy rate and little or none of the wretched poverty and filth that characterize Bombay, Calcutta, Delhi and the other metropolises. It was distinct politically as well: it elected a communist state government in the 1950s, much to the alarm of the U.S. state department; later, when the people voted them out, the communists left peacefully, the first time such an event had ever taken place.

This ancient and still industrially undeveloped land of silks and spices also would have drawn Woodcock because of the way various cultures lay in sedimentary strata. The Chinese were early travellers there, while Christianity along the coast dated to the arrival of St Thomas the Apostle in C.E. 52. In the sixth century, Sephardic Jews settled in Kerala too, establishing the first synagogue in what later became the British Empire; the poet Siegfried Sassoon was descended from this particular part of the diaspora. The arrival of Vasco da Gama, who came in the early sixteenth century (and was buried there for a time), introduced a period of Portuguese Catholicism, superseded by one of Dutch Protestantism. The displacement of the Dutch by the British in 1804 meant that this part of India would remain heavily Christianized, though not to the point where the native culture, including the musical Malayalam language, a part of the Tamil family, would be endangered. Woodcock had always been a student of various imperialisms, as part of his larger cross-examination of the nation-state and its natural enemy, local, indigenous anarchistic culture.

Then there are a few books of Woodcock's that seem to have been his destiny to write. *Anarchism* certainly figured among these, as did *The Crystal Spirit*, his study of Orwell. Orwell's political ideas were part of the baggage Woodcock carried to Canada. Unlike anarchism, however, Orwell was not a subject on which the process of emigration caused Woodcock to refine his views. Writing from Canada may have given Woodcock rather a new viewpoint on anarchism; indeed, spending the rest of his life in Canada, with its national disease of constitutional hypochondria, would help ensure that Woodcock's ideas on anarchism were always in flux, according to changes in the ever-shifting political climate. Orwell was a different sort of topic: a testament and a code: an interest that, as a result of Orwell's death in 1950, would remain fixed in time. All the more ironic and satisfying, then, that publication of *The Crystal Spirit* finally gave Woodcock status as a Canadian author; its official acceptance freed him, in a sense, to write more, and more confidently, about Canada, and to do so from the inside, from the standpoint of one Canadian addressing his fellow citizens.

Even more so than that of *Anarchism*, the publishing history of *The Crystal Spirit* was tangled. For a time, in fact, it looked as though the book might not materialize at all. Woodcock had been writing about Orwell's work since 1946, when he published, in Dwight Macdonald's *Politics*, the first serious essay on the subject, a piece that later formed part of *The Writer and Politics*. Orwell's death sent Woodcock back to writing about his friend again and again. A biography might have seemed the natural next step, but Orwell had left emphatic instructions in his will that no biography of him be published. Still, in 1955, Woodcock wrote to Sonia Bronwell Orwell, the author's widow and literary executrix, about the possibility of writing one anyway. She replied, with perfect courtesy and maddening logic, that she would of course assist in whatever critical book Woodcock wished to write but that she had decided to go ahead and appoint an authorized biographer. The person she had selected, she said, was Malcolm Muggeridge, a former editor of *Punch* and the future Christian gadfly, whose book might be appearing as early as the autumn of 1956.

But years elapsed with no sign of the Muggeridge book, until at length Woodcock came to believe that Muggeridge was allowing himself to be used as a phantom biographer, designed to scare off other suitors. Woodcock waited a few years to make certain that the road to the marketplace was clear, then returned to his project once again. Still, he was careful to use the title "Reflections on George Orwell", suggesting a combination essay and memoir, in the proposal he sent to his London agent, John Smith (who, by a strange coincidence, had been the first person in the publishing world to read Orwell's manuscript of *Nineteen Eighty-Four*, which then bore the working title "The Last Man in Europe").

Smith was a director of Christy & Moore, the firm that had had such success getting Woodcock onto the Faber and Faber list. This time, however, the deal Smith struck was with Jonathan Cape. In an agreement finalized in August 1964, Woodcock would receive an advance of five hundred pounds—one hundred pounds on signing, one hundred pounds on delivery of the manuscript and fifty pounds on publication. Later, Woodcock's U.S. agent placed the book with Little, Brown in Boston for $1,500, half on signing, half on acceptance. Significantly, this was only after the proposal was rejected by William Jovanovich of Harcourt, Brace in New York. Jovanovich was issuing all of Orwell's works in the American market and was a friend of Sonia Orwell.

Woodcock was on spongy ground. Three years earlier, Orwell's papers had gone to University College, London. The deputy librarian there informed Woodcock that six authors, including two with commissions from publishers, had received permission to go through the manuscript and epistolary resources. All six had been discovered in violation of their promises to avoid the purely biographical. In confusion, the college had closed the Orwell Archive for a few months in 1964 in order to review the problem and formulate a policy. That policy, which was now in place, was that writers whose "intentions are predominately biographical"[1] could not use the manuscripts. "On the other hand, every serious student of Orwell whose critical project has been approved by Professor [James] Sutherland [a University College trustee] is allowed to consult the Archive manuscripts, except where the donor has laid down special conditions" limiting access.[2] Only two donors had done so. Sonia Orwell was one.

Rumours about barriers erected to Orwell scholarship had naturally reached Woodcock's ears. In the end, what ensured he would be given access was the fact that, on first learning the Orwell Archive was being established (significantly, before he wrote his book proposal) Woodcock had generously donated copies of his own Orwell correspondence, without waiting to be solicited. Now he was careful to promise that he would make the Archive aware of whatever other privately held letters or documents he might turn up in the course of his research. He had fallen into a wary but cordial professional relationship with Mrs Orwell, and he wasn't about to let it be tainted by direct negotiation. In an unusual role for an author's agent, John Smith secured permission for Woodcock to quote from various published Orwell works.

Appearing in the spring of 1966, *The Crystal Spirit*, one part affectionate memoir to three parts illuminating criticism, proved a wondrous success. It was well promoted. Bill Berger, Woodcock's agent in New York, managed to sell an impressive chunk of it to *Esquire*, which billboarded it on the cover of the August issue; the excerpt paid US$680, which Woodcock thought "a handsome fee".[3] The book had a warm reception, largely because of its sympathetic and seemingly unassailable understanding of the personage, who, when considered as a transatlantic figure, was the subject of remarkably wide disagreement.

As late as 1983 (in the busy run-up to the celebratory 1984, in whose panels, symposia and documentaries Woodcock would take an active role) the right-wing American writer Norman Podhoretz would state, in an article in *Harper's*, perhaps one of the most controversial in that magazine's long history, that if Orwell were alive today he would be a neo-conservative. The piece had the virtue of forensic cheek but not really that of originality. What Podhoretz considered daringly revisionist was actually an attempt at re-revisionism. Orwell even then was still in the early stages of his first re-positioning, the one that got under way with *The Crystal Spirit*, a book which, like *Anarchism*, and somewhat to the author's surprise and bewilderment, found favour with the young people of the sixties generation—people who had been taught a different version of Orwell by their parents.

Since the publication of *Animal Farm* in 1945, Orwell has been claimed by the political right, the American political right in particular, as one of their own, despite all the evidence (such as his service with the Republicans in the Spanish civil war) that he was on the other side. The appearance of *Nineteen Eighty-Four* a few years later only increased the tug-of-war. The tussle goes on still, though it seems rather silly at this late date. Even casual observers have always seen clearly that Orwell stood outside the two power blocs, a resident of a declining Britain, whose decomposition gave off a warmth he liked. His passion instead lay with anti-authoritarianism, one that was more socialistically inclined than the Freedom Press version of anarchism, which he nonetheless viewed with sympathy.

The Crystal Spirit was trounced by Raymond Williams, a rival Orwellist with whom Woodcock would clash again in the future. In general, however, it received highly favourable reviews much to Woodcock's delight: "One was by V. S. Pritchett in the *New York Review of Books* and the other ... a very long one by Malcolm Muggeridge in *Esquire*. I particularly value the fact that both of these are particularly favourable since Pritchett and Muggeridge knew Orwell even better than I did."[4] There was also a highly positive review by Cyril Connolly (the former mentor and employer of Sonia Bronwell at his magazine *Horizon*). In the *Sunday Telegraph*, a review by Nigel Dennis made its points so perfectly that it unwittingly came close to identifying what it was that Woodcock and Orwell had in common as persons. On these grounds it is worth quoting at length:

> Orwell is a difficult and interesting author to write about precisely because his 'literary personality' and his 'private character' usually seem to stick closely together. Orwell appears in every book by Orwell, except *Animal Farm*. Whether he is writing fiction or non-fiction, Orwell is always telling us about Orwell.
>
> Mr. Woodcock is right to warn us that in the fiction, the Orwell we detect is not the whole man. Of course he is not: he has had plastic surgery done on him by his author and been given invented characteristics. But the author's face always shows through. The man who wanted no biography to be written of him spent nearly all his life writing it.

It is this biography that is still being read with interest in the 1960s. Mr. Woodcock believes that younger people read it because they trust it. It tells them what the 1930s and 1940s were like in the opinion of a man who never played safe and never diddled himself or his contemporaries deliberately. Orwell is one of the few writers of the period of whom this can be said.

It would not be said of him if he were not so quirky, so unpredictable, so mixed in his feelings. There is no consistency in his writings; there is consistency in his own character.

He can be understood as ... a 'rebel' rather than a 'revolutionary', as Mr. Woodcock puts it. Unlike a revolutionary, a rebel is one who rejects every 'line' that crosses his way ...

Mr. Woodcock parades all Orwell's rebellions and sets them out clearly and well, as far as possible, in chronological order. But only 'as far as possible' because it was in Orwell's character always to have one rebellion working against another rebellion. That is one of the main reasons why he inspires trust. He says what he feels, not what is currently felt.

Even in his earliest days as a police-officer in Burma, Orwell was not content to rebel only against imperial government. He rebelled against the East and eastern manners, and with the passing years he rebelled against those who rebelled against imperialists. He thought it ridiculous that men who had slaved under appalling conditions should be mocked by stereotyped radicals who would always be too cowardly to think for themselves and too irresponsible to take personal responsibility.

A born humanitarian, he looked to his opposite numbers for correction. 'A humanitarian', he wrote, 'is always a hypocrite, and Kipling's understanding of this is perhaps the central secret of his power to create telling phrases.'

But Orwell's life would not seem nearly so interesting if it were only a series of interacting rebellions. It is his loves and passions that fill out the picture and explain what most of the rebellions were about.

He was convinced that the common people—the 'proles' of *1984* [*sic*]—led a rich life that was beyond the understanding of Socialist reformers. He loathed the birth-controllers who tried to limit the splendid fecundity of the poor, and he abominated the machines that would save them from the physical excellence of manual labour. Mr. Woodcock makes a good point when he compares Orwell's views to those of the radical wing of the Continental Roman Catholics.

He was horrified to imagine an educated, refined, hygienic England
—one in which, as he put it, 'it is hardly likely that Father will still be
a rough man who likes to sit in shirtsleeves and says: 'Ah wur coomin'
oop street.' "[5]

The opposing ideological camps that have tussled over Orwell have
almost come to represent the two warring sides of Orwell's personality; it was from the conflict between the two halves, perhaps, that
Animal Farm and *Nineteen Eighty-Four* sprang.

After listening to a multi-part 1984 radio biography of Orwell in
which he had played a significant role, Woodcock would remark that
he was struck by the diversity of accents among the old friends,
acquaintances and family members who had been recorded. That
underscores the most basic fact about Orwell: he was an upper-
middle-class intellectual who chose to align himself with the caste
below him, and whose politics derived in large part from his conscious
desire to fit in. Some Marxists used to throw about the term *class alien*
to describe those still stuck in the aristocracy come the revolution—
somewhat mistakenly of course, for that is not what Marx and Engels
meant by class alienation at all. Orwell was stuck between two
extremes like a pedestrian trapped forever on a traffic island, unable
to complete crossing the street, equally unable to turn back. The condition now seems characteristic of the dispirited post-war England
where declining expectations were the norm. That Orwell should have
shone in journalism, a field that exists almost as a class of its own, or
a kind of no-man's-land, does not really seem surprising.

Woodcock demonstrated convincingly how the two ends of Orwell's
short life show how far he travelled. Orwell was born in India, the
son of a civil servant, and went to Eton before becoming a colonial
policeman in Burma. Up to that point his life is almost an imperialist cliché. What changed him? The Depression, among other things.
By 1933 Eric Blair, as he was christened, had become George Orwell,
a homely name that could have belonged to a suburban tobacconist,
and had published his first book, *Down and Out in Paris and
London*, describing the poverty and degradation he had sought out
quite deliberately. As already illustrated by Woodcock's experiences
with him in pubs and restaurants, there was still a lot of the upper-
middle-class about him as well as something too studied in his lower-
middle-class affectations. But then he genuinely loved the shabby

middle class. He loved the smell, particularly in the morning perhaps; it smelled not of victory but of peace. Such at least is the suggestion from the novels he wrote in the 1930s.

Woodcock would always entertain a much loftier opinion of the strictly novelistic skills of the pre-*Animal Farm* Orwell than was necessary to appreciate Orwell's greatness as a writer. This is part, a small part, of the story of Woodcock's major role in the shaping of Orwell's posthumous reputation (a process discussed in detail in *The Politics of Literary Reputation: The Making and Claiming of 'St. George' Orwell* by John Rodden, an American teacher of rhetoric—a work both ponderous and vacuous but one which clearly traces Woodcock's role in helping build the idea of Orwell as a rebel rather than a revolutionary).

Orwell himself of course operated on the hopeful assumption that he had gifts as a novelist (as distinct from a writer of parables or fables), though even he was not always blind to the truth of the matter, to judge from his letters. He went along nonetheless, partly because writing novels, if not the task that most attractively displayed his craft, was the one that best suited the twin pieces of his make-up. There was something comfortably literary about the writing in *A Clergyman's Daughter* or *Keep the Aspidistra Flying* that, for all the class consciousness of those books, appealed to his gentility. From the other side of his personality, though, Orwell wrote fiction because fiction was still one of the principal entertainments of clerks and artisans. Had he not worked at an old-fashioned second-hand bookshop, the kind with a lending library at the back, and seen locals carrying off armsful of Ethel M. Dell? Novels were still written by gentlemen and near-gentlemen and read by washerwomen with pretensions. The difficulty is that Orwell's early fiction, extending to *Coming Up for Air* in 1939, was less than riveting at the time and appeals to us now for its period sensibility and its insights into the author of *Animal Farm* and *Nineteen Eighty-Four*. The fiction belongs to a different canon from Orwell's essays and journalism.

This last consideration is crucial. From their publication until the revisionist work of the late 1960s, *Animal Farm* and *Nineteen Eighty-Four* accounted for almost the whole of Orwell's reputation. He was productive as a journalist and writer-of-all-work and even in his lifetime put together three collections of essays (*Inside the Whale, Critical Essays* and *Shooting an Elephant*), but these had been regarded by most as ancillary writing, like the essays of a great novelist; only in

1968, with the appearance of *Collected Essays, Journalism and Letters*, in four volumes edited by Ian Angus and Sonia Orwell, did Orwell's periodical writing form the rightful basis of his attractiveness. This was surely a unique case: a not terribly interesting writer of narrative fiction whose political fables elevated him to the level of a major figure, until he was proven among the most significant journalists of the age.

Orwell had one of the keenest ears of any British prose writer of the day: a fact that somehow helped thwart his ambitions as a novelist. His ear was like his accent, something he often tried eradicating but couldn't, something that continually made him suspect to the proletarians with whom he wished to communicate. It also helped him to blur the lines between the various forms in which he worked. He wrote noble polemics in the language of studied essays and essays with the strident edge of polemics. At its highest, his non-fiction is neither one thing nor the other but can be categorized only according to length. *The Road to Wigan Pier*, his Depression reportage, and *Homage to Catalonia*, his observations from Spain, are not more bookish in their prose than the magazine and newspaper work, which, because of its size, we think of as articles. He wasn't a run-of-the-mill journalist and he wasn't exactly a belletrist; he was a High Journalist. That is one reason he presents such a contemporary face.

Looking back on the course it has taken, one cannot avoid being struck by the lucky timing inherent in Orwell's reputation. His renown as a novelist collapsed as the decent middle-class novel fell into disrepute as a mass vehicle. His fictional manifestoes like *Animal Farm* came at the beginning of a long public fascination with fantasy. His journalism was rediscovered at the height of what probably will be looked back on as a golden era of journalism, if only because the period has no loftier claim to fame. Even without such coat-tails as these to ride on, however, Orwell's essays and miscellaneous non-fiction would probably continue his reputation, because they show him to be a curiously contemporary figure even fifty years after his death.

Reading *The Crystal Spirit* leaves one with the impression that Orwell was perhaps the first important post-war writer on whom all the scars of the war showed plainly. Like most skilled journalists (this is one of their chief faults) he was stuck in the present, preferring it to either of the alternatives. Woodcock's personal reminiscences of Orwell, dating back to 1942, paint him as a person for whom the bad times had the virtue of being real times. The times tended to make a mockery of the old imperialist ideal of which he disapproved. They tended to show the stupidity of class disparity, which he disliked because it was so destructive—and also because he too was, in his way, its victim. In this sense, Orwell was a precursor of John Osborne and Arnold Wesker and even the Beatles: he helped make the wrong side of the tracks fashionable (and a perennial candidate for legitimacy).

Woodcock's Orwell is the most English of Englishmen in so many ways. Unlike Chesterton, say, he had, after all, experience at both ends of the social spectrum: he had been up and about as well as down and out. He had more in common with Defoe than with Dickens, more in common with Cobbett than with journalists of his own time, such as Muggeridge. Yet he contradicted all the stereotypes. He did not seem particularly saddened by the shrunken role of Britain in the world; he simply recognized that Britain would be one of the territories over which the Americans and the Russians would hurl their insults and their bombs. This comes through in *Animal Farm* and *Nineteen Eighty-Four*, but comes through more strongly in almost everything else he wrote in the last years and likewise in how he wrote it.

Much has been made of his confession that he tried to write prose "like a window-pane", free of old-fashioned literary conventions, free even of much of the writer's personality. He was mistaken in what he believed he accomplished. His style is full of his personality and wouldn't be readable if it weren't. But it conspicuously lacks both elements he was no doubt thinking of when he wrote those words: the purple, orotund stuff of the Victorian headmaster or clergyman and the elliptical, stylized stuff of the 1890s aesthete (how French it all was!). He wrote a very English hand, redolent of all things dear to those with ambitions to acknowledge civilization. Not for him the vulgar American ideal of short declarative sentences, marching endlessly like soldiers. His was a more international style than most, more mid-Atlantic, a combination of American economy and British taste, a blend that has not only travelled well but travelled far. He put it to uses that seem even now, on the far side of 1984, surprisingly contemporary.

In another manifestation of the class shifts that lie at the heart of Orwell, he wrote both of high art and of popular culture, in a manner practically unheard of then. He would write of complex linguistic matters and could presume to discuss rhyme schemes. He also could write about Henry Miller, the boys' newspapers and the art of Donald McGill, an illustrator of vulgar post cards. Pop culture was not then a field of study or much of anything other than commerce; but Orwell was interested in it and in the democracy of the marketplace, just as he showed signs of being interested in back-to-the-landism and other branches of self-sufficiency. Likewise, he seemed to have some prescient understanding of international terrorism. Such elements continue to make his work, and the personality that shows so strongly between the lines, reassuringly fresh.

By its very Englishness and its suggestion of pub food, shilling meters and Woodbine cigarettes, there is something comfortably shabby and nostalgic in his work, like a favourite pullover whose elbows have been patched and repatched. At the same time, there is the strong sense he had of living in the nuclear age, a sense that lent fear to his predictions, defiance to his assurances and sometimes even hope to his warnings, even if, as in *Nineteen Eighty-Four*, the hope is there by negative example.

As for *The Crystal Spirit*, its author would note in 1973 that Bernard Crick, another writer on the subject, "must be at least the sixth person who has been 'official biographer'; there was an American professor, and there was Julian Symons, who would have written a very good biography and thought everything was cleared when Sonia turned against him. Fortunately I caught her on an up wave, and she approved everything I'd written up to the time of publication—only to run me down after the book appeared!"[6] (The first true "authorized" biography, Michael Shelden's excellent *Orwell*, did not appear until 1991, more than a decade after Sonia Orwell's death.)

In July 1966, a reporter for the Vancouver *Sun* interviewed Woodcock and found him like "a St. Bernard—big, shaggy, dependable-looking and gentle."[7] Dependable-looking and gentle he would remain, but soon he would be vigorously engaged in losing weight, and giving up tobacco, following the heart attack that autumn that had nearly ended his life at fifty-four. Typically, Woodcock became fascinated by cardiology and also by the psychological effects of heart disease. On the tenth anniversary of his episode he would remember how "when I emerged from hospital and began to totter out on my first walks, as a mild Vancouver winter merged into an early spring, I experienced something near to what I had felt forty years before [presumably, a reference to puberty], a sense of a world totally renewed and sparkling with excitement, a feeling that I had indeed been born again."[8]

Certainly he was about to enter a wonderfully expansive period of creativity and recognition unlike any other he had known previously. This time would denote the real beginning of the astounding productivity that always seemed the central fact of his career to people not attuned to recognizing ideas instead. The books came tumbling out like coins from a fruit-machine that had hit the jackpot: *Selected Poems* (1967); *Hugh MacLennan* (1969); *Odysseus Ever Returning: Essays on Canadian Writers and Writing* (1970); *Mohandas Gandhi, Mordecai Richler* and *Victoria* (all 1971); and, most remarkably of all, *Dawn and the Darkest Hour: A Study of Aldous Huxley, Herbert Read: The Stream and the Source* and *The Rejection of Politics and Other Essays on Canada, Canadians, Anarchism and the World* (all 1972). As the list shows, this period was also the signal for the real beginning of his recognition as a specifically Canadian figure. One of the key players in this second transition was Robert Weaver of the Canadian Broadcasting Corporation and the quarterly journal *Tamarack Review*.

Weaver was himself a gentle, dependable-looking man, a native of Niagara Falls who served in the RCAF and the army during the Second World War and then drifted into talks and literary broadcasting at the CBC in Toronto. He had first met the Woodcocks in the 1950s, when they were briefly in Toronto before beginning the trips to Mexico recounted in *To the City of the Dead.* Weaver had astounded Woodcock by drawing from his bookshelf a treasured copy of *NOW*, volume six of the second series, the one containing Orwell's essay "How the Poor Die".

> George expressed astonishment that this magazine had made it that far across the ocean. I then told him about Roher's Book Store on [the south side of] Bloor Street [just west of Yonge] ... Roher's was the first in a kind of continuing history of primarily magazine stores but with books as well, [places whose virtue was their policy of taking] every kind of magazine. They didn't draw lines. It's the place, I think, where I first saw and bought Dwight Macdonald's *Politics.*[9]

Weaver was now, in 1967, part of the three-person jury charged by the Canada Council with selecting the winners of the Governor General's Awards for the outstanding English-language books published by Canadians during the 1966 calendar year.

> The other judges were [the novelist] Henry Kreisel and Mary Winspear, who ran a school for girls in Montreal. This was two years after [Douglas] LePan had won the fiction award for *The Deserter*, instead of Margaret Laurence for *The Stone Angel*; one of those years in which there was a lot of complaining. Mary was the hold-over judge. [Laurence's] *A Jest of God* was one of the books before us, and there was a certain amount of defensive feeling after what had happened to *The Stone Angel*. As for poetry, it was a very big year, what with Frank Scott, Peggy Atwood [the winner for *The Circle Game*], Miriam Waddington, Gwen MacEwen, Margaret Avison ... there were quite long discussions about all that. So it was a great relief when non-fiction came round that all of us said 'Woodcock' without a second thought. All three of us, from quite different angles, admired the Orwell book, so the choice was easy.[10]

Of course, there would always remain pockets of resistance to Woodcock's claim to being Canadian and indeed native-born. The arch-nationalist academic Robin Mathews became the sort of recurring antagonist for Woodcock in Canada that Albert Meltzer was in Britain, turning up when least expected with some fresh assault. Mostly, though, it was Mathews' opposites—writers in the U.S. orbit—whom Woodcock would seem to offend by his existence. Weaver recalled Morley Callaghan telling him that "Woodcock was a tiny frog in the English literary puddle, who, since he wasn't getting anywhere in England and was having a bad time generally, decided to come to Canada to trade on this sort of mythical reputation, and that we colonial people in Canada, suckers that we are, had taken him at his word, so to speak."[11] Another and equally abiding example was Mordecai Richler, who charged in a 1971 issue of *Saturday Night* that Woodcock was someone who had cultivated the acquaintance of English writers and then "returned here to mine them in memoirs."[12] To which Woodcock replied in the following month's issue: "This is merely absurd, and demonstrates the ignorances and half-truths on which Richlerian journalism is based ... Significantly another of the forty books I have published was a brief account of

Mordecai Richler; equally significantly, it did not consist of unadulterated flattery."[13] And so it went.

≈

All the while that he was basking in completion of *The Crystal Spirit* and recovering from his heart attack, Woodcock was busy on other fronts. He was, for instance, continuing to quarrel with UBC over employment terms that would provide him both a decent stipend and maximum time for travel; at various points, the discussion grew heated. And he was working on another important book, *The Doukhobors*, his last collaboration with Ivan Avakumovic.

The story of the Doukhobors, the dissident sect of Russian Christians who lived communally and refused to recognize the state's moral authority, was one that Woodcock had grown up hearing from his father. Arthur Woodcock apparently had had some casual experience of the nearly 7,500 Doukhobors who, thanks partly to the efforts of Count Tolstoy and Prince Kropotkin (and also those of the Society of Friends), had been permitted to settle in what is now Saskatchewan. Partly because Doukhobors abjured written records along with traditional scripture, the precise origins of the movement are obscure, but it arose in the seventeenth century as a radical fringe, rejecting the elaborate liturgical requirements of the Orthodox Church at about the same time the radical protestants in England were rejecting those of their own country's state religion. The name (meaning, roughly, "spirit-wrestlers") was bestowed on them in the late eighteenth century as a term of derision. Like the "Quakers" they wore the label proudly and, by doing so, neutralized the abuse in which it came wrapped.

Woodcock remembered his father's words about the Doukhobors in the late 1930s, when the young clerk was busily reading about Canada, and he discovered in the Doukhobors traits he admired. They were "Nature's anarchists [with an] anti-militarism ... that appealed to my own pacifism, and I accepted Tolstoy's impression of a libertarian sect who took their Christianity neat and had turned their settlements into Utopian communes."[14] Later, his attitude became less romantic, particularly after he and Inge established themselves in British Columbia and hitchhiked to Hilliers, sixty miles north of Sooke. There they spent time in a small Doukhobor community, part of the Doukhobor migration to B.C. in 1908 under the leadership of Peter Verigen—Peter the Lordly—who had been killed, along with eight of his followers, in a railway explosion in 1924. Many had long believed that the Sons of Freedom, the Doukhobor splinter group given to arson and nude protest marchers, had been behind the murders.

The Doukhobors continued to speak and write (and sing) in the Russian language, which made Avakumovic the ideal partner, in charge of archival research in other than English, while Woodcock, starting in the summer of 1966, and continuing into the autumn, when he was still weak from his heart attack, made more visits to surviving communities and also worked in the provincial archives in Victoria and the Public Archives in Ottawa, documenting some of the Doukhobors' many clashes with the authorities. Previous Canadian writers had concentrated on the Sons of Freedom, and on their more sensational and prurient aspects at that. The most recent example was the 1966 bestseller *Terror in the Name of God* by Simma Holt, a right-wing Vancouver *Sun* reporter and future prickly Liberal MP. In passing on to Avakumovic the preference of Oxford for appropriate illustrations, Woodcock was careful to be precise: "By 'sober pictures' I do not mean that nudes should be excluded. Obviously all phases of Doukhobor life should be in some way represented, but we want to avoid the *emphasis* on the sensational which Simma Holt cultivated and which [her publisher] Jack McClelland for commercial reasons encouraged. Personally, I see no reason not to include the photo of Doukhobor women pulling a plough."[15]

Woodcock wrote the letter from his parents-in-law's home in Germany, one stop on a long eastward journey. The trip included Montreal: "Today we tried Expo; it took us 2½ hours to get through the Montreal traffic james [*sic*]—the result of the transport strike—and when we did arrive the holiday weekend crowds were so enormous that both of us found all our most anti-social hackles rising, decided that we were solitaries by nature, and fled for some clear air at the top of Mount Royal."[16] It also included, en route to a protracted stay in their beloved Switzerland, a hurried business trip to London, about which, in an altogether uncharacteristic slip into what would later be called sexism, Woodcock informed Avakumovic: "I liked the girls: they have better legs for mini-skirts than Vancouver girls."[17] He added: "To the new London my feelings were ambivalent and I walked around rather like a ghost."[18]

Which is not to wander from the story of the Doukhobors or to obscure how much an affinity Woodcock felt with their beliefs, however sceptical he became of the day-to-day reality of Doukhobor life, with its twin propensities for fundamentalism and violence.

In 1989, Woodcock reacted with sadness to a report that the largest band of Doukhobors was considering leaving Canada for Siberia, their ancestral home. The announcement represented not only another vivid illustration of the improvements being made to the Soviet Union in its last days but also a forceful statement on the unfortunate decline of Canada's tolerance and belief in cultural plurality. In sending a delegation to explore the possibility of resettlement there, the Doukhobors were doing more than coming full circle back to the land their forbears had been driven out of in the late nineteenth century. It was the negative aspects of Canada, rather than the positive one of Mikhail Gorbachev's U.S.S.R., that propelled them, their leader stated. Even living as they do, in the remote B.C. interior, where they speak Russian and keep to themselves, they were finding it increasingly difficult to maintain their sovereign traditions, given the all-pervasive nature of modern electronic (that is to say, American) culture.

Since the Depression, which cost many Doukhobors their land in B.C. and nearly ruined others, the sect has struggled to maintain itself in the face of enormous external pressure to conform to rural Canada's usual ways. The largest group, the Union of Spiritual Communities of Christ, has been the most successful, which is perhaps why it is the largest. Experts estimate, however, that only about half of Canada's Doukhobors, perhaps fifteen thousand people, still practise the religion for which their families were seeking a haven when they came to Canada originally. The gradual erosion has been due not only to a lessening of their religious fervour but also to the inexorable homogenizing progress—one uses the word cautiously—of popular culture.

Woodcock and I discussed the matter once. He concluded that if the Doukhobors, or rather the USCC sect specifically, were contemplating emigrating to Russia, it was not necessarily because Russia was enticing; the language they speak, for example, sounds as queer to modern-day Russians as eighteenth-century English would sound to us. Rather, it is a question of Canada having failed them. We talk a good game of multiculturalism, but in fact it seemed in 1989 that Russians might play it better, at least to the extent that they are not in the path of the American monolith that rolls over everything with which it comes into contact. By this time, of course, Woodcock had long since earned his stripes as a trenchant social critic of Canadian life and politics, a part of his public role that grew stronger as he grew older.

10 PHILANTHROPY
SELF-TAUGHT

IN RESPONSE TO a 1989 request from the poet Bronwen Wallace, soliciting a copy of a favourite book for a charity auction, Woodcock
took down from the shelf one of his oldest possessions. It was the
copy of *Naturalist on the Amazons* that his father had given him.
The author was Henry Walter Bates (1825–92), the great English
entomologist, who had discovered eight thousand species of insects
previously unknown to science. Before donating this treasured keepsake to the group called Kingston Literacy, Woodcock inscribed it as
follows:

> This is one of the golden books of my childhood. I was given this copy
> when I was 10, more than six decades ago, and the condition of the
> book shows how often it was read. I was fascinated by its account of
> strange natural phenomena and of a society and a way of life that seems
> natural and free. I also admired the serviceable but eloquent prose
> developed by Bates and the other Victorian naturalists. This book more
> than any other made me a great traveller. But, strangely enough, my
> journeys, which have taken me to all continents and scores of
> countries, never led me to the Amazons. I feared the innocent land of
> the 1840s which Bates had described would be spoilt. And of course
> I was right. The vision Bates created remained in my primitive mind,
> and today I am ordering a copy of a new edition of his book to replace
> this one.[1]

He added a further notation: "The calculations inside the cover have their interest. I was counting up the pages of an issue of *NOW* in the mid-1950s. 'Miller' was Henry Miller, 'Juli' was Julian Symons, 'Savage' was D. S. Savage, and 'K.' was Kenneth Rexroth. The others I am not sure about."[2]

Such acts of generosity were almost legendary, especially among the community of antiquarian booksellers who sometimes stood to gain by them. One dealer noted in his catalogue how Woodcock's "library was sold in sections, year and by, to raise money [for Tibetan refugees]. The annual sale, previewed by no one, was [as] likely to turn up an inscribed George Orwell as a box of paperback textbooks."[3] In later years, at certain seasons, few visitors to McCleery Street could escape Inge's high-pressure sales techniques with regards to boxes of Christmas cards in support of the Woodcocks' causes, the first of which was called the Tibetan Refugee Aid Society and which in time would raise a small fortune for its cause.

Inge Woodcock, that remarkable woman who has remained in the background of the story (always willingly, and often to the point of unbending insistence) had been studying Tibetan culture and language for years. When the Woodcocks lived in Seattle, the task was made easier by the presence of a large Tibetan community, which Vancouver lacked. George, too, took an interest in the language, but never had his wife's gifts as a linguist. Their interests in all things Tibetan was intensified by their extended trip to India and Ceylon, gathering information (and Inge taking photographs) for what became *Faces of India*: a trip Woodcock called "the most important of our early journeys—by boat from Venice to Alexandria, up the Nile to Luxor and the Valley of Kings, and then from Port Said through the Suez Canal, the Red Sea and the Arabian Sea by P&O liner, the classic outward voyage of the Raj."[4] They both admired the courage and determination of the Tibetans still fleeing their homeland after the invasion by the People's Liberation Army from China. The communists effectively colonized Tibet and cracked down on Buddhism and other activities counter to Maoist doctrine, destroying monasteries and persecuting monks with a fervour rarely seen since Henry VIII.

As usual, Woodcock was financing the trip through a complex matrix of freelance assignments, including a series on Gandhi's legacy for CBC Radio and another, on Indian writers, for All India Radio. While the Woodcocks were going through All India Radio's headquarters in Old Delhi with a producer from Kerala

Inge saw a door marked *Tibetan Section*. As soon as he learned of our interest, the producer knocked, and there appeared the director of that section, Lobsang Lhalungpa. Lobsang, the son of the State Oracle of Tibet, had himself seen the perils of the future when the Chinese army first crossed the border into Tibet in 1951, and had made his own flight. He was glad to meet anyone interested in things Tibetan, and he became our lifelong friend. [He] suggested we go to the old hill station at Mussoorie, a Kiplingesque outpost where the British from Delhi used to take cool refuge during the monsoon months when it was so hot and humid.[5]

In following the advice, the Woodcocks ran into the displaced Tibetans, seeing a newly opened school as well as orphanages "to be run on Pestalozzi principles."[6] They were greeted by a thin-faced woman wearing a traditional *chupa*. This was Rinchen Dolma Taring, who had followed the Dalai Lama into exile, taking a vow of poverty and dedicating herself to helping the children. Her spouse, a former aristocrat, had been head of the Dalai Lama's English-trained bodyguards. Taring, Woodcock would recall, "seemed to have some fore-inkling of our coming,"[7] as she was in the process of serving tea to a roomful of English-speakers, including aid-workers and missionaries. Also present was a young Tibetan woman who listened attentively to Inge's fervent interest in Tibetan affairs and said, "You must meet Uncle!" She was the niece of His Holiness the Fourteenth Dalai Lama, a Manifestation of Chenrezig, Bodhisattva of Compassion; Ocean of Wisdom, Protector of the Land of Snows and Learned Defender of the Faith, etc.—and future winner of the Nobel Peace Prize for his Gandhi-like passive resistance to the Chinese occupation of his homeland.

A time was arranged. Uncle sent his driver, who brought the visitors to an old bungalow where langur monkeys disported themselves on the tin roof. Inside, the rooms were "as full of watchful people as a Shakespeare tragedy, and when the draft moved the curtain in the open doorways, one would sometimes see a peering figure retreating into concealment."[8] This was the Dalai Lama's residence, the hub of a community of seventy thousand exiles that had sprung up since 1959, when he fled across the mountains after rebellion broke out in traditionally non-violent Tibet and the Chinese army came to put it down.

During their longish stay in Dharmsala, the Woodcocks had several meetings with the young Dalai Lama, who told them of his hopes of eventually returning to Tibet to establish a democratic system, one that would bring about his own deposition. Woodcock noted the leader's fabled interest in mechanical devices (and disappointed him by repairing a malfunctioning tape recorder before his host could disassemble it and see how it worked).

Of all the Dalai Lama's titles, "Defender of the Faith" is perhaps the most important one to westerners generally, including most western Buddhists. With his saffron robes and the look of a middle-aged science student, the Dalai Lama has long seemed an impossibly naïve and quixotic figure on the religious and political stage: an image that can be easily dismissed but sometimes almost as easily rekindled. One must take the story of his early belief that Chinese communism would somehow bend to accommodate his people's customs and beliefs and set it alongside an understanding of how early he began to preach the sanctity of the environment and the need to see environmental problems globally yet through individual sets of eyes. His power resides partly in the virtue of his simplicity and candour, which are inseparable from the lack of worldliness. His sincerity and extreme intelligence are remarkable. In fact, the latter takes one aback somewhat, as it is the kind of intelligence devoid of worldly cunning, a variety we seldom encounter in public figures.

Thupten Gyatso, the Thirteenth Dalai Lama, had already been dead for five years when, in 1938, members of a search committee, struck to find his rightful successor, reached a small village called Takster. They had gone there to pursue a lead contained in a vision. They met a small boy named Lhamo Thondup who was able to tell them facts about themselves he couldn't possibly have known and, what's more, to pick out objects that had once belonged to the late leader. This boy was chosen to be the next Dalai Lama.

As the monarch of the Tibetan people, the Dalai Lama stood at the head of a culture whose most devout wish was simply to be left alone, a wish shattered on 26 October 1951 when a vanguard of three thousand Chinese troops reached the palace at Lhasa. The Chinese were long in arriving at Lhasa because at that time no road linked Tibet to the outside. The Chinese promptly commenced building one with Tibetan forced labour.

For years, the Dalai Lama harboured hopes that Buddhism and Chinese Marxism could be reconciled. But the Chinese had other priorities, and the rest of the world could have cared less, for Tibet has no natural resources of interest to the Americans or the other major powers, who in any event—then as now—were fearful of offending the Chinese over trifles. In 1954, Jawaharlal Nehru of India signed a peace accord with the People's Republic recognizing the latter's right to conduct its business with Tibet as a purely internal matter. Nehru did, however, permit the Dalai Lama and his followers to live in India as exiles, first at Mussoorie, in the Himalayan foothills north of Delhi, then for the longest period at Dharmsala. In later years, the whole entourage returned to Mussoorie. According to the Tibetan government-in-exile, 1.2 million Tibetans have died to date as a result of the Chinese occupation, 300,000 of them by torture and execution.

As souvenirs of their pilgrimage, the Dalai Lama gave the Woodcocks a *tangka*, a prayer wheel and white "visiting" scarves. In the 1970s, when they met again, in Vancouver, he made them a gift of the sort of silver bowl used during religious observances, to hold the oil in which a lighted wick would float. These articles found pride of place in what the Woodcocks called their Tibetan Room, the upstairs guest bedroom, which they decorated with Tibetan objets. Another prized gift was a *tangka* from western Tibet. "It had belonged to the old Panchen Lama, the one before the one who just died, who gave it to an old nobleman in Sikkim who gave it to us, in thanks for taking care of his daughters at university here", Woodcock told a visitor to McCleery Street in 1991. "We went to Darjeeling, and he came to see us in a weird little hotel called the Windamere—that's W-I-N-D-*A*-M-E-R-E—where you lived in cottages on the grounds. I remember suddenly seeing this figure coming up in a gold brocade robe and his hair in plaits and full of turquoise ornaments. This was the father with the *tangka* in his hand. A servant followed him, also dressed in robes, though not so splendidly, with a basket filled with tangerines on his head! Whenever I look at this, I still think of that nobleman, now long dead."[9] Typically, the Woodcocks were still in touch with the man's daughters decades later.

They saw how five children shared a single blanket during Himalayan winter nights and subsisted largely on *momos* (flour dumplings) and thin vegetable soup, with widespread malnutrition the result. In short, the visit "directed our attention to the poor peoples who are marginal to our European world."[10] Back in Vancouver, they organized.

Their first thought was to seek support from recognized charitable organizations, such as the Bollingen Foundation in New York, which was interested in Asian matters and whose director, Jack Mathews,

Woodcock happened to know. Woodcock wrote explaining that Inge and he had learned of the exiles' plan

> for preserving before it is too late the remains of Tibetan culture—collecting art objects and manuscripts, setting up a museum in Northern India, recording music and orally transmitted traditions, reprinting classic Tibetan texts both in Tibetan and in translations, etc.
>
> Since they themselves have almost no resources, the only way they can do this really effectively is with financial support from abroad ... The project is official in the sense of being approved by the Dalai Lama ...[11]

A cultural preservation scheme similar to the description above did indeed go through (and various other groups were started, such as the Tibetan Cultural Society, in Surrey, B.C.). Woodcock also talked the New York theatrical producer who had brought the Peking Ballet to America into considering the possibility of sponsoring a tour by traditional Tibetan dancers and actors, including an appearance at the world's fair in New York in 1964, as a further means of raising funds for the exile community. At length, the plan came down to a matter of two thousand dollars to send someone to India to appraise the performers' box-office potential. Woodcock wrote seeking the amount, not as a grant but a loan, from Walter Koerner of Vancouver's Koerner Foundation, only to be rebuffed—rudely, he thought. Later, Woodcock created a Koerner-like title character in his play ironically entitled *The Benefactor*. But the Woodcocks' focus soon shifted more to the most immediate human needs of the refugees, including clothing, medical supplies and education.

In a typically Woodcockian burst of energy, the Tibetan Refugee Aid Society (TRAS) was incorporated under B.C.'s Societies Act, with Norman Mackenzie of UBC as chair and Woodcock as vice-chair. Within a month the group had twenty members. It listed its priorities as aiding refugees in Nepal, whose conditions, according to the Red Cross in Katmandu, were especially desperate; assisting with the physical needs of pupils at the nursery at Dharmsala and various refugee schools; and helping to found schools themselves. The first fund-raising scheme was an election (ballots cost twenty-five cents) to choose the ugliest male student at UBC. "I refrained from meeting the victor", Woodcock recalled, "and gratefully received $700 ... which the Dalai Lama asked me to send to roof a school" in Mussoorie.[12] The society was also considering helping to establish a residential school for the Tibetans in Nepal, "and one of our members, Professor Belshaw, who is at present in Geneva, will discuss the possibilities with the International Red Cross there."[13] (The reference was to the Woodcocks' friend Cyril Belshaw, whom Woodcock once suggested be named the president of UBC but who gained notoriety instead, years later, when tried for murdering his wife.) Meanwhile, Woodcock was busily launching a campaign of lectures and radio and television appearances, and in quick order he had raised several thousand dollars. Before the end of the year, the Woodcocks and others, including Doris Shadbolt, had organized an art auction of work donated by Canadian painters as different as Molly and Bruno Bobak and Roy Kiyooka, Gordon Smith and Toni Onley, Jack Shadbolt and Goodridge Roberts. This particular tactic would be repeated, as when the Tibetan Refugee Aid Society assumed the additional obligation of aiding boat people fleeing Vietnam. By 1970, Woodcock could report that the Society had "collected, without any overhead costs, about $230,000, which has been used for feeding and clothing children, for providing medical aid, for building schools, for looking after the old."[14] Inflation has deprived contemporary readers of the knowledge of just how impressive a sum this was, and likewise of how much good it could do when translated into rupees. In any case, matters of overhead and administration were, in the Woodcocks' view, crucial. In time, the Woodcocks would back away from close involvement in the Tibetan Refugee Aid Society (while continuing to support it financially and also serve as honorary officers for various periods). They did so, however, mainly in order to devote more effort to still other charitable causes, both their own and other people's. Eventually, as Woodcock's oeuvre expanded and he grew relatively well off financially, he became a broadly based and experienced donor, but one with high standards. In reply to a typical request, from a group called British Columbians for Mentally Handicapped People, he replied:

Before I support you, even to the extent of a dollar, I would like to know:

1. Whether you are registered as a society under the B.C. Societies Act.

2. Whether you are registered as a charity under the tax regulations and, if so, what your number is.

3. What proportion of your funds is spent on salaries and overheads. I am working with some societies doing very good work whose proportion in this respect is 1%. I never give to groups whose salaries and overheads are more than 5%.

4. I would like *specific* information about the actual projects you are carrying out.

5. I would like a copy of the balance sheet submitted at your last Annual General Meeting.[15]

Many mocked the Woodcocks' fund-raising methods: the endless round of jumble sales and the like. Surely the Woodcocks' time is worth more than that, people would say; surely the great George Woodcock could raise more money through the prestige of his name than through donning an apron and selling donated cakes and pies? But for Woodcock this self-taught philanthropy had a Gandhian flavour, calling to mind the Mahatma's statement, "One step [is] enough for me." It was also applied anarchism. Woodcock operated most effectively from an external position beyond the range of institutional charity, raising small sums month by month (which of course grew impressive when viewed cumulatively) but likewise doling them out to closely targeted projects where the money would produce the most benefit. Such an approach was certainly labour-intensive. But then no one, however dedicated an enemy, ever accused Woodcock of sloth. Nor of lack of persistence.

Woodcock apparently never made the connection publicly, but he may well have been taking heart from the example of his old friend Nancy Macdonald, ex-wife of Dwight Macdonald and the manager of his magazine *Politics* in the 1940s. Following their separation, Mrs Macdonald took up the plight of half a million Spanish loyalists who had fought Franco only to flee over the Pyrenees into southwestern France after the collapse of their cause. By the 1950s, with Franco's fascist dictatorship showing no signs of loosening its grip on Spanish life, this dwindling number of exiles, tolerated by the French, became, in Mrs Macdonald's words, "the legion of the forgotten". A tireless public speaker and fund-raiser, drawing on the connections of her prominent New York family and her Vassar education, she set up Spanish Refugee Aid in 1954 to alleviate conditions among the exiles.

In time, actuarial realities sharply reduced the number of her charges, and of those who survived, many returned home after Franco died in 1975 and the monarchy and democracy were restored in Spain. But even then, she continued to care for about 125 aging refugees from the good fight who could not, or would not, go back. She retired in 1983 and produced a book about her experiences. When she died at eighty-six in 1996, the *New York Times* memorialized her as a "well-born anarchist",[16] a phrase somehow redolent of 1930s Hollywood comedies, with their zany heiresses and madcap debutantes, but one that would have had special significance for Woodcock, who found the combination charming and Kropotkinesque.

By 1972, Woodcock had spent the equivalent of one year in India during four trips. What he saw each time never failed to impress and appal him. The simplest scenes sometimes left the deepest memories. In northeast India one day, he observed an elderly woman fight a pariah dog over a scrap of food in the street. He continued his efforts to help, and broadened their geographical reach, working on a large scheme to resettle refugees in southern parts of the subcontinent.

Reluctant as he was to deal with government, he believed that officials in Ottawa should at least follow the lead of private groups like his, as had happened in other countries where such foundations were performing good works in what was starting to be called the Third World. For seven years, Woodcock and his friends waged a lonely fight. Finally, in 1968, the federal government set up the Canadian International Development Agency, with the remarkable Maurice Strong, an entrepreneur both within and outside government, at its head. Under the banner of CIDA, the authorities would consolidate all the various small foreign-aid funds already in existence and develop long-term strategic plans. Gradually, Canada's official emphasis would shift from its United Nations or World Bank contributions to unilateral help for the most desperate countries, without regard to strictly political considerations. Once CIDA was in operation, Woodcock recalled, "I finally succeeded, with much help from former High Commissioner James George, in persuading the Canadian government to join with Canadian and European voluntary agencies and with some West European governments, in financing a major resettlement programme for these refugees in South India."[17] Having done so, however, he found his efforts frustrated for eighteen months by "the survival of a British civil service system [in India] that is the last and the most durable of the negative heritages of the Raj."[18] Of the Indian bureaucracy, he wrote:

> Where flexibility is needed, it is rigid, operating by rules of thumb laid down by long-departed viceroys, and, charming as its members may be when they ply one with strong Darjeeling tea and imitation English biscuits in their Delhi offices, they make their decisions on a Victorian time scale and only after the ladder of responsibility has been climbed to the top …[19]

for, in Woodcock's subconscious, government would always be the Great Western Railway writ large: an evil that, in this particular instance, was made worse by

> the exactions of the Indian patronage machine, which means that a proportion of public funds regularly finds its way into the folds of politically faithful dhotis (for if corruption lubricates autocracy in Latin America, it tends, as Gandhi foresaw, to clog democracy in India) …[20]

Indeed, it was democracy in India that concerned him, along with the suffering of individuals: the abstract was always inseparable from the practical. In 1975, for example, he would accuse Prime Minister Indira Gandhi of having

> set in motion the same mechanism of irresponsible tyranny which the British used to combat the civil disobedience campaigns led by her namesake, Gandhi, and her father, Nehru. Many of the people she recently imprisoned were imprisoned then. The sole satisfaction Indians could gain from this imitation of the departed and detested viceroys is that they were suffering at the hands of a native autocrat. Indira, God help them, is their own![21]

With CIDA in place, however, it was practical for the Woodcocks and their friends to establish another charity specifically to help "low-caste and tribal people whom progress seems to be trampling underfoot."[22] This was Canada-India Village Aid, or CIVA, founded in August 1981.

Woodcock always excelled at enlisting the support (often *pro bono*) of knowledgeable specialists in various professions. So it was that CIVA's constitution was drawn up by Stephen Owen, later B.C.'s ombudsman. The document set out the purpose of the organization as being to "solicit, receive and disburse funds ... to be used in the establishment and maintenance by qualified persons and organizations in economically underprivileged areas of India ... using the Kabliji Hospital in Haryana State as a nucleus and an example, for medical care, for village development related to the promotion of public health, and for industries, crafts or other activities that may help make such programmes self-supporting ..."[23] The goal of improving the status of women in rural India was added later. All the founding members were India hands. Two, Douglas Forbes and Shirley Rushton, were medical doctors. The first chair, Tony Phillips, was a psychology professor at UBC. Others were Doris Shadbolt, John Friesen and Hari Varshney. A particularly important member, who joined later and served with Woodcockian zeal, was Sarah McAlpine, a former student of Woodcock's.

The great advantage of CIVA, coming along when it did, was that it was in a position to receive matching funds from CIDA, usually at a ratio of three to one. This link, however, did not alter the creative approach to fund-raising that would characterize CIVA as much as it had done with TRAS: the new group hawked hand-painted T-shirts and sold rugs woven by Indian artisans to designs by Vancouver artists. In its single most ambitious project, in 1984, it organized a festival of Indian culture that took over such facilities as the Anna Wyman Dance Theatre, the Pacific Cinematheque and the Vancouver Art Gallery. Woodcock also used his connections to the publishing world to help fund CIVA. The Woodcocks and the Onleys went to India in 1982; the result was a beautiful collaborative book, *Walls of India*, with Woodcock's lyrical prose set to the music of Toni Onley's watercolours; royalties went to CIVA, as did revenues from the sale of Onley's original works; all told, when matched by CIDA funds, the project raised nearly a quarter million dollars. *Bad Trips* was a 1991 anthology of the worst travel experiences of writers such as Graham Greene, John Updike, William Trevor, Peter Matthiessen and Paul Theroux (Sir Victor Pritchett did not acknowledge Woodcock's invitation to contribute). The book was edited by the short-story writer Keath Fraser, another Woodcock friend, and produced $30,000 in royalties for CIVA, a tidy sum when one considers that CIVA's projects, from providing a mobile dispensary or training midwives to backing construction of a dozen small dams, were budgeted at between $20,000 and $150,000. Woodcock often induced literary friends and admirers such as George Bowering or Margaret Atwood (also a generous cash donor, as Margaret Laurence was before her) to lend their names and labour to poetry contests, best-anecdote contests and the like. Again, the methods sometimes drew laughter outside Woodcock's hearing. But the aforementioned dams were built with the proceeds of CIVA's Canadian Poetry Contest, as judged by Atwood and Al Purdy, which raised more than $16,000 in entry fees, a figure then boosted to $65,000 by grants from CIDA. In its tenth year of operation, CIVA was responsible for $120,000 in aid to India and had no paid staff and spent less than 1 per cent of its annual budget on administration.

Woodcock's torrential correspondence during this entire period is peppered with insights into his charitable work, which generally remained unknown compared with the products of his literary labour. In a typical moment, he informed Atwood:

> Your letter came yesterday, and we are very pleased with your donation and your continuing interest. We really do seem now to be getting under way ... CIDA has agreed to put $19,000 into our scheme for a small six-bed obstetrical and family planning ward at Kabliji, which will be the centre from which the obstetrician will go out in the jeep we're buying to train the village midwives over an area with 200,000 population. This means we've been able to telegraph the go-ahead on the building. Also, the gift of a mobile X-ray unit, which I'd negotiated in India, finally came through last week. And, also as a result of our trip, we've been presented with a very interesting scheme in another part of India—a health project in a tribal area where the people live almost entirely by gathering forest products like gums and wild silks, and have been routinely exploited by traders because in their languages—they are mostly Gonds and related groups—there are no numbers over 20, and they accept 20 rupees for almost anything. Mysore Resettlement and Development Agency, which did marvellous things with resettling Tibetan refugees, is moving in to organize a trading co-operative that will prevent these people from being exploited, and they've invited us to provide the health unit they see as the "entry". It's a modest scheme which offers a lot in results, and if CIDA matches generously, we shall certainly be able to do it.[24]

Having no wish to monopolize the limelight, such as it was, the Woodcocks held various positions in the organization at various times, before finally backing away into honorary status. No task was too menial. In 1988, a year when Woodcock published seven books, including *Caves in the Desert: Travels in China, A Social History of Canada* and a collection of original essays on anarchism translated into German, he was also the recording and corresponding secretary of CIVA, taking down and then reading back for approval such meticulous minutes as these:

> Referring back to item 9 of the minutes of the last meeting, G. Woodcock reported that he had followed up the letter from Dawa Dolma Lhewa, asking for help in founding a school for poor Tibetan children. He had received a letter from Nancy McDonald [*sic*] of Spanish Refugee Aid in New York, who sponsored Dawa Dolma's education, testifying to her qualifications as a teacher. He had also received a proposal, with estimates and a plan, from Dawa Dolma herself; the total sum she requests is 906,000 rupees, or approximately $95,000. During discussion it was noted that the building costs were high in Indian terms, and that it was not clear how the school would integrate into and serve the community as a whole. GW was asked to write to Dawa Dolma seeking clarification on the second point, and urging a simplification of plans with the aim of achieving a more realistic estimate. GW will pass on a copy of the proposal, and of the letter he will write, to Tony Phillips so that TRAS, which is considering a joint underwriting of the school, may be kept informed.[25]

One can only marvel at his patience, and shake one's head sadly at how bureaucratization creeps into even applied anarchism.

In the course of working with her in CIVA, Woodcock became especially fond of Sarah McAlpine, who was the age to be the biological daughter the Woodcocks never had. Woodcock describes her to the New Brunswick poet Fred Cogswell as "one of my closest and dearest friends, a woman of great charm, intelligence and character."[26]

Woodcock was typically anarchistic and laissez-faire in his approach to scholarly inquiry. Despite his strong desire for personal privacy, he imposed few access stipulations on what became, through successive donations, his massive private and literary archive at Queen's University in Kingston. Juvenilia, passports, financial records, correspondence with literary agents—all were to be opened for research. The only exceptions were two diaries from late in life (one of which he seemed to censor) and a package marked with the initials S. M., all of which he instructed could not be opened until after his death. S. M. turned out to be Sarah McAlpine, to whom at least once, in 1988, he wrote with genuine intimacy:

Dear S. (if you must) or Sarah dear,

It was sweet and wonderful and astonishing of you to turn up the other days [sic] with gifts of boose [sic] and gold and friendship! I shall open the bottle on Sunday, drink a glass with Tony P[hillips], who will be here to dinner, and think of you striding over the delphium-blue meadow of the Chilcotin (or is delphinium the local flower). The gold I shall probably hoard; I note it comes from Cyprus, and that being the place where Aphrodite rose from the sea, God knows what symbolism Jung—my current favourite among psychoanalysts—might divine from it. And here am I rewarding you with yet more bumph!

I took your point, with some shame, over the last. But with what impeccable ironic gentleness you made it! No wander [sic] I am *pris de toi* ...[27]

11 THE WORD FACTORY ON McCLEERY STREET

IN RETROSPECT, IT seems clear that Woodcock's general state of health was never again so robust as it was before his major heart attack. From 1967 onward, his letters are peppered with reports on the progress of one ailment or another, even though he still had many rigorous travels ahead of him and was just then beginning his most productive writing years. In the 1970s alone he published twenty-five books. Many were minor additions to his shelf but all of them, if only by their range of genres, including drama and bibliography, show him living out his peculiarly anarchistic view of the literary life: writing both to feed and relieve the pressure on his busy mind, publishing as often as he pleased, the market be damned, and working for virtually any editor who asked him or would have him, regardless of the pay.

In 1969, Woodcock was actually planning his phased withdrawal from the world around him. As he confided to his old friend Roy Fuller in England:

> We are halfway into retirement, as it were. We have just bought a house at a village called Mission City up the Fraser Valley, with an acre of grounds dense with bushes and a view up the Fraser itself to the mountains, and in about three years we shall be moving up there more or less permanently—that is with every other winter in Europe or Asia. I have now been ten years editing *Canadian Literature*, and I feel it is soon time to give up.[1]

In fact, though, the Woodcocks would never move from the house on McCleery Street and would never retire. Even his editorship of *Canadian Literature* would go on for almost eight more years. At this time, in fact, Woodcock was just embarking on the most extraordinary part of his career.

Any list of Woodcock titles from the 1970s not mentioned previously would have to include *Who Killed the British Empire? An Inquest*, his final post-mortem on the colonial system that he found repellent but that had opened up the world to him, and *Amor De Cosmos: Journalist and Reformer*, his biography of the eccentric (and later actually mad) first premier of British Columbia. Together, such works show Woodcock paying ever closer attention to his own back garden as, at the same time, he scanned the world with powerful glasses. The momentum would only increase. In the 1980s, the figure was thirty-four published books. Neither total takes into account the staggering bulk of his occasional journalism, except to the extent that he made several collections of previously published essays. More interestingly, neither total acknowledges the way that his journalism sometimes was the egg from which his books would later hatch.

For example, an article in the July 1973 issue of *Saturday Night*, "Gabriel Dumont: The Forgotten Hero", about Louis Riel's military commander in the North-West Rebellion of 1885, grew, almost exponentially, into one of his key books from this period, *Gabriel Dumont: The Métis Chief and His Lost World* (1975). It is key because it is the biography of a semi-nomadic individual who lived in harmony with the land and could neither read nor write (but who did dictate a memoir in 1903) and who, for these and other reasons, seemed to embody the difficult-to-locate anarchist spirit in Canada in a way far different (and, in Woodcock's view, more successfully) than did the Doukhobors. Alas, government and society ate away at Dumont's anarchic naturalness and dignity. For a time, he appeared in Buffalo Bill's Wild West; indeed, he lived long enough to have once met the young John Diefenbaker, his opposite in every way: another of history's cruel ironies. With characteristic concern for bringing his ideas to different audiences, Woodcock later wrote a version of Dumont's life for the adolescent market and then a play about him. A poem, "On Completing a Life of Gabriel Dumont", found its way into *Notes on Visitations* (also 1975), his first collection of new poems in decades, a book that signalled his rebirth as a poet (a contemporary Canadian lyric poet), a creative burst that would last the rest of his life. The way Woodcock wrote so widely on Dumont over the period of a couple of years was not at all a question of simply recycling for profit, in the manner of slick professional journalists such as Pierre Berton. In any case, the splinter works had the effect of herding more readers towards the principal book, one that acquired a mythic significance for many readers, and not just ones in the West. To the Toronto philosopher and novelist John Ralston Saul, *Gabriel Dumont: The Métis Chief and His Lost World*

> had a clarifying effect on me—more than any other book—fiction or non-fiction, because I've always believed that was an artificial division. Perhaps I should call it an effect of revelation about what Canada is. So much of our public debate is lost in imitative concepts which we owe to other places. Woodcock finds in Dumont the perfect expression of the anti-heroic respectable citizen, who nevertheless sees himself as part of an uncontrollable environment. This is a curious mixture— middle-class animism. Technically Dumont and the Metis are destroyed by Middleton's army. But in reality they were chewed up in a European scrap between the European orangemen obsessed by land and Riel, the European saint in the making, obsessed by a profoundly anti-animist god. It seems to me that Dumont's is the quintessential Canadian story and Woodcock finds the truth in it perhaps because he is an anarchist and so does not get caught up in the standard pseudo-European debates which afflict us. Anarchism I suppose— and I'm not a great expert on the subject—could be taken as a rejection of the abstract view of civilization. In that sense it is an intellectual form of animism, which is, as I've seen in countries where it still functions, both a respectable and personally demanding kind of humanism.[2]

The beginning of 1968 found the Woodcocks in Switzerland. The *annus mirabilis* that was about to unfold, one that would promise to equal 1848 in its revolutionary zeal, started with Woodcock bogged down in practical matters, including "a bad bout of flu, which has been followed by badly inflamed eyes."[3] The treatment he prescribed for himself was the sunshine of Sicily, a place then in the news after a series of earthquakes. The Woodcocks, however, saw little devastation, just a few refugees in Palermo, but the whole feeling of the island was depressing, and we stayed just long enough to see the various sites. Actually, Paestum, near Naples, was much more impressive than any of the Greek remains in Sicily. I am thoroughly glad that we decided to sit out the winter in Lugano [in Switzerland]. I could never have written in Sicily.[4]

They would soon push off to Franco's Spain, the focus of so many of their youthful political ideals, dreams and nightmares. There they found

the sun, the scenery, the architecture, the early spring, the great amiability of the people all delightful. The food was about the world's worst, and that was the one drawback. We did not dabble openly in politics, and indeed talked to few Spaniards except in the general way of travel. However, from what we could see, the standard of living was much higher than we had expected. Children well clothed and shod, rarely hungry-looking; field workers on the *latifundia* of Andalucia equipped with bicycles and even motor bikes; new groups of clean, whitewashed cottages for the workers on the large southern farms; extensive workers' housing estates on the outskirts of even small towns. This applied mainly to Andalucia, Levante and Catalonia. In Esthemadura and Old Castile the land is naturally bleaker, and conditions were obviously so much improved over the past decade, particularly in the remoter villages, from which the young are flying, and where the old people look bitter and starved. Indeed, it is among the old and the infirm that one mostly notices the differences between Spain and other countries; the old are desperately poor; the lame go on peg legs or crutches; the blind make a living by selling lottery tickets—it is said to be lucky to buy from a blind man! The police—surprisingly unobtrusive! We were let in without a question—without even a look at our luggage; and the Guardia Civil, apart from running an excellent road emergency service like the [Canadian Automobile Association] patrols, kept in the background and were either fat and elderly or young and bespectacled—by no means the fearsome creatures one had expected; there were far less of them in evidence than of Carabinieri in Italy, and Spanish police in general were much less offensive than Italian or German police. The army—again—rarely to be seen, except for a few conscripts in garrison towns like Seville. These, of course, are superficial observations. But they do suggest that over the past decade the stick, while still held firmly in the hand, is being supplemented by the carrot. Certainly the Spaniards seemed far from a terrorized people, and the general atmosphere was less tense and ominous than, say, Egypt in 1961. The Civil War was mentioned to us only once, by an old guide with whom we were alone in the depths of the Altamira caves, and he merely mentioned the fighting that had taken place in the region, being curiously scrupulous to avoid the appearance of supporting *either* side. And that seems to reflect the attitude of most Spaniards—a plague on the past in general.[5]

Clearly, Woodcock's intellectual honesty won out over what his political and generational sympathies had inclined him to anticipate, perhaps even to wish for. Such respect for the truth would win him many antagonists during the next few years as Canadian revulsion with the American errand in Vietnam—the Spanish civil war of the younger generation—contributed to a rebirth of nationalist sentiment in Canada. That Woodcock was opposed to the American war in Vietnam there was never any doubt at all. Writing in 1967 a review of Mary McCarthy's book *Vietnam*, Woodcock spoke this way to readers of the *Canadian Forum*:

American tourists have taken over from their Edwardian British predecessors the longing to make every place home. From the Nile Hilton in Cairo to its sister hotels in Mexico City and Hong Kong and Istanbul, one sees them, stitching a few coloured beads of exotic memory onto an experience they could have enjoyed just as well in hotels of the same chain in New York or Chicago. The most chilling feature of [McCarthy's book] is that she presents us with tourists at war, Americans trying to create a home away from home in the wretched land which they muddle-headedly imagine they are helping towards freedom. One observes a people ... living in the dreadful moral vacuum, not of calculated wickedness, but of a decaying innocence which even the most harrowing experience does not seem able to break. Just as [President Lyndon] Johnson is more horrifying than Hitler because he is palpably not a monster yet sanctions monstrous acts, so his agents are more chilling than the Nazis because their illusion of acting as moral men is greater.[6]

Yet Woodcock would find himself at loggerheads with the part of the counterculture that involved student radicals on university campuses. This position would prove somewhat bizarre, given not only his own radical past and his abidingly hostile attitude towards the academy generally but also his place within UBC: a university where student radicalism of the California sort was in full flower (as in October 1968, when one thousand students, aroused by the appearance the day before of the American radical Jerry Rubin, stormed the faculty club and held it overnight). But then it was characteristic of Woodcock to be out of step with the world as a matter of proud principle, to be a contrarian.

Much of what we know of Woodcock's private thoughts at this time comes from his letters to Ivan Avakumovic, who foresightedly preserved all those he received, one of Woodcock's few correspondents to do so before the mid-1970s. As it happened, the two collaborators were in frequent communication for a long period beginning in 1968, when they were struggling with their work on the Doukhobors. The book went through many vicissitudes on the road to publication, particularly implied threats, or at least the fear of threats, from various Doukhobor historians and leaders, who felt their sect had been badly smeared by sensationalist reporting in the past. "Do not get depressed about problems", Woodcock wrote Avakumovic. "After all, one does not embark on any subject like the Doukhobors without expecting problems. Inge warned me in the beginning, but I must say she is considerate enough not to say, now, 'I told you so!'"[7]

Eventually, given his detailed knowledge of the publishing business, Woodcock finessed their way through the difficulties, and the co-authors were rewarded by strongly favourable reviews from the *Times Literary Supplement* to the *Listener*. Historians as eminent as J. H. Plumb and E. H. Carr praised them. Even the Freedom Press crowd greeted the book with a positive attitude not typical of their response to Woodcock projects. Another review, in *New Society*, brought Woodcock renewed contact with its writer, Alex Comfort, his old anarchist colleague from the 1940s (who now, in 1969, stood on the threshold of worldwide fame as co-author of *The Joy of Sex*, a publishing phenomenon of the time). Comfort enjoyed *The Doukhobors* so much that he asked Woodcock to contribute a book on the aboriginals of Canada's northwest coast to a series of pop anthropology books he was editing. Woodcock declined, pleading a full load. He was writing *Into Tibet* and a book about the city of Victoria, all the while considering a book on Sir Herbert Read. He also feared he might accidentally spike his ever-more-promising relationship with Alan Pringle at Faber. The work he did eventually write on the subject, in response to his own interest rather than to Comfort's series, did not appear until 1977, as *Peoples of the Coast: The Indians of the Pacific Northwest.* In reading through his extended back-and-forth with Avakumovic one finds Woodcock commenting on internal politics at UBC: "Doubtless you've heard the news from here. Walter Gage is President—and for my money better than the two before him. [Robert] Jordan is Head of the English Department, and there might be many worse choices. He is a really good Chaucer man, and also, I think, very fair-minded."[8] This suggests that when Woodcock began to observe a disturbing strain of authoritarianism in certain segments of the student body, he was also, for once, relatively content with his superiors and colleagues. Believing the methods of *some* student leaders to be doctrinaire and undemocratic and dismissive of (other people's) rights to free speech, he sent an essay on the subject to Robert Fulford of *Saturday Night.* The piece relied heavily on some remarks in the Toronto *Star* supposedly spoken by Robert Rae, a student leader at the University of Toronto. Woodcock entitled the manuscript "Fascism or Freedom? The New Radical Dilemma".

At times, Woodcock could show a keen understanding of the mass media and their needs. Responding to a 1970 request from *Maclean's* that he might like to suggest some articles, he replied at length with four detailed proposals, including one for

> A piece on political safety valves. It seems to me that our democratic processes are too rigid for modern needs, and that they could be opened out in a way which would largely defuse the appeal of violent and extremist groups. I am thinking politically of some modification of the Swiss institutions of the referendum and the initiative. Through these, highly controversial laws can be put to the people *between* elections; more important, demands by significant minorities can be put to the voters directly. If this were done, it would be far less possible for authoritarian minorities to complain that the democratic system is weighted against them, particularly in certain cases, where the issues were local [and] the initiatives were voted on only by the people directly concerned. I do feel that, just as the Americans pay too much reverence to the presidential office, so we pay too much reverence to a parliament

which is becoming steadily less flexible, and we need as many of the institutions of direct democracy as will work in outer [*sic*] to counter the authoritarian tendencies which may creep in through too-rigid a system of cabinet-and-committees.[9]

Significantly, the above was written during the October Crisis.

Despite his years of writing for all types of periodical, however, Woodcock was not quite receptive to an understanding of how, in commercial magazines, the titles of articles are chosen by the editors, because they must be presented visually, as more a piece of graphic design than of mere description. In time, Woodcock's resistance to journalistic reality became one of his quaint writerly charms. In 1989, for example, he could still speak admiringly of what "the French called a *feuilleton* and which the English called a middle, because it appeared customarily as a kind of reflective interlude in a magazine, situated between the main articles and the book reviews"[10]—a way of thinking supplanted generations earlier by the modern magazine article, what would be known as an island piece to editors such as Fulford, who headed Woodcock's contribution to the July 1969 issue "The Ominous Politics of the Student Left" and then trumpeted it on the cover with "Are the Student Rebels Fascists of the Left?"

Saturday Night's wording resulted in a storm of protest from leaders of the student movement, including Rae, explaining that he had been misquoted by the *Star*, and John Warnock of the University of Saskatchewan. Warnock found the piece "typical of what we hear today from those who fear the current student movement" and less accurate a picture of the student movement than even "the reports of J. Edgar Hoover."[11] For his part, Dimitrios Roussopoulos, the editor of *Our Generation*, a radical student publication in Montreal, wrote, "Many of us were truly shocked and disgusted by the piece by George Woodcock." There were some moderating voices as well, including that of Hugh Segal, vice-president of the University of Ottawa student's union. Woodcock accepted Rae's claims that the *Star* had misquoted him, saying, for example, that he (Rae) supported a student veto of professors' private research projects.

An experience of the misreporting of my own oral statements by newsmen [Woodcock wrote] makes me accept Mr. Rae's protest, and I therefore apologize (though apparently the *Star* has not yet done so) for having unwittingly misrepresented his views, for the suggestion of arrogance, and for putting him in a gallery where obviously he does not belong. I make my apology for what was inaccurate in my article all the more gladly because I do not have the prophetic itch to be right, and welcome any sign that things may not be as bad as I had gloomily seen them. Mr. Rae further appears to believe that I imply that he is, to use his words, 'a fascist and a Nazi.' If he re-reads my article carefully, he will see that I am not implying that *anybody* can at present be termed a fascist; I am talking about tendencies and threats. I am concerned with a future I hope we can avoid.[12]

In later years, Bob Rae became Ontario's first New Democratic premier and quickly moved the NDP away from its historic roots. John Warnock became the editor of the pro-labour journal *Canadian Dimension*. Dimitrios Roussopoulos matured from Marxism to anarchism and became the publisher of Black Rose Books, which brought out many of Woodcock's works, including his edition of Kropotkin. Hugh Segal became a key player in the Progressive Conservative Party, provincially and federally. In terms of human rights, most social programmes or the marketplace, they all, to one degree or another, ended up to the right of George Woodcock.

Honours began to pour in. At first, Woodcock reacted with his hallmark ambivalence. In 1968 he was elected a Fellow of the Royal Society of Canada but soon fell to quarrelling over the group's insistence that he attend meetings; by 1974, he wrote that "so as not to embarrass anyone, I formally and reluctantly re-submit my resignation [because] I would not like anyone to be forced into the embarrassing situation of actually expelling me ..."[13] Thereafter he made do with being a Fellow of the Royal Geographical Society in London, which did not seem to demand his physical presence.

In 1971, Woodcock was asked if he would accept membership (the lowest of three ranks) in the Order of Canada. He refused, writing the Governor General's secretary at Rideau Hall in Ottawa:

I am deeply moved by my understanding of the esteem and good will which have led to the recommendation of the Advisory Council, and I am grateful for His Excellency's courtesy in asking you to advise me of that recommendation. But I have regretfully to say that, for reasons which are primarily philosophic, I would not be prepared to accept the award of the Medal of Service. Since I assume that the substance of your letter will not be made public, I do not propose to trespass on your time by recounting those reasons in detail, but I would like to assure you that I appreciate the honour implied in the suggestion ...[14]

In fact, as he would later admit, he refused the award not only because it came from the state (for in 1967 he had accepted a Centennial Medal) but also because he was hurt not to be made an Officer, which would have permitted use of the letters oc after his name—hurt all the more, in fact, because Nancy Greene, a champion downhill skier, had been admitted to the most exclusive tier at twenty-five. In 1968, Woodcock received his first honorary doctorate, from the University of Victoria. Others followed, from Sir George Williams University in Montreal (1970), the University of Ottawa (1973), the University of Winnipeg (1975), Trent University in Peterborough (1976) and UBC (at long last, 1977). He took no undue pride in these honours but was able to use them to good effect when required in an emergency or a good cause. When soliciting a charitable contribution from someone who needed to be suitably impressed, or when writing a letter of support or a reference for a much younger colleague, he could trot out quite a little alphabet after his name: George Woodcock, LL.D., D.Litt., F.R.G.S. He found mention of the honours useful when travelling in India and other developing countries. The tactic also worked for getting the attention of public officials and politicians (or their aides) who might not be familiar with him. Thus the existence in the Woodcock archives of a letter such as the one beginning:

From George Woodcock, Writer, LL.D., D.Litt., F.R.S.C., F.R.G.S., winner of the Molson Prize, the Governor-General's Award for Literature, the Canada Council Killam Fellowship, the Canadian Government Overseas Fellowship, the John Simon Guggenheim Fellowship, late Associate Professor of English and Lecturer in Asian Studies at the University of British Columbia, now Editor of *Canadian Literature*.

To Dr. Sylvia Ostry,
Director, Statistics Canada,
Ottawa, Ont.

Dear Dr. Ostry,

I am writing to object strongly to the methods employed by the
people whom Statistics Canada engages to gather information, to the
growing intrusion into the privacy of citizens which—whether with
your consent or not—is becoming part of the regular routine of
Statistics Canada, and to the diversion of your office's activities to the
harrying of already hard-pressed individuals when it should be using
whatever resources and powers it may have to investigate the short-
comings of corporations whose activities are detrimental to the public
interests ...[15]

By contrast, he felt that "(Dr) George Woodcock, Editor" was enough
to identify himself to Dave Barrett, British Columbia's NDP premier,
when writing to call "attention to what appears to be a flagrant breach
of the pricing policy which was introduced by your government on
October 1st relating to sales to the public in Government Liquor
Stores."[16]

Incidentally, the Molson Prize, to which he alludes in the letter to
Ostry, was, in point of exclusivity and monetary richness, his largest
award, a $50,000 windfall awarded annually by the Canada Council
in recognition of an individual's lifetime contribution to Canadian
culture or science. He felt he could accept the award because it was
not quite government munificence, but resulted from the decision of
a group of fellow writers. The honours, while intended to recognize
past achievements, fell at a time when Woodcock was at his most
fecund. By 1969, wishing to revisit his own past, including the anarchist circle of the 1940s, Woodcock conceived the notion of a book
about Sir Herbert Read. In May, he explained to Sir Herbert's son,
Benedict Read, that he had not yet planned the book in detail, but
envisaged it as being similar to *The Crystal Spirit*, using biographical
material to illuminate criticism and exposition but retaining the quality of a personal appreciation. Even though his subject had recently
died, Woodcock felt obliged to add that the time for the definitive
biography of his old mentor had not yet arrived and that any mere

biography less than the definitive one would suffer sadly from comparison with Read's own 1963 account of his life, *The Contrary Experience: Autobiographies*. Woodcock did research in Britain during the autumn of 1969, but enjoyed the immense advantage of having Sir Herbert's papers open for examination comparatively near to home, at the University of Victoria Library. UVic had acquired the Read *fonds* partly through the initiative of Woodcock's (and Read's) friend Robin Skelton, another poet and writer-of-all-work. Woodcock combined the English journey with another visit to India, where the Tibetan Refugee Aid Society, thanks partly to matching funds from the Canadian government, was suddenly able to "pay half the cost of the school [at the Mundgod resettlement project], maintain the hospital for a year, provide two ratproof godowns and two trucks, purchase several thousand trees for fruit and shade, and set going a small adult training scheme."[17] All this while he was attending to his myriad other duties from wherever he happened to be. The spirit of his life on the road during his richest writing years is conveyed most vividly in a nonetheless routine letter, written from London, to Donald Stephens, an associate editor of *Canadian Literature*.

> A hasty note on the move ... after a wonderful time in England; Inge is converted to the idea of returning—if that were only possible—every year, and we still feel a little frustrated at the thought of all the exhibitions and shows we *didn't* see.
>
> Mrs. [Catherine] Easto [*Canadian Literature*'s part-time secretary] has sent me another list of books [received for review]. They do seem a most miscellaneous lot, and I think that most of them could wait for me to look them over in January. However, we obviously should line someone up for [the poet Ralph] Gustafson's *Ixion's Wheel* and [the poet-diplomat R. A. D.] Ford's *The Solitary City*. Why not offer them to Miriam Waddington for a long double review and, if she doesn't agree, ask Fred Cogswell? The most difficult will probably be [Desmond] Pacey's *Essays in Canadian Criticism*. Since he talked of dedicating it to me, I obviously can't deal with it. Roy Daniells would be the ideal person, but might feel too close. Why not try Roy, though, and if he doesn't agree ask Carl Klinck, who would probably pick out the flaws and virtues very fairly? ...
>
> One idea that does strike me—we should really have a piece on the last decade or so in Vancouver—something about the poets'

conference, the coming of the American group, the foundation of *Tish*,
the little presses, and so on. I'm rather at a loss whom to suggest.
Warren [Tallman] would be the man, but we could probably wait
another decade for the piece. Have you any thoughts on this? We really
should deal with that moment in literary history, particularly now that
it seems, judging from what comes out of Vancouver, to be almost past.
[bill] bissett too should be in it. Who could bring all that together into
a cohesive whole?

Do write if you have a moment. We go to Athens tomorrow and
should get to Delhi about the 1st December. I'd like to see a copy of
No 42 if you could ask Mrs. Easto to airmail me a copy.[18]

The Woodcocks returned to Canada declaring ninety-five dollars
worth of clothing, cigarettes and household furnishings at Customs.
They always prided themselves on being sharp shoppers. In fact,
Woodcock, with clerkly ways drilled into him by the Great Western,
was sometimes penny wise but pound foolish, as when, the same year,
he asked Avakumovic, then in London himself, "if by any chance you
see in a shop or a catalogue Sir Clements Markham's *Narrative[s] of
the Mission of G[eorge] Bogle to Tibet, and [of] the Journey of T[homas]
Manning to Lhasa, with Notes and Lives, London, 1879* [*sic* 1876], I shall
be very grateful to hear of it—and to pay up to 7 guineas for a copy!"[19]
An absurd request of a friend and an arbitrarily absurd price-ceiling,
especially as "There is one in the London Library, and I suppose at a
pinch they would xerox it for me."[20] In his letters, particularly his
business correspondence, he seems eager to enjoin people to do unto
others' accounts receivable as they would wish done unto their own;
only very rarely does he give in to the freelance's natural frustration,
as in a 1976 letter to John Robert Colombo, the managing editor of
the *Tamarack Review*:

Must I keep going the rounds, like a Buddhist touring the Wheel of
Existence, in search of my fair and honest fees? For poems published
in *Tamarack* more than six months ago, you promised me—I seem to
remember—$140. I waited patiently for a long time—no cheque. Then
I wrote to remind you—no reply. Bill Toye [another of the editors]
came to Vancouver, so I thought I'd ask him. Bill told me it wasn't *his*
province—I should write to Bob Weaver. To Bob I did write, a month
ago yesterday—no cheque and no reply! So now I've started on the

rounds again, my annoyance somewhat fuelled by the reports a visitor brought from Toronto two days ago about the kind of subsidies *Tamarack* is getting from the combined Canada Council and Ontario Arts Council. Round about double, I gather, what *Canadian Literature* gets from its combined Canada Council and UBC subsidies. Yet I pay fees on the dot and make that the first call of funds. So I feel a real justification in complaining when I am not paid—and particularly when the non-payee is a free-lancer like myself with no fat university or CBC pension to look forward to. Please, John, don't force me to continue beyond you in the second round of cheque-chasing![21]

The honours bestowed on him did not ameliorate Woodcock's willingness to engage in controversy: society was not buying his silence. Some controversies were intramural and literary, others were more public. A young poet, writing in a rival journal, committed a pyrotechnic attack on *Canadian Literature*'s editorial policies and received the following response:

> In the White Russian restaurants of Hong Kong, they produce a dessert of the most glittering visual appeal, crowned by a tower of spun sugar in a flickering blue nimbus of flaming brandy. The splendid structure burns and melts away, and what is left is a little brown, toffee-like substance covering a very humble kind of millet porridge. [His attacker's sally] was a performance of the same kind, decorative, entertaining, but burning down, if one waits long enough, to a couple of simple and quite unacceptable propositions: (a) that the quality of criticism is related to word count; (b) that the critic should devote himself to the appreciation of what he finds good, and should ignore whatever he finds bad.[22]

While often disdainful of career academics and what he considered their lifeless pedantry, Woodcock was easily stung by aspersions on his own scholarly practices, the sort of complaint he faced repeatedly through his later career and usually responded to heatedly. A particularly vivid example, running to many closely argued pages of accusation, counter-accusation and reply, came in the autumn of 1972 and ended, after much negotiation and hard-fought compromise, in the following announcement in the *University of Toronto Quarterly*:

The Summer 1972 issue of 'Letters in Canada' contained a review of *Wyndham Lewis in Canada,* edited by Professor George Woodcock. In it Professor Woodcock was sharply criticized for his editing of a Lewis manuscript, 'Nature's Place in Canadian Culture', published in the volume identified there as being in the Cornell University Library. Professor Woodcock has since advised the Editors of the *Quarterly* that the manuscript published by him was not in fact the Cornell one, but another version, in the possession of Mrs Lewis, which differs from the Cornell manuscript in several particulars.

As a result of this misunderstanding, the *Quarterly* review was principally concerned with the Cornell manuscript and with its apparently faulty reproduction in the volume, and Professor Woodcock was mistakenly accused of having in his edition altered Lewis's text.

The Editors deeply regret the embarrassment caused to Professor Woodcock by this accusation. In drawing the attention of the *Quarterly*'s readers to the error and its unhappy sequel, they wish to retract any suggestion of editorial tampering on Professor Woodcock's part, and to express to him their sincere apologies.[23]

Tempests and teapots, one might suppose, but arguments about writers on the far right, such as Wyndham Lewis or Ezra Pound, tend to be essentially political. In that sense, this one fitted the pattern of Woodcock's more public stand-offs during the 1970s, most of which involved the rising tide of Canadian nationalism and his own role in shaping it or reacting to it.

In April 1972, the *Canadian Forum* published a short Woodcock essay, "Plea for the Anti-Nation" (it appeared later that year in Woodcock's essay collection *The Rejection of Politics* as "Up the Anti-Nation" and under that name became one of his most frequently anthologized pieces). It was an explanation of how he had come to reconcile his personal belief in anarchism with a growing sympathy for nationalism based on being a British Columbian first, a western Canadian second and a Canadian third. He explained his stance with special force and clarity, however, when the matter came before an American audience the following year:

I have never in the past thought of myself as a nationalist; if I were asked to devise an appropriate label, I would reluctantly describe myself as a federalist patriot, by patriot implying no more than lover of a land

and people within which and among whom I choose to live my life, and by federalist an attitude of deep distrust for the centralizing, homogenizing tendencies of the nation-state.

Even so, such reactions, at this point in the 20th century when it has become evident to Canadians that 60 per cent of their industry is owned by alien interests, and that their land is quickly following their industry into foreign ownership, are as much those of concern merging into defence and defiance as are the reactions of many of my fellow writers who actually call themselves nationalists, and of many Canadian artists and academics who do the same.

I read the signs and realize that I have to take sides on basic issues of local independence just as people in the 13 colonies did 200 years ago.[24]

The *Forum*'s editors saw that "A Plea for the Anti-Nation", for all its brevity, was pungent and controversial and might easily provoke rebuttals from a number of different well-articulated positions. So they turned the issue into a symposium, with responses to Woodcock by a variety of left or leftish intellectuals, from Desmond Morton, the military historian, to Patrick MacFadden, one of the editors of the radical magazine *Last Post*, to Edward Broadbent, the New Democratic MP for Oshawa-Whitby (and future federal leader). The results were republished the following year as a book, *Nationalism or Local Control: Responses to George Woodcock*. Before this could be published, however, some of the responses had turned into attacks, with the focus shifting and the diction turning nasty. Others joined in, among them Woodcock's old antagonist Robin Mathews, whom Woodcock credited with an entirely new literary genre

> which I propose to call the *roman à serrure*, since its function is strictly complementary to that of the *roman à clef*. The *roman à clef*, of course, is a novel in which a character is based on a person in real life and only the character's name is a matter of fiction. The *roman à serrure* takes only the name of the character from real life; the rest is invention.
>
> The *roman à serrure* as practised by Robin Mathews is built up step by step in a series of fictional insights, revealing aspect after aspect of the invented character, which he ingeniously secreted in reviews, articles and letters ... Consider this character as he is now displayed— "George Woodcock, a man at the heart of the Canadian capitalist

establishment ..." Implied in such a statement are of course a number of interesting facts about character, which immediately reveal how distant is the humble being whose name has been borrowed from the "ideal" man Mathews creates. [The fictional Woodcock would no doubt be] the well-paid director of several important companies; I am merely a director of a charitable society so modest that it cannot afford paid office help. [The fictional Woodcock] is obviously on first name terms with the leaders of the land [whereas] Mr. Trudeau did not even answer "Fuck you!" when I wrote him a recent angry letter ...

In earlier Mathews texts there are further interesting features of this George Woodcock who is his fictional creation. In *Canadian Dimension* (1967), he was revealed to be a "former Englishman" (I am a mere native of Winnipeg), a "neo-Aesthete" (an odd thing for a man from the heart of capitalism to be) and involved in the "Woodcock-Frye game" (whereas [Northrop] Frye and I—when we meet at roughly five-yearly intervals—merely look at each other with guarded amiability).[25]

Mathews also had accused Woodcock, accurately, of having been kind to Warren Tallman, the influential American-born professor, the father-figure of the *Tish* movement that, in the eyes of those opposed to it, was said to have sabotaged Canadian poetry with imported ideas and techniques. Indeed, Tallman would eventually dedicate part of a book to Woodcock "with great gratitude ... for all the personal kindnesses over the years, for the great help this has been to my literary self, such as it is, and in a larger sense of course for all that you have done in 20 quick years to push literature in this Canadian place such long steps forward."[26] Mathews and Tallman were key figures at opposite poles of one of the great public questions of the day, the high proportion of American-born academics (and thus, it was argued, of American-bred ideas) in Canadian universities. This was an issue about which Woodcock had no ambivalence but only common sense.

As Woodcock explained to the executive secretary of the Canadian Association of University Teachers, who was seeking consensus about possible guidelines:

There is no doubt at all that in the past we had too many unCanadian and particularly American teachers in our universities, and I doubt whether the balance has yet been adjusted satisfactorily. I am no [conventional] nationalist, and if I thought that the interests of Canadian education were served by the presence of a large number of foreign teachers, I would have no objection in principle. However I think that—considered on a purely practical level—those interests have not been served by the foreign teachers we have had ...

Over the past twenty years (though perhaps to a diminishing degree in the last year or so) we have been subjected to a flood of American teachers who have come to Canada because they are not good enough for American universities. Some have been unable to get work in the United States of any kind; others have calculated—and experience has justified them—that they would get promotion more easily in Canadian universities than in American institutions of comparable standing. The result has been a *qualitative* lowering of standards in addition to limitations in the extent of knowledge in relation to Canadian needs.

The latter fact makes me doubt the value of any system based on Canadian citizenship or on intent to take up Canadian citizenship, since the incompetents who have given up the hope of making a good career for themselves in the United States are precisely the people who will accept Canadian citizenship out of sheer calculation ...

There are, however, two types of situation which should be carefully avoided. The first is that in which a brilliant and original scholar in any field might be excluded because he is initially not a Canadian or expelled because he fails to become one. The other is that in which a scholar comes as a refugee and for very understandable reasons wishes to keep the citizenship of his original country—in so far as that is allowed him—in the hope of one day returning. To force such a man into the situation of accepting Canadian citizenship would be particularly repellent.

Only slightly less repellent, in that it would be a form of coercion, would be imposing citizenship as a condition of tenure. If a test is to be made at all, it should be made before a teacher joins the faculty of a university, and then, I reiterate, I believe it should be a test of competence—including competence to teach courses with Canadian content where necessary—modified by a rule that where a Canadian is available who will fill the post adequately a non-Canadian should not be appointed. However, I would be strongly opposed to this becoming a matter of legislation. The academic community should be self-regulating, and decisions under such a policy as I have outlined should be reached within the university in question, with a faculty review board to hear objections to all appointments, whether of Canadians or non-Canadians.[27]

≈

In January 1972 the Woodcocks departed for the South Pacific. There, accompanied by a CBC film crew, they would spend "a gruelling five months wandering by all kinds of hard forms of transport—police boats, copra boats, even canoes—from island to island"[28] in the Melanesians, using a supply base set up by the crew in Fiji. "The preparations have been vast and consequently everything else [in my life] has been done in a fragmentary way", he informed Sir Herbert Read's son, Ben.[29] The result was a multi-part travelogue for television—a rare event in Woodcock's professional life, for, comfortable as he was in front of radio microphones, he shied away from cameras, motion-picture as well as still. Of course the scripts he wrote, to his way of thinking, simply subsidized *South Sea Journey*, the book that followed in its own time (1976). Woodcock kept obsessively detailed records of his expenditures for the CBC accountants, noting such out-of-pocket items as "Taxi to explore Ovalau"[30] (one of the Fiji group). In fact, however, he spent less than the CBC's none-too-generous per diem. The trip provided him an opportunity to study in close detail the dregs of the French colonial system, a sobering complement to his long discontinuous examination of the British equivalent.

It may also have been during the long trip in the southwestern Pacific, with its seascapes and climate quite new to him, that he first conceived the idea of writing his autobiography. Research for such a project was certainly on the go before a year had elapsed. Late in 1973, he wrote an old friend from his Seattle days that he expected to be in Britain in the spring: "I shall be beginning my life of George Woodcock, the agitator, and visiting old haunts and old friends. I'm getting into the climacteric mood of the autobiographer!"[31] Not surprisingly, Woodcock would grapple with his own biography using much the same methodology he had employed in coming to terms with Orwell, Read or, most recently, in *Dawn and the Darkest Hour*, Huxley, by first writing various trial pieces, such as the private document that appeared in *Northern Journey* as "Notes from an Eleventh-Hour Journal" or, more publicly, reminiscent essays on various personalities and places associated with his English self. As he told a British correspondent, "My autobiography—there are many factors involved here, and [the] manuscript of the first volume ... may or may not reach Red Lion Street,"[32] that is, may or may not reach the story of Marie Louise Berneri and the trial at the Old Bailey. In any event, he stated hopefully that a manuscript would be "ready before the end of this year—and probably not before about March 1972, which would bring us to a date of winter 1975 for the earliest possible publication."[33] In fact, *Letter to the Past* did not appear until 1982. If the gestation period was especially long, the fact can no doubt be attributed to the difficulties—emotional and diplomatic—inherent in the task. In assessing his life honestly, Woodcock could not always convince himself that he had made the correct decisions. "I suppose I should have stayed in London", he wrote to another acquaintance during this period of intense self-examination. "But if I had I would never have travelled nearly as far as I managed to do from Canada, and now I've come to the stage when it doesn't matter a great deal where one is physically, and indeed when life among painters and mathematicians and almost anyone but writers has become more interesting than the literary ambience. I like to meet writers now as Stanley met Livingstone, great events in the jungle ..."[34]

When the Huxley book appeared, Alex Comfort wrote to congratulate him, saying that—as a gerontologist and a convert to Hinduism —the three of them shared a belief that learning how to face death was a primary virtue yet that they all had a sad understanding of just how much such knowledge was underrated in western culture.

By October 1973, Woodcock could inform yet another correspondent, "I've pulled out entirely from teaching, and now spend my time writing, travelling and editing *Canadian Literature*, my only remaining contact with the University."[35]

While planning the approach to his memoirs, Woodcock was busy narrating the film from the South Pacific and frantically trying to cut down the length of *Who Killed the British Empire?*

> which should have had Gibbon's eight volumes ... Now having got the book in nearly three months late on deadline, I've fled with Inge for three weeks['] holiday with her parents in a Bavarian village, with side tours into Austria and Switzerland ...
>
> This is an odd part of Germany—just over the Inn from Austria, a

brand new spa town in the midst of villages that are still largely mediaeval in feeling. The spa itself reminds me of Huxley's *After the Fire-Works*, but a bit also of [Thomas Mann's] *The Magic Mountain*, since it's filled with old rheumatic people like my parents-in-law, who in a curious way identify with the growing town and by a kind of unconscious magic transfer its youth to themselves, so that vicariously their lives begin again at eighty with the sense that the gardens and the trees will take at least fifteen years to grow into maturity and somehow they'll be preserved to see the town—with all its clear white buildings and its poplar alleys and birch-copsed parts all complete. One has exactly the same feeling of people living in a world of self-created and necessary phantasms as Mann's character have. I think I'll do a play on it, linking it up with the villages around, which are very earthy, and where they're busy putting up the Maypoles for the Mayday saturnalia —tall peeled fir trees sixty feet high, with their wreaths and garlands made out of the tree's own twigs. The biggest of all we saw in a village on the Austrian side of the Inn, called Oberfucking. That's where I'll be heading on May Day. I'll try and tempt Fulford with an article on "May Day at Oberfucking"![36]

The piece duly appeared in *Saturday Night* (under Woodcock's title this time).

Insomnia was one of Woodcock's troubling ailments. He turned it into an asset by sleeping late and withdrawing to his office at about 9 P.M. every evening to spend long hours writing. One secret of the productivity that always astounded others (and blinded them to the underlying unity of his work) was the fact that he could work with furious concentration through the night in his office at the back of the first floor while Inge—herself a night-owl but perhaps not to the same extent—slept undisturbed upstairs. Such was the schedule at 6429 McCleery Street in Vancouver, an address famous among his global correspondents, who apparently tended to picture it differently than it was.

Before Julian Symons and his wife Katherine visited the Woodcocks *in situ* in 1976 during a tour of western North America, they were cautioned by Roy Fuller, who already had made the trip to Vancouver to relive old times, not to get off the bus at the wrong end of McCleery Street. British visitors were often puzzled that the numbers of the houses should run into the four digits on what was only, in Symons's words,

> a short tree-lined street of considerable charm. The houses are detached and of varying design, with largish gardens kept green by sprinklers, and the architecture has the anonymous pleasantness of affluent suburbia. George and Inge's house was among the smallest in the street. There were splendid things in it, wall hangings given them by the Dalai Lama as a result of their visits to the Himalayas, a fine collection of Indian masks and artefacts. Everything had an air of settled and comfortable charm, an impression enhanced by the food put out each night for the family of raccoons which crept up to the back porch, and the cat adopted because its claws had been removed by a previous owner so that it was unable to defend itself.[37]

The Woodcock routine was to mix "a pitcher of powerful martinis with a certain slow gravity at six o'clock every evening"[38] and entertain guests—guests ofttimes in contrapuntal and intriguing combinations—with food and conversation. Both were memorable. I myself recall one evening in which Woodcock's table-talk ranged from arts patronage in fifteenth-century Germany to the iconography of the wild roses on Hornby Island as distinct from the iconography of those on the B.C. mainland. Indeed, his grasp of botanical subjects and of ecology in general surprised many, who expected no scientific knowledge from a literary personage. When he talked so wonderfully, in the speech patterns of the Thames Valley and the Welsh border intertwined and not much dimmed by time, it was with a joyous sense that he was sharing information rather than pontificating. In fact, as Symons observed, Woodcock "made no attempt to dominate the conversation, sitting for the most part like Buddha, foursquare and sympathetic, sometimes gently smiling."[39]

It was during this period, when he was researching his own memory for his projected autobiography, that he seemed finally to let go of any British literary ambitions. Yet he remained restless to a degree that would have surprised most of his Canadian friends if they could have read his mind: restless to find some new challenge or at least a new landscape that would take the place of the settled life of the word factory on McCleery Street, which seemed so idyllic to other writers looking in. In August 1975, he wrote to Fuller: "We are, I suppose, settling down, not planning great travels; indeed, I find my Shropshire yeoman blood welling up, and most of this summer we have been looking for land, without yet finding the right place."[40] By early October, he could report to a Canadian acquaintance on the frustration of "dickering over the little shack"[41] near Chilliwack on the Fraser, beyond the usual commuting range to Vancouver, which lay one hundred miles to the west.

> We put in an offer nearly three weeks ago, and the bloody man won't say yes or no. But we have heard that other land on Vedder Mountain is falling in price. One piece of 20 acres for which we were asked $55,000 has now dropped—asking price—to $43,900; if it's still on the market by late October it might easily be obtainable for about $35,000. In fact, we've now decided to wait until the really bad weather and then to attack the people who've had property on the market all summer. Frightful how one even talks of it in terms of military strategy![42]

The dream apparently collapsed after speculators "built a vast barn right on our boundary",[43] blocking the view of the flats. A year after beginning the search, they located another country property: "Talking about it on our way, we had thought $45,000 sufficient for the land, plus about $10,000 for the buildings in their present condition and perhaps $10,000 for the water pipes and power connections and the road. Just a little less than half of what [the vendor] asks!"[44]

At this time, Woodcock reached the most active point in his fight to save the CBC's regional radio production centres, a campaign that was of course doomed to the evil of centralization. "Indeed," he confided to Fuller, "after having enjoyed a decade of rising fortunes, many literary ventures here are withering in the twin blasts of inflation and government austerity, and I'm rather glad I [have] decided to withdraw next year from the editorship of *Canadian Literature*",[45] which he had been putting out for eighteen years. He added that he didn't know how much longer his financial luck might hold.

Always the soul of diplomacy in person and almost always elaborately polite in any public role, he was nonetheless given to acerbity and even despair in his private letters, which sometimes deal in candour approaching libel. There was talk of the Toronto literary establishment. The more pretentious they are, the more mediocre. But they hang together, and in this way keep themselves above the surface. Think of the scandalous way in which they kept up [Morley] Callaghan's reputation when all his bath water ran out thirty years ago. And the way they're buoying Richler up—a limited and worked-out talent if ever there was one. A good thing for [Torontonians that Wyndham] Lewis departed—not a good thing for *us*.[46]

He was finding that though

I get continual requests for articles from London, New York, San Francisco, Holland, even Mexico, as well as doing my regular work for Canadian magazines and newspapers ... I'm not publishing [books] in England as much as I used to. The publishing trade there is in a dither, and won't make solid commitments or pay good advances, while the fall in the pound has sharply reduced the value of royalties in Canadian dollars. So I'm now originating my books with Canadian publishers, some of whom are excellent salesmen and good in their financial dealings. In fact two of my three most recent books have been published here, and it looks as though the same thing will be happening with the books I am now working on or contemplating—two for Canada and one—perhaps—for England.[47]

Another factor, of course, was that his contacts and contemporaries in Britain were dying out. One who continued to prosper and be productive, though, was Roy Fuller. When Fuller sent him one of his recent poetry collections, Woodcock returned the compliment, as, in this otherwise darkening period, Woodcock discovered that, to use the metaphor that he himself enjoyed, he was being revisited by Euterpe, the muse of lyric poetry. He sent Fuller a copy of *Notes on Visitations* (shipping it via the U.S., because Canada was undergoing a grueling postal strike at the time) and warning him that it

will really seem a thin offering in comparison with your record. I wonder if it has anything to do with the fact that I have dissipated my life on so many travels and so many kinds of writing while you have conserved yourself for poetry. There's no doubt that great binges of prose are bad for verse writers, but I'm not so sure about the travels, provided one keeps them for one's poems. Three of the best Canadian poets—Birney, Purdy and Layton—are monstrous travellers—geo-poets one could call them.[48]

The strike against Canada Post forced the Governor General's office to telegraph an invitation to Woodcock to travel to Ottawa for a conference on the twenty-fifth anniversary of the Massey Commission, out of which the Canada Council and other cultural initiatives had come. Woodcock reported to his cousin in England that staying at Rideau Hall was

> rather like being at a Victorian country house party, the meetings of the symposium broken by two receptions and two enormous formal meals a day, with endless protocol, aides-de-camp always at one's elbow, and guards locking and unlocking the doors whenever one went out into the grounds. High life indeed! By the end I'd put on ten pounds and made myself unpleasant to at least three cabinet ministers with whom I disagreed sharply on government policies.[49]

To Avakumovic, he spoke cryptically of "desiccated phantoms of the empire!"[50]

When the Symonses arrived in the summer of 1976, their visit, Woodcock reported back to Fuller,

> was delightful for us—I think they enjoyed it too—and many other visitors turned up, and then we had to go to the Kootenays to do a joint CBC-National Film Board couple of documentaries on the Doukhobors, and then up far north, seven hundred miles from Vancouver, to the Indian villages of the Skeena River, for one of the chapters of the book I'm now on, and then another 200 miles down river to the sea at Prince Rupert, and then back into the Rockies to the Alberta border to load the car with booze—such being about 18% cheaper owing to the variations in our provincial taxes—and then back home after a total of 3,500 miles on the road, which all shows what a bloody big empty place we live in.[51]

For his part, Symons (whose letters are full of whining but whose published work is more careful) remembered the visit to Vancouver differently.

A certain tolerance is necessary when old friends meet again after a long lapse of time [he wrote]. One's ideas have solidified or, as one might less kindly say, ossified and opposite points of view seem evidently wrong. During the week in which K and I were with George and Inge, I had clearly brought home to me the immense difference in viewpoint between a Western materialist like me with no faith in the perfectability of man, and a romantic idealist like George, whose whole adult life has been based on a belief in the naturalness of voluntary cooperation among individuals within a group. As I listened to George outlining his hopes of social change in Canada, and saying that the first step was a questionnaire that would be issued in a popular magazine, as Inge told me of the spellbinding revelations in Jung's autobiography which was her current reading, I began to feel a strong kinship with almost any kind of organized society. I had an inclination to sing the praises even of Macdonald [*sic*] and Burger King, and to praise the architecture of Howard Johnson's.[52]

Symons also observed that Woodcock "appeared on any slightly formal occasion wearing a suit".[53] The visitor thought that he perceived his host looking somewhat disconcerted when he himself dressed more casually.

12 A GREEN OLD AGE

WOODCOCK WOULD BE turning sixty-four on 8 May 1976 and was anxious about putting his financial affairs in order. He would be receiving a small seniors' benefit from the federal government. In addition, his connection to UBC had allowed him to purchase units of the Teachers' Insurance and Annuity Association, a New York bond fund. These he now cashed in and bought an annuity with another New York firm, the College Retirement Equities Fund. As a prolific freelance broadcaster and scriptwriter he was also part of the pension scheme at ACTRA, the Association of Canadian Television and Radio Artists. One year after the epochal anniversary of his birth, he wrote to the relevant official at the union: "Clearly, as I still earn quite substantial amounts from CBC it would be in my interest to allow my contribution to accumulate in the fund, at least for the time being, and to review the situation in another few years' time."[1]

The Woodcocks had always conducted their lives on a modest financial scale so that they might indulge themselves in travel and practise charity. Yet Woodcock was so prolific a writer, and so careful in his expenditures, that he found himself quite comfortable financially —and quite conservative in his investments, too, preferring guaranteed income certificates for the predictability inherent in the word *guaranteed.*

Woodcock would be handing over *Canadian Literature* to William New, a friend and UBC colleague and a Malcolm Lowry scholar, who was also specialist in both Canadian and Commonwealth literature generally as well as in the relationship between the two. The loyal Ivan

Avakumovic conceived the idea of a Festschrift to celebrate Woodcock's achievement, and New volunteered to edit the volume, soliciting memoirs from Woodcock's old colleagues, tributes from his writer friends and images from those in the visual arts. Avakumovic also proposed to New a special Woodcock issue of *Canadian Literature* for 1982, when Woodcock would reach seventy. "As you know," Woodcock responded, "while I was editor I never commissioned pieces on myself and even steered people who wrote pieces to other magazines. But now it would be appropriate to run an issue. However, it's something I can't talk to Bill about, so that I'm glad you have mentioned it."[2] Yet he also felt such a plan "would probably take away from ... the magazine's *own* celebration when its hundredth issue comes out at the end of 25 years of life, which will be in the summer of 1984 ..."[3] In fact, the special Woodcock number did not materialize until 1992, when Woodcock was eighty. But the Festschrift, entitled *A Political Art: Essays and Images in Honour of George Woodcock* and aided by grants from the Koerners of Vancouver and the Bronfmans of Montreal, appeared in 1978 from UBC Press. Indeed, it came out after only moderate delays (and some unstated small crisis of diplomacy in which Woodcock had to intervene without spoiling the surprise). What pleased the honoree was

> the way in which each contributor seemed to be acting very characteristically, [with] Julian [Symons] taking the ironic pose of *l'homme moyen sensuel*, Roy Fuller obsessed with mortality, Bob Heilman defending a New Critical position, Derek Savage being as amiably cantankerous as I remember him when we tried to found a community together in 1941, Kathleen Raine being luminous but oblique ...[4]

Woodcock added that, what with "pieces by people from so many pasts and places, [and] with the names of dead friends tolling like bells through the book, I found a strange and new configuration of my life emerging, and emerging in splendid print, for I thought the design and workmanship by Dick Morriss [the son of Charles] were superb."[5] He called Avakumovic's own contribution, a detailed bibliographical listing of Woodcock's work, "obviously the greatest labour of all, and perhaps in the long run the most useful."[6] He reported to Fuller that two of his artist-friends who contributed "turned up this week with the original drawings, so that it has been a kind of birthday as well as a Festschrift, with a presentation dinner still to come!"[7] He went on that he hoped to see Fuller in Britain in September. "And there are possibilities of being sent on a new film assignment to Panama, Papua and Indonesia—which I am sure will be the last big journey, if it comes off!"[8]

That particular trip never got beyond the planning stage, no doubt because the film project collapsed. Like most literary writers, Woodcock had only mixed success with filmmakers. He was frequently frustrated when scripts written and paid for failed to be produced. As recently as 1977, he had been commissioned to write a proposal for "It Seems We Are Dying Beyond Our Means: A Film about Britain Today"; similar disappointments littered the past. Yet, again like so many other authors, he enjoyed occasional windfalls from films as well, one of them quite large. "I once earned £10,000 for doing a mere chronology of Orwell for a British-Spanish consortium that was never produced, several thousand dollars for a treatment of a film on the Sepik River in New Guinea, odd thousands from the NFB for outlines—all paid for and none produced."[9] In any event, the trip that did in fact take place was by no means Woodcock's last chance to travel.

In Colombo in 1962, the Woodcocks had become friendly with James George, who was then Canada's high commissioner to Ceylon and would later serve at the same level in India and then in the Persian Gulf states. The relationship persisted when the Woodcocks returned to Vancouver. When the diplomat retired in 1977 (and became a dedicated environmentalist), Woodcock wrote him that in his own experience retirement "doesn't seem to make much difference, since editors and publishers seem to sense when one has spare time, and I have commissions to last me a good time, and then other works which I want to do for my own sake and which are likely to fill an indefinitely extendable future. (Perhaps I didn't tell you that one of them is a shortish book on Thomas Merton, which I am finding, apart from anything else, a great extension of my own education.)"[10] That was in December 1977. In March 1978, the Woodcocks came home from an extended journey to New Zealand, where they had been entertained by Bill New, who was doing research there. Six weeks after returning, still struggling with the residual effects of jet lag and correspondence backlog, Woodcock wrote New to tell him of events in Canada, including the deaths of two writer-friends, Roy Daniells and Patrick Anderson. Daniells

died last Saturday, a week ago today, having had a bad heart, and refused
to go into hospital; he died, I gather, in full consciousness and seren-
ity, writing almost to the end and completing an extraordinary little
Bunyanesque parable. Altogether, as near as one can get in our day to
a holy dying in the classic sense. There was a great memorial service,
with about a thousand people attending, hundreds of whom one had
never seen before, which gave one an idea of the strange ramifications
of Roy's world ... It is only now, days afterwards, that one realizes how
much has gone out of one's life with Roy and how much one—
there is no other word as Jack Shadbolt and I agreed last night—*loved*
the man.[11]

Another matter preyed on Woodcock's mind: the disappearance, in
Switzerland, of Betty Belshaw, the wife of another UBC colleague, Cyril
Belshaw. Woodcock told New

I fear there has been no news of Betty. We have had three letters from
Cyril, telling of his frustrations. One promising trail from the French
police, which led to nothing, and a similar experience with the Swiss
police. No real clue of any kind has emerged. Now Cyril has decided
to accept our suggestion of making contact with two Dutch psychics
who have helped the European police a great deal in connection with
missing people. Though every day does make it seem less likely that
any good news will materialize.[12]

In time, Belshaw was tried for the murder of his wife, only to be
released. One of the most poignant documents in the Woodcock
archive is a 1980 letter from Woodcock to Belshaw, who was then in
prison in Woodcock's beloved and idealized Switzerland. Knowing that
one cannot write too long a letter to a prisoner, Woodcock brought
Belshaw up to date on such matters as the Woodcocks' work with the
boat people: refugees from Vietnam, often ethnic Chinese.

Our life goes on its course, but through no will of ours. There have
been difficulties all over the summer with our refugees, particularly one
very scared family who had been through all the more sensational experiences of robbery, beating and raping by Thai pirates. However, after
about two months of very difficult work we seem to have got them
into a calmer state of mind and on the way to fitting in here. From

other parts of Canada we hear reports of refugees who are just incap-
able of finding their feet here, and we begin to realize how fortunate
we are to have Chinatown as a source of practical help (though by no
means all Vancouver Chinese *are* friendly to the cause) and also a kind
of cultural half-way house on the way to accepting Canadian society.
But we're beginning to feel a little too old for such arduous and anxious tasks, and this fall we intend to make something of a break by
going off to Australia and Asia and perhaps Europe for two or three
months, which will give our associates time to get used to doing
without our expertise in such matters, on which they have really been
relying too much. I begin to feel now that I must concentrate on the
works I want to finish—for after all I have a major programme involving five long volumes of writing, and I *am* 68 and not imperishable.
Inge also finds the refugee work much more tiring than she did, yet,
being Inge, cannot be other than thorough about it, and so tends to
get nervously and physically exhausted. We have at last, I think, to
withdraw from that aspect of our lives, which after all has been a
dominant aspect of them for nearly twenty years.[13]

Inge was taken ill in January 1981 and the couple, as Woodcock
reported in a chatty letter to Margaret Atwood, "went to Victoria to
hole up in a hotel and rest for a couple of weeks."[14] They were intending to travel to India by way of Greece and what Woodcock still
referred to as the Levant. Now he worried that the local cuisines would
"hardly [be] the food for an ulcer patient" like Inge, who had "reacted
negatively to the new quick-cure drug, so she has to get better the
slow way."[15] The occasion for the correspondence was Woodcock's
decision to rejoin the Writers' Union of Canada, from which he had
resigned earlier, to protest a multi-tiered fee structure that he thought
was unbecoming and undemocratic. He told Atwood now that

as soon as I hear what I must do, I'm willing to start in again, since
I really would like to support you in whatever you have a mind to do.
Even I, who've had a wide range of publishers to pick and choose from,
and have managed to keep my independence from tieups, am finding
things far less easy than three or four years ago ... And I hear of young
writers with books and projects that would have been snapped up five

years ago, but who now can't find a publisher to give them a start. So I think the union is necessary to protect what we have and try and get publishing going again.[16]

In a slightly later letter, however, he could not promise to attend the annual general meeting, citing Inge, whose recovery had "been disappointingly up and down until a herbalist recently put her on to Slippery Elm which really seems to be working . . ."[17] His concern was genuine (but so was his fear and detestation of meetings). Of course, this did not mean that his interest in good works had abated or would ever do so. At this particular time, he was actively propagandizing for abolition of the seal hunt in the North, a cause to which he had become attached through Inge's influence. Typical were these remarks in the Vancouver *Sun* (for Woodcock was a tireless believer in local discussion in local media):

> First, we have been assured that our ideas of what goes on in the seal hunt are exaggerated. It is untrue, we are told, that cruelties that would lead to immediate arrest if they took place in a city street are being enacted on the ice floes. The talk of baby seals being skinned while they are still alive and conscious must be absurd, we are assured, since the government is now regulating the hunt.
>
> Nobody in the government has successfully answered the question of why, if the hunt is so humanely carried out, independent observers were prevented from witnessing it.[18]

Privately, he told Margaret Atwood that

> Farley Mowat is probably right in saying that the main objective of the Department of Fisheries is the destruction of all species of marine mammals. So we're selling stamps and bumper stickers (stamps at 50 for $1) to raise funds to pay the expenses for a nationwide manifestation by Canadian artists in November, with simultaneous shows from Victoria to Halifax and, we hope, musicians and poets also participating in the events.[19]

Before long, Woodcock was using his access to magazines such as *Saturday Night* to write about the issue, and he and Inge helped to organize a large protest at the Arts Club Theatre on Granville Island.

Inge did in fact recover in time for the Woodcocks to travel ("Greece [was] swarming with tourists and Turkey swarming with soldiers").[20] Once he returned to "the relative unpopulation and unpollution of Vancouver",[21] Woodcock was again in close communication with Atwood. She had initiated a benevolent conspiracy to get the Canada Council to award the Molson Prize to the poet Al Purdy (the literary figure with whom Woodcock had the most frequent correspondence of all). This was a difficult proposition given that Purdy did not boast of middle-class heritage. Woodcock in turn enlisted support from other friends, such as George Galt, a youngish Anglo-Montreal travel writer and man of letters, now exiled in Toronto; Galt was one of the original board members of the Woodcock Trust, which Woodcock established to help Canadian writers in need. The Council instead gave the Molson this time to Atwood, leaving Woodcock "divided in mind",[22] as Atwood herself doubtless was. Relaunching the campaign would prove difficult, given new calamities. Woodcock experienced another "bit of minor heart trouble ('premature heart beat' they said after thinking at first it was fibrillations); I'd gone a little wild in the garden, shifting nearly a ton of compost in one afternoon."[23] But he and Purdy's other friends persisted year after year, to no avail. Woodcock later succeeded, however, in eliciting Atwood's moral and financial support for the Canada-India Village Association.

All this while, the Woodcocks were privately discussing another more permanent escape from the climate they found so hard on them. For a time, they entertained the possibility of Bermuda or the Bahamas, though Inge, Woodcock reported, felt generally uncomfortable living on small islands. This was late in 1981. By this time, bits of Woodcock's autobiography-in-progress had begun appearing in print.

≈

Long before May 1982 drew near, Woodcock developed "what I suppose is a superstitious feeling that my 70th birthday is the one milestone I really don't want to celebrate very highly—tempting Providence, etc. etc."[24] His own presents to himself included two new books, each in its way highly controversial.

As early as 1978, in discussions with Jim Polk and Ann Wall at House of Anansi Press, Woodcock had toyed with their idea for a selection of his letters to other Canadian writers. Woodcock had hesitated, because "I'm a little bewildered by two problems. The first is an ethical one: Should one publish one's letters before one dies? Perhaps that is a matter less of ethics than of pudeur ... [The] other problem remains how to select from the vast mass of letters I have been going through ..."[25] This project now finally appeared but with Quadrant Editions, another Ontario small press, one regarding which Woodcock would eventually go to the Canada Council complaining of non-payment of royalties. Some in Can lit circles were offended to find themselves the subject of Woodcock's candid comments in letters not originally intended for publication. Woodcock's defence was that "at least I don't say behind anyone's back what I'm afraid to have them hear!"[26] On quite another level, in its mosaic of references to deadlines and outlines, publishers and reviewers, *Taking It to the Letter* gave a true likeness of the writer's life and of the drudgery involved—and of the peculiar personalities one is forever trying to soothe. It is also a moving book on the subject of friendship, something which, in Woodcock's case, as he tended to be shy in person and uncomfortable on the telephone, often found its most intensive expression through the post. In its much more personal way, the book was also a sort of explication of his essay collections *The World of Canadian Writing: Critiques and Recollections* (1980) and *Northern Spring: The Flowering of Canadian Literature* (1987).

The other controversial book, *Confederation Betrayed!*, harked back to Woodcock's beginnings as a radical pamphleteer. The argument this time was western separatism or at least the threat of western separatism as a lever for use against the authority of central Canada. Woodcock argued that the original intention of Confederation, as it existed in the land prior to passage of the British North America Act, was betrayed early on by the *fact* of the BNA Act, "by which the provinces emerged as looking like glorified municipalities", at the mercy "of the centralist and authoritarian elements" that find expression (he was of course writing during the long Trudeau era) in the "servile and disciplined Liberal parliamentary majority, composed almost entirely of Central Canadians."[27] Sometimes his specific argument became obscured in the storm of wider principle, but the book displayed a rare gift for outrage and logic combined.

If his seventieth birthday was not the turning-point he dreaded, it was a signal for various strands of his existence to come together somehow. An exiled Iranian commissioned him to write a script for a proposed feature film to be called *Lupus*. Woodcock described it as being "about revolutionary ethics, part didactic, part symbolic, and [it] will be done, if the finances work out, in British Columbia."[28] He was enthusiastic at first. Of course, the project did not materialize. But as he confessed to Atwood, "One of the advantages of getting old is that it no longer seems to matter a great deal either way. The work itself is what finally matters. Sententious again!"[29] At other times he was less accepting of his fate with films. "I shall certainly be willing to meet you," he told a Los Angeles producer who approached him the following year about the possibility of a television series based on one section of *Peoples of the Coast*, "as long as there is some understanding beforehand about the framework in which our conversations take place. To be frank, I have on occasion had a good deal of my time wasted to no purpose by film developers, and have had to establish the rule that in any conversations relating to fields in which I have written I shall be treated as a professional consultant and remunerated accordingly."[30]

Proof of inexorable mortality was all round. Kenneth Rexroth died in California. Woodcock eulogized him for the *London Review of Books*, in verse as well as prose. In the former genre, Woodcock returned to his elegiac mode.

> Hearing you were dead,
> I went out to
> look at mountains.
> Forty years
> we had been friends,
> writing between cities,
> meeting in cities,
> talking of anarchist
> persons and principles
> and never climbing
> a mountain together.
> Yet all it meant
> was mountains, and always
> in your poems
> the mountains rose, bright
> as freedom, crystalline

as science. Kenneth,
you were like Shaw. None
of your friends liked you.
They loved and sometimes
hated you, and were held
in the spell of a
harsh voice reading
lines as crystal as
runnels of sweet water
under the flower-edged
snowfields of the
high Sierra.[31]

A whiff of the inevitable was in the air perhaps. He wrote to Atwood:

> I always smile a little wryly when you exhort me to slow down! I'd
> just find it impossible to undertake those vast marathon journeys across
> the continent which you embark on. With me I think it's less hard
> work that's the trouble so much as an increasingly creaky body that
> finds coastal winters less and less endurable. After all, [I am nearly]
> seventy ... though I feel a little ashamed to use that as an excuse for
> weakness when I remember the appalling vitality and the destructive
> wit my mother-in-law was showing on her ninetieth birthday a couple
> of weeks ago.[32]

Nineteen eighty-two was also a time when Woodcock was intricately
and intimately involved with a number of public and semi-public
crusades, among them the cause of Canadian artists persecuted by
Revenue Canada. Another, longer-lived one was the possibility of
founding, along with, at various times, Gary Geddes or Mike Doyle,
a journal of comment that would avoid what he termed the compla-
cencies of *Saturday Night* and *Maclean's*, magazines which, it should
be said in fairness, often gave Woodcock space to air his grievances
and champion his beliefs, particularly under the editorships of Robert
Fulford and Peter C. Newman, respectively. While Woodcock vehe-
mently opposed Ottawa's decision to allow the United States to test
its cruise missiles over Canadian territory, he remained firm in warning fellow protesters about what he had once called the folly of
revolutionary violence, in particular that perpetrated by a group that

came to be known as the Squamish Five. "The bombing of the Litton Industries plant in Toronto because of its involvement in the development of the cruise missile is the most recent example of such counter-productive action", he told readers of the Vancouver *Sun*. "The act has done no good to the peace movement, it has harmed a number of people in no way responsible for the planning or construction of the missile, and it leaves us, as the dust of the explosion drifts away, still facing the problem of Canada's involvement in this highly controversial project and the need to consider it with logic as well as passion."[33]

His autobiography, *Letter to the Past*, appeared in the middle of all this, and although the reviews it garnered were positive, it received far fewer than most of his other major books and, despite dealing only with his British years, failed to find a publisher in the U.K. The changing of the guard at Faber, for example, left Woodcock without a major publisher in London. Indeed, the last generation in Canada that felt at home in British culture was fading rapidly. Much of the autobiographer's art resides in knowing the moment to publish, and Woodcock had missed his moment of maximum opportunity, which would have been sometime in the 1970s, when he first became such a figure of popular recognition that he was the subject of profiles in competing national magazines, for instance. He must have been disappointed in the response, but his reaction is not recorded in his correspondence, except in such remarks as this one to Atwood, to whom he sent a copy: "You may find it curious, if nothing else."[34] He threw himself into other matters. Before the end of the year, he could write Atwood a

note in haste and chaos, since we're leaving the day after tomorrow for India. Partly we're going to have a good look at the Kabiliji Hospital and the villages ... CIVA has been accepted as a non-governmental organization by CIDA, and, because of the years Inge and I put into Tibetan relief, they have immediately given us the highest ratio—$3 to every $1 we raise! What we are especially concerned with is the small revolution that the hospital seems to be carrying out in the status of women in this highly purdah-oriented region, but when we get back there'll be more to tell you and the other sponsors. And then Toni Onley and I will be wandering over the country—Rajesthan, Kerala, Oriss, Darjeeling, doing parallel visual and verbal diaries which perhaps will make up into an interesting book. We'll be back on the 30th January, with a week in Burma on the way back.[35]

The book, perhaps the most visually appealing one in which Woodcock was ever involved, was published as *The Walls of India* in 1985. The royalties, along with proceeds from the sale of Onley's original watercolours, went to Canada-India Village Aid. The book's physical beauty contrasted with the fact that Woodcock found India this time "rather depressing, since I know and rather love the country, and now, under the frightful Mrs. [Indira] Gandhi, it's deteriorating in almost every way. Perhaps, at 70, it's time I gave up wandering. There are so many places I can only compare with what they were one, two, three decades ago, and nowhere is the world improving."[36] In fact, he still had travels ahead of him, and battles as well.

Nineteen eighty-three was the eightieth anniversary of George Orwell's birth and the fiftieth anniversary of his first book. More importantly, of course, it was also the run-up to the chronological 1984, a year in which academics, critics and journalists would bombard the landscape with books, articles, papers and reviews comparing and contrasting the present reality with the society that Orwell had imagined in *Nineteen Eighty-Four*. As one of the few true Orwell authorities, and perhaps the only one who had been Orwell's friend, Woodcock was ready for the onslaught. To one request, from an American journal called *College Literature*, he replied that he was

> being widely sought by both editors and [by] the organizers of symposia. I have decided not to take part in symposia, since such occasions inordinately waste a writer's time and sap his energy. With regard to articles, I do not "submit"; I only work on definite commissions. And I would, if we were to agree on a suitable topic and you were to commission a piece, expect the payment appropriate to a professional writer, though, realising you edit a scholarly journal with a small circulation, I would be willing to accept something in the neighourhood of $300-400, which is considerably less than I ask of most magazines.[37]

The tone was entirely out of character and requires contextualization.

For Woodcock, the 1984 celebrations had begun in 1982, when the producer of the *Lupus* film project commissioned him to write a treatment for a dramatized film biography of Orwell. By 1983, Woodcock was being "invited to involve myself in Orwell [festivities] from London and Chicago, where they're reprinting *The Crystal Spirit* with a new introduction, from Toronto, where I'm doing a 5-hour CBC programme and have written a great article for *Quest*, from Paris and Waterloo, in connection with other articles, and even from Madeira Park, B.C., where Harbour Publishing has commissioned a further book on GO."[38] He was proud of his contribution—and hurt by the fact that he wasn't asked to take part in an Orwell conference in Vancouver, saying bravely that the situation "suits me well; I like the role of the prophet in his own country."[39] So the tone of Woodcock's reply to *College Literature* was provoked no doubt by overwork and the creeping cragginess that accompanied old age with its multiplying physical ailments.

The CBC production, for which he made one of his rare trips to Toronto, a destination he dreaded above all others, was entitled "George Orwell: A Radio Biography" and was sold to Public Broadcasting in the U.S. Woodcock was the narrator and one of sixty people who gave their reminiscences of Orwell. Later he wrote an introduction to the book that resulted, *Remembering Orwell*, which competed for attention with Woodcock's own book from Harbour Publishing, *Orwell's Message: 1984 and the Present.* That was a book he thoroughly enjoyed writing, to judge by these comments in a letter to David Koven, his old anarchist colleague in the Bay Area:

> I've spent this weekend writing the first chapter of a new book—the Orwell and 1984 book—and feel the kind of high I always do when I start something and it goes well from the first word. I did 4,500 words in two days with hardly a revision needed. I only hope it keeps on that way. I'd like to get a good chunk done before we go to Australia. The plans are finally set, after much trouble with an Indian travel agent who kept us dangling for three weeks and then did nothing. We go on the 24th December, which means we shall avoid most of the Christmas and New Year shit, and we shall be back on the 31st January. I've had such good reports from such a variety of people of a culture much more vital than the Canadian that I'm looking forward to seeing what can have aroused such enthusiasm. And even if we're disappointed on that

score, it will be summer, the wine will be cheap, and one gathers the fruit and fish are superb.[40]

He added in an aside: "Inge is busily painting the house."[41]

≈

Beginning in the 1970s, Woodcock's letters are full of references to visiting the United States, either on short holidays or on shopping trips. In 1979, for example, in a newsy letter to the New family, William and Margaret, he writes: "We are off on Tuesday for a brief trip, to the Shadbolts' place on Hornby, then to Vancouver Island friends, then over to Port Angeles [Washington] for a trip to the Olympic Peninsula and the Oregon Coast, back on the 4th May."[42] Since the debacle at the University of Washington in the 1950s, he had experienced no recurrence of official United States hostility, and he crossed the frontier freely. Now, suddenly and dramatically, the situation changed when he found himself "in a real 1984 situation, in which Big Brother is the U.S. Immigration Service."[43]

As he related to an academic at Washington State University in Pullman, who had asked him to attend the inevitable Orwell conference, he and Inge had landed in Hawaii on Christmas Eve 1983,

> passing through Honolulu on the way to Sydney [when I discovered that] I was not allowed to land because, to my astonishment, my name was still, 28 years later, in the *lookout book*, a literal black book, which the immigration officer was using ... Until the matter is cleared up, I cannot be sure enough of getting through to make any commitments. I have tried to get the American authorities to rectify the situation, but so far have experienced only stonewalling from them, represented in this case by the U.S. Consul General in Vancouver.[44]

Word spread quickly, and the case became a *cause célèbre*. Hearing the news, Robert Fulford of *Saturday Night* wrote to Woodcock:

> God, that's an appalling story about U.S. immigration. I've had various friends who were on the list and then briefly hired lawyers to get them off—but all that happened eighteen or twenty years ago. I believed (though now that I think of it, I had no real reason to) that

the immigration service had long since given up most of that nonsense. But apparently once you go on the list you stay on forever, unless you arrange to be taken off. The list must include quite a few people who are long-ago deceased—unless, of course, they informed the immigration service when they died.[45]

Fulford went on to commission an article from Woodcock about the whole affair. The piece filled in many of the details, such as the fact that Inge was declared free to enter the U.S. while George was not and that he was in some danger of being jailed for three days until a helpful agent of QANTAS Airways got the couple on another Sydney-bound flight an hour later. Ironically, while public reaction was building, Woodcock, settled back in Vancouver, graciously played host, at the suggestion of the Department of External Affairs in Ottawa, to a luncheon for visiting American academics: Fellows of the Harvard Center for International Affairs. The following day, George Woodcock, menace to America, turned seventy-two.

He found himself in the eye of a storm. He was also the central clearing-house for information about the case, and he sought to keep all parties informed, including the person who had invited him to the Orwell conference in Pullman, to whom he reported that

> the head of the United States section in our Ministry of External Affairs in Ottawa was in touch with the United States Embassy there which assured him the US Consul in Vancouver would arrange some kind of travel permit. However, when I did talk to the local consul, [Maynard] Winge, he said that this was not for him to do, but volunteered to ask the local Immigration and Nationalization [*sic*] man at Vancouver Airport, one Carney, to send me the necessary forms to apply for a waiver. Carney has done nothing. So I feel that I am caught in a grand buck-passing exercise, like [Kafka's character] K trying to find out where he stands in relation to the Castle. I have a feeling a word from a legislator might help greatly. With regard to Congressman Foley's assistant's remark that there was no such thing as a black book, I saw it from a distance of two feet and while I stood there the immigration officer was checking it for every person entering at Honolulu. Also, the spokesman for the I&N in Washington admitted to a correspondent of the Anchorage *Times*, which heard of the case, that such a book, known in the service as the "lookout book", does exist.[46]

Of course, many other writers, from Graham Greene to Gabriel Garcia Marquez to Carlos Fuentes, had been kept out of the United States. But this instance seemed a remarkable new advance in that Woodcock was being kept out on the grounds that he had been kept out once before.

The Trudeau government, which Woodcock had so recently excoriated throughout his book *Confederation Betrayed!*, came to his defence on principle. Trudeau himself had once been on the list, owing to his attendance at an economic conference in Moscow in 1952. One estimate suggested that three thousand Canadians remained on the exclusion lists because of such facts as that or because of ideas they had voiced or written. As a result of the Woodcock case, their names were eventually made known to Ottawa. They included a large number of harmless figures such as Barker Fairley, the Goethe scholar, portrait painter and co-founder long ago (in 1920) of the *Canadian Forum*.

Toronto MP David Crombie found the episode "quite shocking" and feared that "other scholars and writers are quite likely being subjected to similar experiences".[47] Crombie brought the matter to the attention of Allan MacEachen, the External Affairs minister, who expressed alarm "that such a distinguished Canadian has been excluded from entering the United States."[48] MacEachen then got some of his officials at work whittling away at their American counterparts. Canada's ambassador to the U.S., Allan Gotlieb, wrote Woodcock that he personally was "seeing what can be done to repair the situation", adding: "It will reinforce your sense of unreality to learn that the *Images of Canada* booklet you wrote for us on Canadian literature has been extremely popular in the United States. We are still inundated with requests following the distribution of the full printing of 10,000 copies and are now considering whether it should be reprinted."[49]

The case achieved greater recognition in international academic circles in September 1984 when the *New York Review of Books* published Woodcock's *Saturday Night* essay under the title "On Being 'Inadmissible'". Other American journals, such as the *New Leader*, also took up the cause. Woodcock wrote to the U.S. consul-general in Vancouver "formally to request you, under the Freedom of Information legislation of the United States, to allow me access to the file regarding me on which the decision of the Consul in 1955 was based."[50] This was one of those occasions on which he found it prudent to inform the addressee of his pedigree, and signed himself "Yours faithfully, George Woodcock. D.Litt., University of British Columbia. D.Litt., Université d'Ottawa. D.Litt., Concordia University. LL.D., University of Victoria. LL.D., University of Winnipeg. FRGS. FRSC. Holder of the Molson Award of the Canada Council. Holder of the Governor-General's Award for Literature. Guggenheim Fellow."[51] The consul was "unable to comply with your request inasmuch as the records of the Department of State and of diplomatic and consular offices of the United States pertaining to the issuance or refusal of visas or permits to enter the United States are considered confidential and may be used only for the formulation, amendment, administration, or enforcement, of the immigration, nationality, and other laws of the United States."[52] As for the Freedom of Information Act, "it is applicable only to United States citizens and to legal resident aliens of the United States."[53] The consul suggested that Woodcock simply apply for his exemption. A later telephone call from a U.S. official suggested that Woodcock "let them know of special occasions, such as conferences, that might require my presence in the United States [so that the authorities could] issue specific visas. My position was that this did not constitute a proper waiver"[54] and that in any event the matter was a principle of free expression. In this, Woodcock was not merely insistent but actually consistent as well.

For example, in 1993, when a controversy arose about whether David Irving, a Holocaust-revisionist from the U.S., should be allowed to speak in Canada, Woodcock came to his defence—a minority position in the writing community—saying that Irving should be allowed to

> wander where he will and spout his pseudo-history where he will on the grounds of principle but also of practicality ... I am concerned for the moral state of a society that restricts liberties, even to a small extent, under the specious reasoning that in this way freedom or decency can be protected. Freedom and decency can only be protected if people in a society fight for them against governments and Pecksniffs of every kind, including the literary kind. That is why I am [also] opposed to the anti-hate laws just as I am to the anti-pornography laws; people will hate as much and lust as much as ever, whatever the laws, and negative emotions are less dangerous when they are not repressed by the regulators.[55]

The sections of the notorious McCarran-Walter Act used to exclude Woodcock originally in 1955, and again three decades later, had, in fact, been liberalized somewhat in the interim. Woodcock drew attention to the fact that such exclusions as his contradicted an agreement the U.S. signed in Helsinki in 1975, which discouraged limits on the flow of people and information between and among countries: an agreement in which the United States government officially put great store. In practice, this meant that the Department of State granted waivers, such as the one offered Woodcock, instead of banning persons outright without appeal or redress. In 1976, for example, the U.S. received 47,788 such waiver applications and acceded to 47,572 of them. (Although as the *Economist* remarked, "Impressive as they are, the figures do not appease the friends of the 216 who either were refused, or gave up in disgust.")[56]

In 1985, Farley Mowat, a far more famous Canadian author than George Woodcock, was refused entry by the U.S. immigration authorities when he attempted to board a Toronto-to-Los Angeles flight for a book-promotion tour. The uproar was deafening. Mowat was offered a waiver but declined it. In December 1987, the U.S. finally replaced the offensive provisions of the McCarran-Walter Act; the victory, which affected only visitors to the U.S., was bolstered in November 1995 when, in a landmark decision, a federal appeals court in the U.S. ruled that immigrants to the U.S. enjoyed the same travel rights as both citizens and visitors.

What role Woodcock's file played in this process is difficult to assess, particularly without access to internal U.S. government documents. But one must be careful not to overstate the importance of the case except as a particularly vivid and well-publicized example among many. Woodcock, for his part, continued to slip across the border between B.C. and Washington State without incident, and found the climate of the U.S. Southwest in particular to be conducive to relief from his growing list of physical ailments.

≈

While the melodrama with the U.S. authorities was playing itself out publicly, another and more private one was running its course. It concerned the disposition of Woodcock's personal and literary papers, including letters, documents, book manuscripts, typescripts of articles,

essays and reviews, and one category that Woodcock called *Invitations*
—*mostly declined*. The extent of his pack-ratting was extraordinary.
"I doubt if many writers' archives are quite so massive",[57] he wrote
modestly to the librarian of UBC, which, given Woodcock's long if not
always happy connection to the university, seemed the logical pur-
chaser, though Woodcock had first been approached by the University
of Victoria, where he worked in the Sir Herbert Read papers. Indeed,
a circle of people at the library in Victoria who were interested in the
book-arts were slowly working away on a publishing project entitled
*Letters from Sooke: A Correspondence between Sir Herbert Read and
George Woodcock*. The book was hand-set and hand-printed in an edition of eighty-one copies, designed by Dick Morriss and bound in
quarter-leather.

To illustrate how carefully papers were filed and stored in a special-
collections environment, the librarian at UBC lent Woodcock a copy
of the finding-aid for the papers of *Prism International*, a long-
established literary magazine on campus. Woodcock responded:

> If you take as good care of my papers, I shall certainly be pleased.
> I suppose part of any idea might involve my willingness to give any
> information necessary for assisting the compilation of a similar inven-
> tory. You refer to the original order of the archive being preserved. The
> order of mine will certainly seem haphazard, but it does represent the
> order in which items were stuffed into cupboards and filing cabinets,
> and though I personally see no significance in the order, others might.
> Sometimes, as you will see, sets of items, like volumes of specific diaries,
> are scattered, and such matters perhaps *should* be adjusted.[58]

But the proposed transaction took a sour turn when senior UBC
officials objected to spending money on what they felt they must surely
already have a claim to, given Woodcock's association with the institution. Woodcock became angry and, in a letter to the librarian,
recounted his entire tangled history with the institution:

> I was first engaged in 1956 as a Lecturer in English, resigned in 1957 to
> take up a Canadian Overseas Fellowship, and then returned as Assis-
> tant Professor in 1958, becoming Associate Professor in 1960. I had a
> year's sabbatical in 1961–2, and then in 1963 resigned owing to a dis-
> pute [when the university] refused to allow me a year's *unpaid* study

leave. A compromise was worked out [by Roy Daniells and others] by which I became a *part-time* employee of the University, with the nominal status of Lecturer; it was understood that my duties would be restricted to editing *Canadian Literature*, and that for this I would be paid approximately 40% of the salary I had been receiving before. Later on the salary increased in proportion to the rank I might be expected to hold if I had stayed on, and by the time I resigned was somewhat less than half what a full professor with seniority (which was what I would have been if I stayed on as a full-time faculty member) would have received. In other words, thinking in terms of a 40 hour week, I was being paid for between 16 and 18 hours of work a week which is about what editing *Canadian Literature* took up. Since in fact I work at least 70 hours a week, the University was paying me for about a quarter of my time; the papers for sale represent almost entirely work done in the remaining three-quarters of my time, plus writing done in the many years before I ever reached UBC ...

My need to sell my papers results from the arrangement ... offered me in 1963. I was to be a yearly temporary appointee, and the University would not contribute to a pension scheme. This situation continued until the time of my resignation, with the result that I have a pension based only on what was contributed during the 5 years' [full-time] teaching plus one year's sabbatical between 1956 and 1963. In cash terms I am getting for many years of much praised contributions to the university an amount of just over $120 a month! I have to *sell* my papers, and I do find it rather appalling that the heirs of administrations who put me in this position now try to find reasons to get them at a cut rate![59]

Such was his letter to a *friend*. With the president of the university, Douglas Kenny, he reported that after a month or more of fruitless negotiations

The fine edge of my patience has been worn away, and the purpose of this letter is to let you know personally and formally that I am withdrawing my offer to sell my papers to the University of British Columbia. I would very much have liked them to be housed there; I can think of no more appropriate home. But I fear what I hear of recent developments on your side makes it impossible for me to continue the negotiations; I am not a huckster willing to sacrifice all shreds of dignity in order to make a sale.[60]

Reviewing the situation a couple of months later, after a mind-clearing trip to New Zealand, Woodcock felt that his past political activities had once again reared their head and that the university administrators "are thoroughly scared of what certain newspaper columnists may say if they do anything daring of any kind."[61]

There the matter rested for a couple of years until Woodcock, having just turned sixty-nine and feeling that he needed the income to support his work and his charities, renewed contact with Victoria. He wrote that he "would be happy to open negotiations" again, so long as they "should at all times be carried out through the library. The discussions with UBC broke down because too many people who knew nothing about archives insisted on involving themselves."[62] Before sending his own inventory of the collection, he tantalized the librarian with some random core samplings of his correspondence, finding that "up to 1977 there are 129 letters from Al Purdy, 85 from Dorothy Livesay, 45 from P.K. Page, 48 from Herbert Read, 54 from Roy Fuller, 22 from George Orwell, 23 from Hugh MacLennan, 36 from [Roderick] Haig-Brown, and so it goes on for literally hundreds of names [including, more recently] large batches from new and younger correspondents like, for example, Matt Cohen."[63] Before the breakdown of talks, UBC and Woodcock had been speaking of a purchase price in the $100,000 range. Woodcock saw no reason to increase, or indeed to lower, the figure now.

> Of course you would expect a valuation, and, thinking a little ahead, it seems to me that, in the event of your wanting to carry it that far, this should probably take place in your Library, where there will be more space than in my own basement room. My feeling is that we might reach an agreement by which the papers were handed over to the University against an advance payment of $25,000, and that the final figure be agreed after the valuation, though there should doubtless be some understanding as to the limits within which the payment might range. I.e. I would have a lower limit based on my own knowledge of the papers and you would probably have an upper limit based on available funds. But I am sure all of this can be discussed amicably ...[64]

Woodcock then received an approach from the archives of Queen's University in faraway Kingston. Woodcock politely kept both potential bidders informed and begged Queen's patience until Victoria, which had the earlier claim, made up its mind.

Suddenly the mood at Victoria changed, with the university librarian deciding that a Woodcock archive did not fit into the library's development criteria and that the best offer that could be made was to ask Woodcock to donate the material in return for tax relief. Then came a letter from the archivist at Queen's regretting "to have to tell you that although our request to purchase your personal papers was unanimously accepted by the most senior officers of Queen's University, the private donors whom the university approached found that the amount requested was beyond their scope at this stage, chiefly because of the difficult economic ills from which our country presently suffers, and which have unfortunately transmitted themselves to the private sector."[65] The archivist suggested donating the collections under the Cultural Properties Act. Woodcock replied that his income was insufficient to the enticements of the tax-saving scheme. Yet he was still somewhat sanguine.

> But does this in fact mean that the hope of an arrangement between us is ended? I do remember that at one stage in our correspondence you asked me whether I would be willing, if your hopes of finding a private patron were disappointed, to accept payment over a number of years from university funds. I believe I said that I would be willing to consider this, and indeed, if that were feasible, I would still do so. I don't know what arrangement you had in mind at that time, but something like $20,000 a year over five years, tied in to a Cultural Property tax benefit, would be acceptable to me. It may be, of course, that present financial conditions have made even this suggestion less feasible.[66]

He went on to say that the heartbeat of a deal in B.C. had revived, but "I can assure you that I am not deliberately creating a competition situation."[67] Indeed, he was resigned if necessary "to start again in what I know from experience is the slow business of finding another possible buyer"—one in Canada, because "I am too innately patriotic to consider selling to a repository outside Canada, though I may be going against my own interests in maintaining that attitude", as indeed he had had an approach from Boston University.[68]

Throughout this period and until his death, Woodcock maintained a sort of kitchen-cabinet, an informal circle of advisers and helpers drawn from the relevant disciplines but also from his wide circle of friends (the two frequently overlapped). The members ranged from Paula Brook, the editor of *Western Living* (and one of a number of young women who seemed cast in the role of surrogate daughter on visits to McCleery Street) to what Woodcock always insisted was the best cardiologist in Vancouver. One of the most important portfolios was that of Frank Low-Beer, the Woodcocks' long-time solicitor (and also a poet). Before leaving on a trip on December 1982, Woodcock was able to inform Low-Beer that Queen's had just telegraphed him to say it had found "a patron to pay for the purchase of my papers up to mid-1981, for $100,000 to be paid in five yearly instalments ... This is an arrangement which, in the event of my death, I would want to have sustained, since I think Queen's is an excellent home for the papers, while the proceeds of the sale would notably increase the residuary part of the estate which would be devoted to scholarships for native peoples ... I thought that, as Executor, you should know of this."[69]

Six months later, in June 1983, an archivist at UBC wrote to Woodcock asking where the records were for the first seventy-three issues of *Canadian Literature*, the ones Woodcock had edited.

13 ANARCHIST MOUNTAIN

"WE'RE NOT LIKELY to be travelling for a while now",[1] Woodcock wrote late in 1985 to the producer who was struggling to make a film of Woodcock's script *Lupus*. This, after just returning from what began as a journey to Israel, though "the Israeli bombing of Tunis just before our departure made us change our minds and [we] decided not to go, as a kind of protest against an unjustifiable act which showed that the generals are still an irresponsible force in Israeli actions."[2] Instead, the Woodcocks went to reliable old Switzerland and then meandered down Germany and France to Spain, "finding them much worse than remembered. I was constantly reminded of Proust's maxim—never to revisit a place that had given one pleasure!"[3] Now the same producer toyed with the idea of making a television series from Woodcock's *Canada and the Canadians*, a travel book Woodcock had produced in 1970 and revised subsequently, one that crystalized his West Coast bias as he sorted out precisely what it was he so distrusted about central Canada (mainly, the power embodied in the world *central*). Meanwhile yet another filmmaker was teasing him with a plan for a film based on *Gabriel Dumont and the Lost World of the Métis*.

As the 1990s approached, the flow of books from McCleery Street did not diminish but rather took on what seems, in retrospect at least, two new directions. The first was a renewed dedication to Canadian literature; to this period belong his long codifications of the subject as well as individual monographs on various figures he admired, including Margaret Atwood, Matt Cohen and Patrick Lane. Another aspect of his work, however, was the determination not to neglect books he had been mulling over for years but had always let slip amid the press of other demands on his time. These tend to be works *on* history as much as ones *of* history. Foremost perhaps was *The Marvellous Century: Archaic Man and the Awakening of Reason*. The century in question was the sixth century C.E., in which Christianity, Islam, modern Judaism and Zoroastrianism have their roots, the point at which such figures as Sappho and Pythagoras, Confucius and Buddha, Lao-tzu and Nebuchadnezzar were coevals, or very nearly so. The book finally appeared in 1989, with the same Toronto publisher that two seasons earlier had continued Woodcock's memoirs with *Beyond the Blue Mountains*, a sequel (but not an equal) to *Letter to the Past*, from which it differs markedly in tone, with a livelier though no less precise style.

Beyond the Blue Mountains, which he might have subtitled "The North American Years", abounds in sights, sounds and qualities of light, all vividly remembered, as well as sharply drawn sketches of contemporaries. Kenneth Rexroth, for example, was "like a decrepit Metro Goldwyn Mayer lion" and in conversation "tended to be cantankerous towards the absent."[4] The prose is especially evocative when Woodcock recalls extended periods in Mexico (an experience he says opened his mind to existentialism) and India. But while it can be read for its anecdotes or its travelogues, the book is more than that: it is a brutally honest piece of self-examination. With a brave air of clinical detachment, Woodcock reconstructs nagging financial worries, health problems, periods of depression and writer's block as he steers readers through his professional life. If he has a role, he claims, it is "as a teacher and propagandist, trying to show people how to bring about their own freedom, and salvation from oppression and want."[5] His political opinions, however, have never "been acceptable to the majority of Canadians",[6] and so have contributed to the sense of isolation he says he felt until well into the late 1960s (another startling instance of how someone whom others feel is at or near the centre can nonetheless believe himself to be on the outer reaches). The overall impression is that of a committed, humane and of course fiercely intelligent man who refuses to be humbled by quirks of fortune but is willing to show how they have channelled his energy in certain directions. He would confess to a correspondent that in writing the book it was the portrayal of the writer's life … I most wanted to convey—that life with all its splendours and miseries, as Balzac would say, with its vanities and pettinesses, its small triumphs, great failures, ultimate inexplicable satisfactions. I've always been haunted by Hazlitt's reputed last words. What a marvellous prose writer he was, what a model of dedication to the craft, yet what a wretched life he had—poverty, appalling relations with women, endless betrayed friendships! And yet, there on his deathbed, he could raise himself up at the last moment and gasp, "By God, I've had a happy life!" How wonderfully that glosses the remark of Sophocles, "Call no man happy until the day he dies!" But not merely writers. Think of blind old Handel, of Beethoven, so stone-deaf, with the glory whirling around in his closed head, that he had to be turned round on the podium to *see* the Viennese applauding the *Ninth*![7]

Not surprisingly, given their focus on Canada, neither *The Century That Made Us* nor *Beyond the Blue Mountains* found a publisher outside Canada. Nor, the following year, could another decidedly internationalist Woodcock title, *Caves in the Desert: Travels in China*. Yet this last one is most important as it permitted Woodcock to put faces and places to some of the concerns obvious throughout his career.

Can one be a Buddhist/Existentialist/Nihilist? [he asked in response to a question from the poet Phyllis Webb.] I am sure one can. I think true Buddhism—and here I am not talking of lamaist Buddhism—is to my mind both existentialist—rigorously so in that it proceeds from experience and not from metaphysical assumptions, which the Buddha rejected—and ultimately nihilist. I suppose my triad would be Taoism/Existentialism/Anarchism. Taoism suits me better because I love the visible world so much, and in that aesthetic sense am attached, which I think Taoism allows but Buddhism hardly does. Though there are ambiguities here, for once one has given up desire, is one not free to enjoy Maya for what it is? Have you ever reflected on the curious fact that Maya means the visible world of illusion, but that according to the legend the Buddha's mother was called Maya?[8]

Caves in the Desert, and perhaps the effusion above, originated from a trip to the People's Republic of China offered by that country's government, with fewer than normal restrictions, for Woodcock fell into the "distinguished visitor" category rather than that of a mere foreign writer. The adventure took Woodcock to some spots that had been of concern to him through all the years he was reading for *The Marvellous Century*. The Woodcocks travelled with two Vancouver friends, the husband-and-wife art dealers Paul and Xisa Huang, and were in China a full month. In June 1987, shortly after their return, Woodcock wrote to Earle Birney and his wife Wailan Low:

> A month ago I celebrated my 75th birthday, with much toasting of Mao Tai and other formidable liquors, at Lanzhou, the beginning of the Silk Road, down which we afterwards travelled to Tun Huang and the southern verges of the Gobi Desert. We had a wonderful time in China, and never for a moment felt we were in a foreign country, so immediately and naturally we took to the people. The caves at Yangarn and Tun Huang are marvellous and on the way between we found all kinds of remarkable places, vast mountain ranges we had never heard of, ancient temples filled with splendid statuary and preserved for a millennium in the desert climate, camels, people, people, people![9]

To the biographer James King he added:

> I liked the Chinese immensely and marvelled at the way their individuality had asserted itself as soon as the political system gave a little. I remember Herbert Read once, long ago, visiting China and telling me, "It's as near anarchism as anything we'll see in *our* lifetimes." I laughed at him then, but a great deal that I saw, considered in social, cultural and economic rather than political terms, seemed to me pretty near what Proudhon stood for. It struck me that the political masters were riding an increasingly restive dragon on a road where it would be hard for them to turn.[10]

He wrote that almost exactly two years before the massacre of pro-democracy students in Tiananmen Square. As for *Caves in the Desert*, it did not fare particularly well. One young critic described it sourly as the jottings of an elderly literary gent.

But friends delighted at how productive Woodcock's old age was.

> Age doesn't seem to make me relax into retirement. At the age of 75 I'm conscious that there is so much to be done and so little time, so

I work harder than ever, and so do quite a number of septuagenarians
I know, notably Jack Shadbolt. I'm ... polishing a book of essays on
19th century cultural attitudes for Oxford [*The Century that Made Us:
Canada 1814–1914*], and doing a social history of Canada for Penguin,
with a few articles and reviews here and there. And, as this letter shows
only too well, I'm still using my old manual typewriter none too
accurately, but very productively.[11]

Woodcock hoped to return to China in 1988 but was forced to
cancel the trip because "I have been smitten with a most persistent
arthritis in the hip. I think it is really writer's bum, since I spent long
hours finishing a couple of books, but it means I am unable to walk
more than three hundred yards without pain ... Just now the phys-
iotherapists are pulling and hauling on me and vibrating me ..."[12]

The fact that this particular problem was later diagnosed as disc
trouble did not alter the fact that he was indeed a martyr to a wors-
ening arthritic condition, which forced him to spend some of that
winter in New Mexico and Arizona. While in the latter state, however, he had a serious medical emergency. His "heart began to fail ...
pumping at a wild rate (120 per minute) and sluicing fluid all round
my body so that my legs were swollen in a fearsome dropsy. I got
home just in time ..."[13] He narrowly missed death by congestive heart
failure, in the opinion of his "marvellous cardiologist who is highly
devoted to the arts and treating me as a special case."[14] Woodcock was
incapacitated and bedfast for a month, losing nineteen pounds in only
six days.

There seemed little to be done to relieve the cumulative ailments
of old age, to which Woodcock reacted variously. On occasion he
would give in to a certain irritability. The Woodcock Archive for this
period is peppered with such pieces of correspondence as a letter to
the president of Canadian Airlines, resigning as a customer after thirty-
two years to protest both rising fares and "your recent decision to
forbid smoking on all your flights. Personally, I am not a smoker, but
like many other non-smokers I feel strongly about civil liberties ...
My personal opinion, as a Director of the British Columbia Civil
Liberties Association, is that your action is discriminatory and in violation of the Charter of Rights and Freedoms ..."[15] Which is quite
different in tone from his detailed outrage on such major public issues
as the Free Trade Agreement.

Behind it all lay a growing sense of the inevitable. Woodcock writes in a letter to a friend of living in the valley of the shadow of death for several years; this was long before he gave the title *Walking through the Valley: An Autobiography* to his third and final volume of memoirs, published in 1994.

In 1988, Earle Birney, eight years Woodcock's senior, suffered a heart attack and stroke that left him unable to communicate or to recognize his friends. Wailan Low reported that her husband now travelled mostly in his imagination—often to Australia, for some reason. Woodcock wrote back:

> Your description of Earle's present condition fills me with pleasure and sadness. It is wonderful he has survived and that so much of his originality delightfully survives, even if in a transformed manifestation. I keep on thinking what wonderful things we would have if he were suddenly able to start writing down what happens in his mind at this stage—all those strange Odysseys at which you hint! But it still must be immensely trying for you ... and we wish you courage and patience, and thank you continually for all you have done and been for Earle.
>
> P.S. As I write a raccoon mother has just brought to our backdoor the first litter of babies for this season, delightful, fist-sized things with fully marked black and white masks tumbling about the steps as Inge feeds them.[16]

Contemplating death, Woodcock wrote of the competing comforts of Buddhism and Anglican Christianity: on the one hand, lessons learned in adult life; on the other, his own heritage, much despised yet much loved all the same. Like many other elderly people with a gift for organization, he sometimes seemed on the brink of estate-planning hypochondria. He more than once changed his will and even his literary executor. But slowly a sound plan began to emerge.

Surveying the philanthropic landscape as it pertained to Canadian literature, he saw the obvious spot on which to build. Quasi-government bodies, such as the Canada Council and the various provincial equivalents, were geared more to literary product than to its producers, he believed. Typical of the public sector, he doubtless said to himself. The only charity in the entire field was the Canadian

Writers' Foundation, now driven solely by private contributions but begun in 1933 with a grant from Parliament to rescue Charles G. D. Roberts (afterwards Sir Charles, when he became the first and only person knighted for his services to Canadian literature). The foundation was a minuscule and rather secretive affair that helped to support a small handful of writers who, once their creative years were past, found themselves on their uppers. By contrast, Woodcock would assist Canadian writers young and old who found themselves "in sudden distress",[17] especially distress that interrupted their current work or actually prevented them from completing it.

Such a move was "rather logical" for him and Inge, Woodcock confided to a friend, "since neither of us has any close relatives who are in need, and we have no children. We have been fortunate in recent years—partly through Inge's inheritances—so that we are able to start the fund, which we had thought of originally as posthumous, with contributions up to $12,000 to $15,000 a year. When we die our house ... will probably alone fetch $600,000, and altogether more than $100,000 a year should be available [and so] it seemed a good idea to start now, even in a modest way, so that everything will be in place when the survivor among us does die."[18]

Accordingly, the Woodcock Trust was established late in 1988. It would be administered by the Writers' Development Trust, a Toronto-based umbrella charity that oversees the granting of various writing prizes and maintains a number of programmes to promote Canadian literature and reading. Such a structure would allow the WDT to enlarge on the Woodcocks' generosity by soliciting outside contributions specifically earmarked for the Woodcock Trust, issuing tax receipts to the donors.

At first, the Woodcock Trust's relations with the WDT were not always harmonious. In November 1989 Woodcock would report that he was

> feeling totally frustrated ... *Nothing* has been done to call together the jury to determine the guidelines. *Nothing* has been done to give the modest publicity we had agreed on—in outlets like the bulletins of the Writers' Union, the League of Canadian Poets, etc.,—so that writers would know such a fund existed. We went through all the labour of setting it up, and now it stands like some machine on a distant headland—unused [as] nobody is benefitting.[19]

The tax laws stipulated that the original settlors in such a trust maintain an arm's-length relationship with the trustees, and

> Inge and I are in the difficult and frustrating position of being the donors, and therefore, under the Revenue regulations, being unable to take part *directly* in the operation of the fund, so that all we can do is suggest and stimulate, and just now I am trying to stimulate someone to get the jury together ... We *have* to get things moving if the fund is to be any use.[20]

Gradually, however, the Woodcocks' plans began to be realized. A board was established that included three of Woodcock's literary friends: Silver Donald Cameron from Nova Scotia and Dennis Lee and George Galt from Toronto. The group also included representatives of the WDT, including Eric Wright, the crime novelist. In the first granting period, the Woodcock Trust disbursed $20,000 to four very disparate writers whose difficult circumstances (in one instance, inoperable cancer) had caused others to recommend them. At this writing, the Woodcock Trust has awarded $136,000 to forty-three writers.

Cameron called the trust "a magnificent autumnal gift to a community of writers who already owe a great deal to you both directly and by example", also noting Woodcock's "ability to do it, of course, also implies that you've been as effective managing the business side of your life as you have in the literary and artistic side—and that's no small achievement, either, as I know very well."[21] Galt called the Woodcock Trust "an unusually selfless gesture in this world gone half mad with greed and consumerism."[22]

By his charitable enterprise, Woodcock sometimes left himself financially deflated. For example, when David Koven, his old anarchist colleague in San Francisco, wrote asking for a contribution to a Spanish anarchist commune, Woodcock had to reply that while "both of us ... are sympathetic and willing to do what we can ... we have stripped ourselves right down [with the Woodcock Trust and] a fund for acquiring habitat in BC for rare species that are endangered, and odd things like Amnesty International and our own Canada-India Village Aid."[23] He could only promise a thousand dollars in two months' time.

≈

As the turn of the new decade approached, Woodcock had to apologize to one correspondent for being six weeks late in replying to a letter about the Trust. He pled "a heavy summer, [coping] with visitors and getting my present book over the hump, and since my recent illness the time I can work has been somewhat reduced. No epic nighttime efforts, slipping off to bed just before dawn! It does make a difference."[24] He vowed to take two weeks off from book-writing to bring his correspondence up to date. The book-writing in question included two of his last titles, both appearing in 1992: the one a hymn to his involvement with the present, the other a reminder of his equally abiding quarrel with the past. *Power to Us All: Constitution or Social Contract?* was written in the heat of Canada's discontinuous constitutional crisis and recalled Proudhon's remark that he was opposed to the French constitution *because* it was a constitution. The other book was a work Woodcock wished to call *The Possibility of the Impossible* but was published instead as *The Monk and His Message: Undermining the Myth of History*. In a letter to Koven, he wrote that he had "managed to finish my anti-history [and] the publisher seems delighted with it, and it is due out in the Fall, with a crazy title—though many people will consider it a crazy book. Also I've finished my translation of [Kropotkin's] *Paroles d'un Révolte* ... Now I'm putting together a couple of volumes of essays that I'd like to see put between covers before I am."[25] Such black humour came naturally to him now: "I had a day of doctors and tests, made alarming because that day the vampire girls in the lab couldn't induce blood out of either arm. (The next day it flowed!)"[26] It was at this point in his life that this remarkable man began to translate Marcel Proust's *A la Recherche du Temps Perdu*, reporting to the same correspondent that by 7 November 1991 he had already completed nine of 3,474 pages. To adopt one of Woodcock's favourite marks of punctuation: !

Written in seven volumes, Proust's sprawling masterpiece appeared between 1913 and 1928. A good portion had already been published in Britain when, shortly before his death in 1922, Proust complained to C. K. Scott-Moncrieff, the first of his English-language translators, that his rendering was too ornate (not to say too quick to miss French slang and sexual references). Proust also disliked the English title used for the six-volume translation, *In Search of Lost Time*. Indeed, the phrase *temps perdu* is almost untranslatable, referring as it does to time that is *wasted* as well as *lost*. Subsequently Scott-Moncrieff's edition was revised by Terence Kilmartin; when Woodcock began his version, a new translation, by D. J. Enright, had appeared, and another, by Enright's fellow poet Richard Howard, was well under way. But then Woodcock was motivated not (for once) by the desire to publish but simply by love of the work. The project was one that Inge, for once, could not endorse. She sent him a memo setting out her reasons. First off, she acknowledged that:

> Proust's prose is at times breathtakingly beautiful, filled with essences which must appeal to anyone who has lived in Europe. He is a magician of the sensitive, the subtle, the enchanter of moods. No one can dispute this, in my opinion.
>
> But now, let me put forward the negative side—my "fury", my "disgust", my absolute rejection of this writer. Tell me how anyone in the beginning of his century (in France) can be such an advocate of the defunct aristocracy. One knows that aristocrats exist. (I am in a mild way one myself), but surely to list several hundred or more in the text, which really have no connection with the intrinsic story, is pointless, vapid, stupid.
>
> Then there are the footprints of his social conscience; every 500 pages there is a one-sentence remark that he really has nothing but a luke-warm admiration for the working man. Christ Almighty!
>
> The entire work reads like a gossip column in one of the cheapest tabloids, interspersed with lukewarm philosophical spritzers, some totally obscure, ephemeral political comments, which only applied in his day and have no meaning in 1990.
>
> Final analysis: The man is a spoilt brat in his youth, a hypocrite as he grows up. An egomaniac in any case, at any time. And ultimately a mega-lomaniac. I will not comment on his sexual misalliances and what ulti-mately is his topsy-turvy perception of the time and world he inhabits.[27]

Woodcock went ahead regardless.

In the spring of 1992 he became seriously ill with "kidney, bladder and liver infections that have in combination so sapped my energy".[28] By late July, he was in Vancouver General Hospital awaiting a prostate operation. Following his release on 3 August, he would complain that he "was half starving to death there, and am now plumping out with [Inge's] excellent cooking, and taking [word indecipherable] doses of alcohol."[29]

He bade the year farewell with some relief.

The first half was splendid, with publications and celebrations. The second was truly a chunk of *tempus horribilis,* for I barely had time to recover [from my] perilous illness (and recover with a characteristic loss of stamina) when our beloved Mozart [the Woodcocks' cat] was killed barbarously by the very racoon clan we have fed and fostered over the years. Even our Taoist friend Paul Huang tells us that "this is nature", but I find myself, like Ivan Karamazov [in Dostoevsky's novel], wanting to give God back my ticket. In real terms the shock of the occasion brought on a bad sciatica from which Inge is still suffering, and in me a sudden return of the edema—swelling legs—which I suffered from so badly 3 years ago, but this time I know what to do immediately and the doctors approved in hindsight.[30]

In its last issue of 1992, *Maclean's*, which had once dismissed Woodcock as its regular book reviewer, ran his photograph on the cover, as one of a dozen Canadians who made up its honour roll for the year.

His health problems continued in 1993. So did his determination to work until the end. "Had a cataract operation, and the bad eye is recovering slowly", he wrote. "I am writing a novel [and plugging away] at Proust."[31] Several times during his final years he was visited by the desire to attempt fiction once again, as he had done as a young man, but if he completed a novel he destroyed it (again, repeating a familiar pattern). He did publish a number of short stories during this period, however, including some constructed from dreams.

In May 1994, Woodcock's friends and admirers gathered to celebrate his eighty-second birthday with a symposium at Simon Fraser University's Harbour Centre campus and various other events, including a large art exhibition in his honour at Bau-xi Gallery. Mayor Philip Owen officially proclaimed 7 May as "George Woodcock Day" (prompting Pierre Berton to say that evening, at the B.C. Book Awards dinner at which he was master of ceremonies, that he never thought he would see the time when Vancouver extended such an honour to an anarchist). The next evening, hundreds of people gathered at the Law Courts in downtown Vancouver on the eighth, the actual birth anniversary, at a party in Woodcock's honour. Had he been well, Woodcock might have been too shy to attend. As it happened, he was too ill, and Margaret Atwood, acting in his stead, read the remarks he had written acknowledging the toast to his life and career.

The summer was difficult.

> It has been an odd time, a time of decline, I fear. My walking has become so bad that I no longer go out and rely on people coming to see me or phoning me, which they fortunately quite often do. I had one of those small imperceptible strokes about a month ago which damaged my right hand temporarily but had no other apparent effect; this is why I am hand writing, for therapy.
>
> I am not all that productive at present, though I'm preparing a volume of fiction to send to publishers in Jan. Otherwise keeping a journal for a while and doing a few book reviews.[32]

One of his last articles, for the *Sewanee Review*, was a brief history of love in literature.

Woodcock discussed his pending death fully with Inge. He asked that he be cremated, and his ashes scattered on the face of Anarchist Mountain, a peak in the southern Interior whose name he had always fancied. During the last few weeks of his life, Woodcock was confined to a new bed that Inge had had installed in his ground-floor office, as he could no longer climb the stairs. In the final days, he seemed to return to England in his mind, an England that no longer existed in any other dimension.

≈

Before his last slow decline picked up speed, Woodcock enjoyed a revival of his spirits when an old overseas friend visited Canada once more. I begged Woodcock to write me an account of the meeting, which he did, three months later, though it was clear that by this time his writing days were dwindling to a handful. Telephone calls would follow, but this was my last letter from him. I quote from it here.

> We had expected a call from the Dalai Lama's entourage, because early in the spring of this year his niece, Khando Chatdotsang, a friend of thirty years, came to Vancouver in order to see us once again. She said that she would urge "Uncle" to give us an audience and, if I were too unwell, to visit us in our home.

No invitation came until the Saturday he was actually here (26th June). Then a local Tibetan rang from the Hotel Vancouver to find out where we were, as we had been scheduled to meet His H. at 12.20, as he had a Reception-Lunch at 1.00. (We heard later from people who went to the reception that word got out he was delayed because the Woodcocks had not turned up at a special audience.) We told whoever was on the line that we had not been invited, and an hour later someone else rang up to ask if we could come at 5 p.m. (We only learnt later that His H. had given up his daily meditation in order to meet us.) We rang Tony Phillips and he took us down to the hotel, which was a good thing, since that day it was the locus of many graduation and wedding parties and parking would have been difficult.

There were apparently RCMP guards around, but we never recognized them. However, we immediately encountered local Tibetans on watch in the lobby. Among them was [an old friend of ours] whom we have always suspected of having been a bandit in Tibet, and who was dressed in full traditional rig of chupa, embroidered felt boots and an embroidered white silk shirt; he told us that at night, in the traditional Tibetan manner, he slept on the floor of the corridor across His H's door. All the rest of the Tibetans wore black suits, as I did, and the women traditional blouses and chupas. We went into an anteroom for about ten minutes and chatted with Tibetans we knew, and then the word came for us to go to His H's room. His secretary had come to fetch us, a young Tibetan nobleman from Dharamsala whom we had met a decade ago.

As we turned the corner of the corridor to his room, the Dalai Lama came through the door and walked a few steps towards us; he laughed a greeting to his "old friends", embraced Inge, and took my shoulders in his hands and pulled me towards him so that our brows touched. I was in another way touched, since in Tibet such a greeting was an honour accorded only to great scholars or great spiritual leaders.

We went into his room, offered our white silk khatas (ceremonial scarves) and a little 14th-century Burmese figure of the Buddha. His secretary, who is also his interpreter, accompanied us, but all the time the Dalai Lama spoke in excellent English, laughing and jesting a great deal; the comedy of the world of illusion seemed to please him. I had a slightly bloodshot eye, the final trace of a cataract operation, and immediately he said, very solicitously, "What's wrong with your eye?" To give another example of his awareness, during our conservation he pointed to a minute brownish object on the black cloth of my trouser knee; it looked to me like a tiny piece of bark. I was about to sweep it aside, when he gestured a warning to me, and then I saw that in fact it was a minute ladybird. The secretary fetched a piece of letter paper, he and the Dalai Lama carefully scooped the little insect on to it, and the secretary released it out the window.

We talked of a number of subjects—karma and historical determinism, the situation of the Tibetan refugees and the future of Tibet, as well as his own future, the links between environmental movements and the basic teachings of Buddhism.

The Dalai Lama had read my book, *The Monk and the Message*, of which I sent him a copy through Khando-la, and he agreed with me that the doctrine of karma really had nothing to do with historical determinism. We live within the consequence of our own actions in this and past lives, but there is no ineluctable fatality about it. By right thought and right action we can change the pattern of consequences. "It is difficult, but it is possible" remarked the Dalai Lama, whose own life is an example of the possibility of the impossible, for he still has dreams that other people consider naif.

For example, he is confident that he will return to Tibet on his own terms and within two or three years. He agrees with me that the events which will make possible his return will take place within two or three years and in Beijing rather than in Tibet, and that the passing of the Chinese gerontocrats will provoke a struggle among the successors, and perhaps even between the Party and the PLA [People's Liberation Army], that Chinese forces will be withdrawn from Tibet because of regional tensions elsewhere, and the country will become virtually independent, as it was after the Chinese revolution of 1910–11. When he returns, he will rule for just two years as a temporal leader, during which time he would call a constituent assembly to devise a form of democratic government. When this was established, he would withdraw into his life as a monk.

Inge asked him what he will do with the Chinese who have been settled in Tibet. "Most of them will want to leave when they are not under compulsion, for they do not like our climate", he answered. "Those who want to stay will be welcome ..."

Regarding the Tibetan refugees, he speaks with optimism and satisfaction at what has been achieved with the help of so many good friends. The Tibetans are well integrated into the mosaic of Indian life, yet remain resolute in their loyalty to Tibet and their intent to return. Education among them is now virtually universal, and they have adapted well to new agricultural patterns.

We begin to talk about his ideals of making Tibet an environmentally protected zone, and then Inge tells him of the Tatshenshini decision by which a million square miles of territory in northern Canada and Alaska will be made into a vast wilderness park. He throws up his hands in delight. "What? No animals killed! No trees cut down?" And then he lets out one of his great laughs.

When we leave, he gives us a copy of his newest book, *Freedom in Exile*, and inscribes it in U-Me, the old sacerdotal script of Tibet which even few Tibetans know: "Dr. Woodcock and Mrs. Woodcock, my two old friends, I pray for your good health and success always. May all your hopes be fulfilled. A Tibetan monk who follows Sakamuni, [signed] Dalai Lama. 6/26/93."

He then hung around our necks the white scarves we had given him, recharged with manna, and walked a few steps down the corridor with us before we shook hands and he turned back to his room. He remained standing in the doorway and as we turned the corner of the corridor we looked back, and waved, and he waved back. We felt no sadness at that parting, for we knew we were in his mind as he in ours, and mindfulness is the essence of Buddhism.[33]

EPILOGUE
AND
ACKNOWLEDGEMENTS

THIS WAS NEVER intended as an authorized or official biography but neither has it been a secret one. I enjoyed George Woodcock's friendship for almost a quarter-century. In his last years, with his health declining, he asked me if I would write a book about him and his work. I was honoured to be selected, but I believe that he could have made a wiser choice—someone with more ability perhaps. This is not false modesty, it's blinding hindsight. In any case, the offer being tendered and the promise given, I pushed ahead.

At first, I reasoned that great difficulties would arise in writing a life of someone who, after all, published three volumes of autobiography in the past dozen years. This turned out not to be the case, not in that sense. Our understanding was that George would not look at or attempt to influence the manuscript but instead would allow me carte blanche to quote from his writings, particularly his papers at Queen's University. I soon saw that this repository is so rich in unpublished material that I ran little risk of merely repeating his memoirs. Especially valuable were the thousands of letters dating back as far as 1928. I knew that quoting from them extensively would give, in one way, a disadvantageous picture of the person who wrote them. Woodcock believed that anything written in a book had to be more polished than anything written for a magazine or journal and that anything written for a magazine or journal had to be more polished than a simple letter. He was a craftsman, whose prose, in the cream of his books, sometimes attains considerable beauty. *Belles lettres* indeed. Relying so much on his letters might obscure this fact, because the letters, of course, were almost always produced in haste. Yet for this very reason they usually show us the writer with his celebrated defences down, chronicling events and issues of the moment, passing on news of current work and current travels, conducting business and performing good works, achieving the kind of epistolary intimacy that was one of the states of friendship he prized most highly.

For a while, I actually thought of writing a two-volume biography. I soon abandoned the plan, however, for the very reasons I speak of in the Prologue: my wish to erase, not exaggerate, the fault line that runs through the middle of George Woodcock's chronological life. No, a short biography seemed the best reasoned approach, particularly as this probably won't be the last book on the subject, given the central role Woodcock played in the Canadian literary world and the extent of the Woodcock Archive.

The latter continues to grow even after Woodcock's death. Inge Woodcock, for example, intends to donate a series of letters between her husband and herself dating from one of the few periods when they were not together: the brief time, immediately after the Second World War, when she was the *Peace News* correspondent in Berlin.

This raises another question. Why is there not more Inge Woodcock in this book? Quite simply, she wouldn't hear of it. When Woodcock was writing *Letter to the Past*, he wished to give her full partnership status in the story from the time of their meeting, as indeed seemed proper, since any book about George Woodcock's life must also to some extent be a portrait of a strong and unusual marriage, marked by influences in both directions and ideas freely exchanged. Inge refused, as he points out in the book. When I was working on *The Gentle Anarchist*, I encountered her fairness and generosity, in the way she unhesitatingly extended the exact terms of my agreement with George about the Archive and the manuscript. But I, too, ran up against her horror of being interviewed. At one point, George intervened on my behalf but was rebuffed. "I have talked to Inge again," he wrote me, "but the answer is the same as before. She is not willing to talk, and sets the same conditions for you as for me. Her past before she met me is her own. Where we have done things together, such as building houses, travelling, setting up societies, she is obviously there, as she is in my autobiographies and travel books. I respect her desire for privacy regarding herself, even if my pudeur is more limited ... It seems to me that this is one of the biographer's difficulties ... you can add a touch of the tantalising to your tale."[1]

As for the title, the phrase "gentle anarchist" is not an oxymoron (virtually all the anarchists I know are gentle people) but neither is it a tautology (some figures in anarchist history were anything but meek and docile). In any event, the phrase does not originate with me. A profile of Woodcock in the *Canadian Magazine* by Paul Grescoe (17 May 1975) was headed "Gentle Anarchist", and Woodcock applied the term to another Canadian author ("On the Verge", *Canadian Literature*, No. 121, Summer 1989). Subsequently, the CBC producer Don Mowatt chose "George Woodcock: Gentle Anarchist" for his excellent three-part series on *Ideas* (17 and 24 February and 2 March 1992). Yet for all its drawbacks, the title still seems to be perfect.

As always in the case of a project such as this, many people who tendered their assistance deserve to have their kindness acknowledged. For sharing their knowledge and insight or offering their support I am grateful (in purely alphabetical order) to Scott Anderson, Thomas Axworthy, Paul Banfield, Roger Burford Mason, Duncan Cameron, Boris Castel, Karen Corsano, Ann Cowan, Ann Dadson, Michael Davies, Ramsay Derry, Kildare Dobbs, Dennis Duffy, Sandra Djwa, Janet Fetherling, Robert Fulford, Janet Hamilton, Tom Hawthorn, George Henderson, Larry Hoffman, Michael Holmes, James King, Maria Kubacki, Don Le Pan, Malcolm Lester, the late Charles Lillard, Joan Lyndon, Anne McClelland, Anne MacDermaid, Sarah McAlpine, Albert Moritz, Ted Mumford, Gerald Newman, Gerald Owen, Tony Phillips, Janis Rapoport, Derek Savage, the late Shirley Spragge, Don Stewart, Rosemary Sullivan, Alan Twigg, Deborah Viets, Jan Walter, David Watmough, Janice Weaver, Bruce Whiteman and Daniel Williman.

NOTES

In the following notes, "Queen's" refers to the George Woodcock Archive at Queen's University, Kingston, Ontario, and "U OF T", unless specified otherwise, refers to the author's collection at the Thomas Fisher Rare Book Library, University of Toronto.

PROLOGUE: *George Woodcock and the Necrologists*

1 GW to Frances Eger of Pulp Press, 31 August 1984, Queen's.

2 Jeffrey Simpson, "George Woodcock Was a Major Writer in a Culture of Minority Taste", *Globe and Mail*, 1 February 1995.

3 Trevor Lautens, "George Woodcock's Wish", Vancouver *Sun*, 2 February 1995.

4 Philip Marchand, "Woodcock Major Literary Force", Toronto *Star*, 31 January 1995.

5 [David Twiston-Davies], "George Woodcock", *Daily Telegraph*, 20 February 1995.

6 Colin Ward, "Fringe Benefits", *New Statesman & Society*, 24 February 1995.

7 Nicholas Walter, "George Woodcock", *Independent*, 13 February 1995.

8 Tony Gibson, "George Woodcock: A Tribute", *Freedom*, 25 February 1995.

9 *Ibid.*

10 *Ibid.*

11 NW, "George Woodcock (1912–1995)", *Freedom*, 25 February 1995.

12 *Ibid.*

13 Colin Ward, "Fringe Benefits", *op. cit.*

14 Derek Stanford, *Inside the Forties: Literary Memoirs 1937–1957* (London: Sidgwick & Jackson, 1977).

15 Roy Porter, *London: A Social History* (London: Hamish Hamilton, 1994).

16 NW, "George Woodcock (1912–1995)", *op. cit.*

17 Tony Gibson, "George Woodcock: A Tribute", *op. cit.*

18 Robert Graham, untitled obituary, *Freedom*, 25 February 1995.

19 *Ibid.*

ONE: *A Dream That Failed*

1 Patrick Whitehouse and David St John Thomas, *The Great Western Railway: 150 Glorious Years* (London: David & Charles, 1984).

2 *Ibid.*

3 GW, "Victorian Custom", in *Notes on Visitations: Poems, 1936–1975* (Toronto: Anansi, 1975).

4 See Jack Tracy, ed., *Strange Studies from Life and Other Narratives: The Complete True Crime Writings of Sir Arthur Conan Doyle* (Bloomington, Indiana: Gaslight Publications, 1988).

5 GW autobiographical sketch in Adele Sarkissian, ed., *Contemporary Authors Autobiography Series*, vol. 6 (Detroit: Gale Research, 1988).

6 GW to author, 23 February 1993, U OF T.

7 *Ibid.*

8 GW to James King, 26 May 1990, courtesy of James King.

9 GW to author, 14 November 1993, U OF T.

10 GW, *The Cherry Tree on Cherry Street* (Kingston: Quarry Press, 1994).

11 Lewis Cooke interview, 12 October 1992.

12 *Ibid.*

13 Lance Godwin interview, 10 October 1992.

14 *Ibid.*

15 *Ibid.*

16 GW to Lance Godwin, 28 March 1929, Queen's.

17 GW to Lance Godwin, 2 July 1929, Queen's.

18 GW to Lance Godwin, 1 January 1931, Queen's.

19 *Ibid.*

20 GW to Lance Godwin, 11 March 1932, Queen's.

21 GW to Lance Godwin, 5 June 1933, Queen's.

22 GW to Lance Godwin, 11 May 1930, Queen's.

23 GW to Lance Godwin, 26 October 1930, Queen's.

24 GW to Lance Godwin, 19 September 1932, Queen's.

25 GW to Lance Godwin, 26 October 1930, *op. cit.*

TWO: *A Preference for Paradox*

1 GW, "Fragments from a Tenth-hour Journal", *Northern Journey*, No. 3, 1973.

2 GW, "Gentle Anarchist: George Woodcock", CBC Radio, *Ideas*, 17 and 24 February and 2 March 1992.

3 Walter Allen. *As I Walked Down New Grub Street: Memoirs of a Writing Life* (London: Heinemann, 1981).

4 GW to author, 31 January 1993, U OF T.

5 GW to Lance Godwin, 2 July 1932, Queen's.

6 GW to author, 31 January 1993, *op. cit.*

7 Julian Symons interview, 13 October 1992.

8 GW to author, 28 April 1993, U OF T.

9 GW to author, 23 February 1993, *op. cit.*

10 Julian Symons interview, *op. cit.*

11 Tony Gibson to author, 14 November 1992, U OF T.

12 *Ibid.*

13 Julian Symons interview, *op. cit.*

14 Lewis Cooke interview, *op. cit.*

15 GW to author, 23 February 1993, *op. cit.*

16 *Ibid.*

17 *Ibid.*

18 *Ibid.*

19 GW, *Letter to the Past: An Autobiography* (Don Mills: Fitzhenry & Whiteside, 1982).

20 GW to author, 23 February 1993, *op. cit.*

THREE: *NOW*

1 GW autobiographical sketch in *Contemporary Authors Autobiography Series.*

2 GW, *NOW*, No. 1 (First Series), Easter 1940.

3 *Ibid.*

4 *Ibid.*

5 Colin Ward, *Influences: Voices of Creative Dissent* (Bideford, Devon: Green books, 1991).

6 Paul Goodman, "Introduction" to Kropotkin's *Memoirs of a Revolutionist* (New York: Horizon Press, 1969).

7 GW to James King, 26 May 1990.

8 GW to author, 8 October 1993, U OF T.

9 GW to Victor N. Pasanen, 1 October 1980, Queen's.

10 GW, "Memoirs of Red Lion Street", unidentifiable clipping from an anarchist publication, *c* 1980, Queen's.

11 Inge Woodcock interview, 30 March 1995.

12 GW, "A Tribute from George Woodcock", in *Marie Louise Berneri 1918–1949: A Tribute* (London: Marie Louise Berneri Memorial Committee, 1949).

13 *Ibid.*

14 Eléire Zolla, "Storie de danze e cerimonie segrete di tribù della Columbia Britannica", *Corriere della Fera*, 31 October 1983.

15 GW, "A Tribute from George Woodcock", *op. cit.*

16 Vernon Richards interview, 8 October 1992.

17 Philip Sansom interview, 11 October 1992.

18 GW, "To M., Twenty-Eight Years Dead", in *The Kestrel and Other Poems of Past and Present* (Sunderland, Durham: Ceolfrith Press, 1978).

19 GW, *The Cherry Tree on Cherry Street* (Kingston: Quarry Press, 1994).

20 GW to Lance Godwin, 7 February 1941, Queen's.

21 *Ibid.*

22 GW to Lance Godwin, 25 August 1941, Queen's.

23 George Melly, *Rum, Bum and Concertina* (London: Weidenfeld and Nicolson, 1977).

24 *Daily Telegraph*, 30 March 1954.

FOUR: *Going Underground*

1 GW, "Note to Readers", *NOW*, No. 1 (Second Series), 1943.

2 *Ibid.*

3 GW to Victor N. Pasanen, 1 October 1980, Queen's.

4 Albert Meltzer, *The Anarchists in London 1935–1955: A Personal Memoir* (Sanday, Orkney Islands: Cienfuegos Press, 1976).

5 *Ibid.*

6 GW to Peter Buitenhuis, 9 February 1978, Queen's.

7 Derek Stanford, *Inside the Forties: Literary Memoirs 1937–1957* (London: Sidgwick & Jackson, 1977).

8 GW to author, 31 January 1993, U OF T.

9 GW to author, 8 October 1993, U OF T.

10 GW, "Gentle Anarchist: George Woodcock", CBC Radio, *Ideas*, 17 and 24 February and 2 March 1992.

11 *Ibid.*

12 GW, "Big Ben and the Anarchists", *Tamarack Review*, Nos. 83-84, Winter 1982.

13 *Ibid.*

14 *News Chronicle*, 24 April 1945.

15 GW, "Big Ben and the Anarchists", *op. cit.*

16 *Ibid.*

17 *Ibid.*

18 Colin Ward interview, 12 October 1992.

19 Colin Ward, "Witness for the Prosecution", *Wildcat Inside Story*, London, *c* 1980.

FIVE: *Starting Over in the New World*

1 Quoted in Judith Summers, *Soho: A History of London's Most Colourful Neighbourhood* (London: Bloomsbury, 1989).

2 *Ibid.*

3 *Ibid.*

4 Andrew Sinclair, *War Like a Wasp: The Lost Decade of the Forties* (London: Hamish Hamilton, 1989).

5 Hugh David, *The Fitzrovians: A Portrait of Bohemian Society 1900–55* (London: Michael Joseph, 1988).

6 William St Clair, *The Godwins and the Shelleys: The Biography of a Family* (London: Faber and Faber, 1989).

7 *Ibid.*

8 Quoted in William St Clair, *The Godwins and the Shelleys*, *op. cit.*

9 Harold Nicolson, "Biography of the Author of 'Political Justice'," *Daily Telegraph*, 20 January 1947.

10 GW, "The English Hymn," *The Writer and Politics* (London: Porcupine Press, 1948).

11 GW to author, 23 February 1993, U OF T.

12 Derek Stanford, *Inside the Forties* (London: Sidgwick & Jackson, 1977).

13 *Ibid.*

14 GW, "Poetry Magazines of the Thirties: A Personal Note", *Tamarack Review* No. 60, October 1973.

15 *Ibid.*

16 Alfred Kazin, *A Lifetime Burning in Every Moment: Journals* (New York: HarperCollins, 1996).

17 GW, introduction to *Writers and Politics* (Montreal: Black Rose Books, 1990), a reprint of *The Writer and Politics* (London: Porcupine Press, 1948).

18 *Ibid.*

19 GW, *The Incomparable Aphra* (London: T. V. Boardman, 1948).

20 *Ibid.*

21 *Ibid.*

22 *Ibid.*

23 Doug Worthington interview conducted for author by Charles Lillard, 26 January 1994.

24 Divorce certificate dated 29 November 1948, Queen's.

SIX: *Blacklisted*

1 GW to Eva and Harold Orlans, 13 May 1949, Queen's.

2 *Victoria City & Vancouver Island Directory, 1950–1951* (Victoria: B.C. Directories, 1950).

3 Doug Worthington interview, conducted for author by Charles Lillard, 26 January 1994.

4 *Ibid.*

5 GW to Eva and Harold Orlans, 13 May 1949, *op. cit.*

6 GW to Ivan Avakumovic, 17 May 1949, Queen's.

7 GW to Earle Birney, 22 May 1949, Birney papers, U OF T.

8 Earle Birney, *Spreading Time: Remarks on Canadian Writing and Writers 1904–1949*, revised ed. (Montreal: Véhicule Press, 1989).

9 GW to Ivan Avakumovic, 20 June 1949, Queen's.

10 Doug Worthington interview, *op. cit.*

11 GW to Eva and Harold Orlans, 24 July 1949, Queen's.

12 GW to Ivan Avakumovic, 11 August 1949, Queen's.

13 *Ibid.*

14 *Ibid.*

15 Earle Birney, *Spreading Time, op. cit.*

16 *Ibid.*

17 GW to Ivan Avakumovic, February 1951, Queen's.

18 David Koven, "George Woodcock 1912–1995", unpublished MS, U OF T.

19 *Ibid.*

20 *Ibid.*

21 GW, *Letters from Sooke: A Correspondence between Sir Herbert Read and George Woodcock* (Victoria: Victoria Arts Club, 1982).

22 Quoted in Douglas Fetherling, "At Home with George Woodcock", *Western Living* (Vancouver), August 1991.

23 GW, *Beyond the Blue Mountains: An Autobiography* (Markham: Fitzhenry & Whiteside, 1987).

24 GW, *Pierre-Joseph Proudhon: A Biography* (London: Routledge & Keagan Paul, 1956).

25 Quoted by GW in *Beyond the Blue Mountains, op. cit.*

26 David Koven, "George Woodcock 1912–1995", *op. cit.*

27 GW to author, 8 October 1992, *op. cit.*

28 Doug Worthington interview, *op. cit.*

29 *Ibid.*

30 Jack Shadbolt interview, 6 November 1992.

31 Doris Shadbolt interview, 6 November 1992.

32 GW to author, 23 February 1993, U OF T.

33 GW to Doug Beardsley, 1 February 1974, Queen's.

34 GW to Robert Heilman, 6 February 1955, Queen's.

35 Doris Shadbolt interview, *op. cit.*

36 Jack Shadbolt interview, *op. cit.*

37 GW, *Anarchy or Chaos* (London: Freedom Press, 1944).

38 GW to Robert Heilman, 6 February 1955, *op. cit.*

39 Charles H. Stephan to GW, 12 September 1955, Queen's.

40 GW to John Foster Dulles, 21 September 1955, Queen's.

41 *Ibid.*

42 *Ibid.*

43 Charles H. Stephan to GW, 5 October 1955, Queen's.

44 GW to author, 23 February 1993, *op. cit.*

45 Quoted in Douglas Fetherling in "At Home with George Woodcock", *Western Living*, August 1991.

SEVEN: *Canadian Literature*

1 GW to Ivan Avakumovic, 8 April 1957, Queen's.

2 *Ibid.*

3 "2 Vancouver Men Win Fellowships", Vancouver *Province*, 5 June 1957.

4 GW to Ivan Avakumovic, 9 October 1957, Queen's.

5 *Ibid.*

6 GW to author, 23 February 1993, U OF T.

7 GW to Ivan Avakumovic, 13 May 1958, Queen's.

8 Wayson Choy interview, 19 March 1996.

9 *Ibid.*

10 *Ibid.*

11 *Ibid.*

12 *Ibid.*

13 *Ibid.*

14 Judy Stoffman to author, 22 April 1966, U OF T.

15 GW to John Metcalf, 7 November 1982, Queen's.

16 Carl F. Klinck, *Giving Canada a Literary History: A Memoir*, ed. by Sandra Djwa (Ottawa: Carleton University Press, 1991).

17 GW to Earle Birney, 17 January 1959, Birney papers, U OF T.

18 GW to Ivan Avakumovic, 17 January 1959, Queen's.

19 GW to Ivan Avakumovic, 8 February 1959, Queen's.

20 GW to Ivan Avakumovic, 9 July 1959, Queen's.

21 GW to Ivan Avakumovic, 2 July 1959, Queen's.

22 Quoted in Douglas Fetherling in "At Home with George Woodcock", *Western Living,* August 1991.

23 *Ibid.*

24 *Ibid.*

25 GW to Ivan Avakumovic, 27 August 1959, Queen's.

26 GW to Margaret Stobie, 13 October 1976, Queen's.

27 GW, "*Canadian Literature*—A New Magazine for Canadian Readers", unpublished? typescript, 1960, Queen's.

28 *Ibid.*

29 GW to R. D. MacDonald, 29 July 1973, Queen's.

30 GW, "A Report on the First 3½ years of *Canadian Literature*", undated, unpublished typescript [1963], Queen's.

EIGHT: *Anarchism*

1 Donald Rooum, "George Woodcock's Anarchism" (review of *Anarchism and Anarchists*), *Freedom,* 3 October 1992.

2 Dimitri Roussopoulos, "Woodcock's Anarchist Legacy Defies Media Whitewashing", *Now* (Toronto), 9 February 1995.

3 GW, *Anarchy or Chaos* (London: Freedom Press, 1944).

4 GW, "The Ending Century: Prospects and Retrospect", *Raven* (London), March 1990.

5 GW, *Anarchism: A History of Libertarian Ideas and Movements,* revised ed. (Harmondsworth: Penguin, 1986).

6 GW to Ivan Avakumovic, 12 January 1962 [misdated 1961], Queen's.

7 *Ibid.*

8 P. K. Page interview, 2 November 1992.

9 GW to Ivan Avakumovic, 20 January 1963, Queen's.

10 GW to Ivan Avakumovic, 31 May 1963, Queen's.

11 John Macdonald to GW, 26 June 1963, Queen's.

12 GW to Ivan Avakumovic, 29 February 1964.

13 Eleanor McKechnie to GW, 10 June 1982, Queen's.

14 GW to Chris Scott, 7 September 1983, Queen's.

15 GW to Chris Scott, 10 August 1984, Queen's.

16 GW to Ivan Avakumovic, 20 December 1965, Queen's.

17 GW, *Beyond the Blue Mountains: An Autobiography* (Markham: Fitzhenry & Whiteside, 1987).

NINE: *From Orwell to the Doukhobors*

1 Ian Angus to GW, 23 June 1966, Queen's.

2 *Ibid.*

3 GW to Ivan Avakumovic, 23 June 1966, Queen's.

4 GW to Bill Berger, 22 April 1967, Queen's.

5 Nigel Dennis, "Animal Farm", *Sunday Telegraph*, 28 May 1967.

6 GW to ? Rostetter, 29 November 1973, Queen's.

7 Nadine Asante, "George Woodcock—Portrait of a Literate Man", Vancouver *Sun*, 15 July 1966.

8 GW, "After a Heart Attack: A World Totally Renewed", Vancouver *Sun*, 14 February 1976.

9 Robert Weaver interview, 27 February 1993.

10 *Ibid.*

11 *Ibid.*

12 Letter-to-the-editor, *Saturday Night*, October 1971.

13 GW, letter-to-the-editor, *Saturday Night*, November 1971.

14 GW, "Encounter with an Archangel", *Tamarack Review*, Winter 1963.

15 GW to Ivan Avakumovic, 21 October 1967, Queen's.

16 GW to Ivan Avakumovic, 7 October 1967, Queen's.

17 GW to Ivan Avakumovic, 9 November 1967, Queen's.

18 *Ibid.*

TEN: *Philanthropy Self-taught*

1 GW, undated draft inscription [1989], Queen's.

2 *Ibid.*

3 William Hoffer, *Catalogue 80*, 1992.

4 GW, "The Man Called Uncle", *Western Living*, May 1993.

5 *Ibid.*

6 *Ibid.*

7 *Ibid.*

8 *Ibid.*

9 Quoted in Douglas Fetherling, "At Home with George Woodcock", *Western Living*, August 1991.

10 *Ibid.*

11 GW to Jack Mathews, 2 April 1962, Queen's.

12 *Ibid.*

13 GW to the Dalai Lama, 3 July 1962, Queen's.

14 GW to Anne Wyndham Lewis, 1 March 1970, Queen's.

15 GW to Doug Walls, 6 September 1986, Queen's.

16 Robert McG. Thomas, Jr, "Nancy Macdonald Dies at 86; Aided Spain's Loyalist Exiles", *New York Times*, 16 December 1996.

17 GW, "Aid to India Presents Some Special Problems", *Saturday Night*, December 1972.

18 *Ibid.*

19 *Ibid.*

20 *Ibid.*

21 GW, "The Perils of Freedom in India", *Saturday Night*, October 1975.

22 GW, "The Man Called Uncle", *op. cit.*

23 CIVA *Tenth Anniversary Annual Report.* Vancouver: 1991.

24 GW to Margaret Atwood, 10 March 1983, Queen's.

25 GW, "Minutes of the Forty-sixth Meeting of the Directors of Canada-India Village Aid Society, Held at 6429 McCleery Street, Vancouver, 30 August 1988", Queen's.

26 GW to Fred Cogswell, 19 March 1989, Queen's.

27 GW to Sarah McAlpine, 8 July 1988, Queen's.

ELEVEN: *The Word Factory on McCleery Street*

1 GW to Roy Fuller, 8 June 1969, Queen's.

2 John Ralston Saul to author, 21 March 1993, U OF T. Used by permission of John Ralston Saul.

3 GW to Ivan Avakumovic, 24 January 1968, Queen's.

4 GW to Ivan Avakumovic, 7 February 1968, Queen's.

5 GW to Ivan Avakumovic, 2 April 1968, Queen's.

6 GW, "The Other War", *Canadian Forum*, February 1968.

7 GW to Ivan Avakumovic, 29 February 1968.

8 GW to Ivan Avakumovic, 2 May 1969, Queen's.

9 GW to Cathy Wismer, 25 October 1970, Queen's.

10 GW, *Powers of Observation* (Kingston: Quarry Press, 1989).

11 John Warnock, "Letters", *Saturday Night,* September 1969.

12 GW, "Letters", *Saturday Night,* September 1969.

13 GW to J. R. Mallory, 4 March 1974, Queen's.

14 GW to Esmond Butler, 16 April 1972, Queen's.

15 GW to Sylvia Ostry, 8 August 1973, Queen's.

16 GW to Dave Barrett, 14 December 1973, Queen's.

17 GW to Hugh Richardson, 14 August 1969, Queen's.

18 GW to Donald Stephens, 14 November 1969, Queen's.

19 GW to Ivan Avakumovic, 15 April 1969, Queen's.

20 *Ibid.*

21 GW to John Robert Colombo, 19 June 1976, Queen's.

22 GW, "An Editor Replies", undated typescript, Queen's.

23 "An Apology from the Editors", *University of Toronto Quarterly,* Spring 1973.

24 GW, "The Americans as our George III", Vancouver *Sun,* 12 October 1973, abridged from the *Nation* (New York).

25 GW, "Correspondence", *Canadian Forum,* January 1973.

26 Warren Tallman, *In the Midst: Writings 1962–1992* (Vancouver: Talon-books, 1992).

27 GW to Donald C. Savage, 9 April 1973, Queen's.

28 GW, "After My Heart Attack", Vancouver *Sun,* 14 February 1976.

29 GW to Benedict Read, 4 January 1972, Queen's.

30 GW, undated expense sheet, Queen's.

31 GW to unidentified correspondent ["Dear Betty"], 29 November 1973, Queen's.

32 GW to David Goodway, 9 February 1974, Queen's.

33 *Ibid.*

34 GW to J. F. Hendry, 22 February 1973, Queen's.

35 GW to unidentified correspondent ["Dear Paul"], 26 October 1973, Queen's.

36 GW to author, 29 April 1973, U OF T.

37 Julian Symons, "George Woodcock: An Old Friend", in *Critical Observations* (London: Faber and Faber, 1981).

38 *Ibid.*

39 *Ibid.*

40 GW to Roy Fuller, 26 August 1975, Queen's.

41 GW to [Kathleen O'Connell?], 4 October 1975, Queen's.

42 *Ibid.*

43 GW to Roy Fuller, 24 June 1976, Queen's.

44 GW to [Kathleen O'Connell?], 5 August 1976, Queen's.

45 GW to Roy Fuller, 1 May 1976, Queen's.

46 GW to Linda Sandler, 16 July 1976, Queen's.

47 GW to Lewis and Rene Cooke, 27 November 1976, Queen's.

48 GW to Roy Fuller, 15 November 1975, Queen's.

49 GW to Lewis and Rene Cooke, *op. cit.*

50 GW to Ivan Avakumovic, 30 October 1976, Queen's.

51 GW to Roy Fuller, 7 October 1976, Queen's.

52 Julian Symons, "George Woodcock: An Old Friend", *op. cit.*

53 *Ibid.*

TWELVE: *A Green Old Age*

1   GW to Lynn de Boulay, 17 June 1977, Queen's.

2   GW to Ivan Avakumovic, 20 June 1978, Queen's.

3   GW to Ivan Avakumovic, 8 June 1981, Queen's.

4   GW to Ivan Avakumovic, 7 June 1978, Queen's.

5   *Ibid.*

6   *Ibid.*

7   GW to Roy Fuller, 7 June 1978, Queen's.

8   *Ibid.*

9   GW to author, 14 February 1993, U OF T.

10 GW to James Carol George, 28 December 1977, Queen's.

11 GW to William and Margaret New, 21 April 1979, Queen's.

12 *Ibid.*

13 GW to Cyril Belshaw, 29 August 1980, Queen's.

14 GW to Margaret Atwood, 20 January 1981, Queen's.

15 *Ibid.*

16 *Ibid.*

17 GW to Margaret Atwood, 7 February 1981, Queen's.

18 GW, "A Mighty Affront", Vancouver *Sun*, 27 April 1981.

19 GW to Margaret Atwood, 26 March 1982, Queen's.

20 GW to Margaret Atwood, 26 May 1981, Queen's.

21 *Ibid.*

22 *Ibid.*

23 GW to Margaret Atwood, 3 November 1981, Queen's.

24 GW to Ivan Avakumovic, 8 June 1981, *op. cit.*

25 GW to Ann Wall, 14 November 1978, Queen's.

26 GW to Mike Doyle, 2 February 1983, Queen's.

27 GW, *Confederation Betrayed!* (Madeira Park: Harbour Publishing, 1981).

28 GW to Margaret Atwood, 26 March 1982, Queen's.

29 GW to Margaret Atwood, 19 April 1982, Queen's.

30 GW to Wolfgang H. Richter, 6 September 1983, Queen's.

31 GW, "For Kenneth Rexroth, 1905–1982", typescript poem, Queen's.

32 GW to Margaret Atwood, 19 April 1982, *op. cit.*

33 GW, "Cruise Missile Controversy Calls for Logic as Well as Passion", Vancouver *Sun*, 25 October 1982.

34 GW to Margaret Atwood, 10 March 1983, Queen's.

35 GW to Margaret Atwood, 7 December 1982, Queen's.

36 GW to Mike Doyle, 2 February 1983, *op. cit.*

37 GW to Bernard Oldsey, ? May 1983, Queen's.

38 GW to Mike Doyle, 29 September 1983, Queen's.

39 *Ibid.*

40 GW to David Koven, 27 November 1983, courtesy of David Koven.

41 *Ibid.*

42 GW to William and Margaret New, 21 April 1979, *op. cit.*

43 GW to Allan Kachelmeier, 15 April 1984, Queen's.

44 *Ibid.*

45 Robert Fulford to GW, 20 February 1984, Queen's. Reproduced with permission of Robert Fulford.

46 GW to Allan Kachelmeier, 6 June 1984, Queen's.

47 David Crombie to GW, 6 June 1984, Queen's.

48 Allan MacEachen to David Crombie, 29 June 1984, Queen's.

49 Allan Gotlieb to GW, 8 March 1984, Queen's.

50 GW to George W. Ogg, 22 February 1984, Queen's.

51 *Ibid.*

52 Maynard Winge to GW, 5 April 1984, Queen's.

53 *Ibid.*

54 GW to Frank Low-Beer, 26 April 1988, Queen's.

55 GW, Writers' Union of Canada *Newsletter*, April 1993.

56 "Fairer Entry for Free Thinkers", *Economist*, 15 February 1996.

57 GW to Basil Stuart-Stubbs, 16 August 1978, Queen's.

58 *Ibid.*

59 GW to Basil Stuart-Stubbs, 26 December 1978, Queen's.

60 GW to Douglas T. Kenny, 16 January 1979, Queen's.

61 GW to Alan Twigg, 30 March 1979, Queen's.

62 GW to Howard Gerwing, 7 May 1981, Queen's.

63 GW to D. W. Halliwell, 22 May 1981, Queen's.

64 *Ibid.*

65 Anne MacDermaid to GW, 15 July 1982, Queen's.

66 GW to Anne MacDermaid, 20 July 1982, Queen's.

67 *Ibid.*

68 *Ibid.*

69 GW to Frank Low-Beer, 3 December 1982.

THIRTEEN: *Anarchist Mountain*

1 GW to Bahman Farmanara, 5 November 1985, Queen's.

2 *Ibid.*

3 *Ibid.*

4 GW, *Beyond the Blue Mountains, op. cit.*

5 *Ibid.*

6 *Ibid.*

7 GW to author, 25 December 1987, U OF T.

8 GW to Phyllis Webb, 28 February 1987, Queen's.

9 GW to Earle Birney and Wailan Low, 10 June 1987, Queen's.

10 GW to James King, 24 May 1987, courtesy of James King.

11 GW to author, 15 November 1987, U OF T.

12 GW to Wailan Low, 17 February 1988, Queen's.

13 GW to author, 25 November 1988, U OF T.

14 GW to Wailan Low, 2 December 1988, Queen's.

15 GW to Rhys T. Eyton, 4 May 1988, Queen's.

16 GW to Wailan Low, 16 July 1988, Queen's.

17 "Proposed Draft Press Release Re: Woodcock Trust", undated document, Queen's.

18 GW to Silver Donald Cameron, 3 July 1989, Queen's.

19 GW to Silver Donald Cameron, 6 September 1989, Queen's.

20 *Ibid.*

21 Silver Donald Cameron to GW, 11 July 1989, Queen's. Reproduced with permission of Silver Donald Cameron.

22 George Galt to GW, 28 September 1989, Queen's. Reproduced with permission of George Galt.

23 GW to David Koven, 10 December 1990, courtesy of David Koven.

24 GW to Dennis Lee, 16 September 1989, Queen's.

25 GW to David Koven, 29 June 1991, courtesy of David Koven.

26 GW to author, 7 November 1991, Queen's.

27 Inge Woodcock to GW, undated memo [1990], Queen's. Reproduced by permission of Inge Woodcock.

28 GW to author, 24 July 1992, U OF T.

29 GW to author, 18 August 1992, U OF T.

30 GW to author 18 December 1992, U OF T.

31 GW to author, undated [1993], U OF T.

32 GW to author, undated [December 1993], U OF T.

33 GW to author, 22 September 1993, U OF T.

Epilogue

1 GW to author, 22 June 1993, U OF T.

BIBLIOGRAPHY

A. BOOKS AND PAMPHLETS BY GEORGE WOODCOCK.

Solstice. London: C. Lahr, 1937.

Six Poems. London: Blue Moon Press, 1938.

Ballad of an Orphan Hand. London: C. Lahr, 1939.

The White Island. London: Fortune Press, 1940.

New Life to the Land. London: Freedom Press, 1942.

The Centre Cannot Hold. London: Routledge, 1943.

Railways and Society. London: Freedom Press, 1943.

(Ed.) *Revolutionary Government* by Peter Kropotkin. London: Freedom Press, 1943.

(Ed.) *Selections from* Political Justice by William Godwin. London: Freedom Press, 1943.

(Ed.) *The State—Its Historic Role* by Peter Kropotkin. London: Freedom Press, 1943.

Anarchy or Chaos. London: Freedom Press, 1944. Reprinted with a new introduction by GW. Wilimantic, Connecticut: Ziesing, 1992.

Homes or Hovels: The Housing Problem & its Solution. London: Freedom Press, 1944.

(Ed.) *The Wage System* by Peter Kropotkin. London: Freedom Press, 1944.

Anarchism and Morality. London: Freedom Press, 1945.

What Is Anarchism? London: Freedom Press, 1945.

The Basis of Communal Living. London: Freedom Press, 1947.

Imagine the South. Pasadena: Untide Press, 1947.

(Trans.) *Anny* by Marc Bernard, translated by GW and Marie Louise Berneri as "M. L. George". London: T. V. Boardman, 1948.

(Ed.) *A Defence of Poetry & a Letter to Lord Ellenborough* by Percy Bysshe Shelley. London: Porcupine Press, 1948.

The Incomparable Aphra. London: T. V. Boardman, 1948. Reprinted as *Aphra Behn: The English Sappho*, with a new introduction by GW. Montreal: Black Rose Books, 1989.

(Ed.) *The Soul of Man Under Socialism* by Oscar Wilde. London: Porcupine Press, 1948.

(Ed.) *A Hundred Years of Revolution—1848 and After.* London: Porcupine Press, 1948.

(Ed.) *The Slavery of Our Times* by Leo Tolstoy. London: Porcupine Press, 1948. Reprint. London: John Lawrence, 1972.

William Godwin: A Biographical Study. London: Porcupine Press, 1948. Reprint. Norwood, Pennsylvania: Norwood Editions, 1976. Reprinted with a new introduction by GW. Montreal: Black Rose Books, 1989.

The Writer and Politics. London: Porcupine Press, 1948. Reprinted as *Writers and Politics*, with a new introduction by GW. Montreal: Black Rose Books, 1990.

(With Ivan Avakumovic.) *The Anarchist Prince: A Biographical Study of Peter Kropotkin.* London: T. V. Boardman, 1950. Reprint. New York: Schocken Books, 1971. Reprinted as *From Prince to Rebel*, with a new introduction by GW. Montreal: Black Rose Books, 1990.

British Poetry Today. Vancouver: University of British Columbia, 1950.

(Ed.) *The Letters of Charles Lamb.* London: Grey Walls Press, 1950.

The Paradox of Oscar Wilde. London: T. V. Boardman, 1950. New York: Macmillan, 1950. Reprinted as *Oscar Wilde: The Double Image*, with new introduction by GW. Montreal: Black Rose Books, 1989.

Ravens and Prophets: An Account of Journeys in British Columbia, Alberta and Southern Alaska. London: Allan Wingate, 1952. Reprint: Sono Nis, 1993.

Pierre-Joseph Proudhon: A Biography. London: Routledge & Kegan Paul, 1956. Reprinted as *Pierre-Joseph Proudhon: His Life and Works.* New York: Schocken Books, 1972. Reprinted with a new introduction and bibliographical supplement by GW. Montreal: Black Rose Books, 1987.

To the City of the Dead: An Account of Travels in Mexico. London: Faber and Faber, 1957.

Incas and Other Men: Travels in the Andes. London: Faber and Faber, 1959.

Anarchism: A History of Libertarian Ideas and Movements. Cleveland: World Publishing, 1962. Harmondsworth: Penguin Books, 1963. Reprint. Harmondsworth: Pelican edition with a postscript by GW, 1975. Reprint. Harmondsworth: Pelican edition with a new introduction and bibliography by GW, 1986.

Faces of India: A Travel Narrative. London: Faber and Faber, 1964.

Asia, Gods and Cities: Aden to Tokyo. London: Faber and Faber, 1966.

(Ed.) *A Choice of Critics: Selections from Canadian Literature.* Toronto: Oxford University Press, 1966.

Civil Disobedience. Toronto: Canadian Broadcasting Corporation, 1966.

The Crystal Spirit: A Study of George Orwell. Boston: Little, Brown, 1966. London: Jonathan Cape, 1967. Reprint. Harmondsworth: Penguin Books, 1970. Reprinted with a new introduction by GW. London: Fourth Estate, 1984. New York: Schocken Books, 1984.

The Greeks in India. London: Faber and Faber, 1966.

Variations on a Human Theme. Toronto: Ryerson Press, 1966.

Kerala: A Portrait of the Malabar Coast. London: Faber and Faber, 1967.

(Ed.) *Rural Rides* by William Cobbett. Harmondsworth: Penguin Books, 1967.

Selected Poems of George Woodcock. Toronto: Clarke, Irwin, 1967.

(With Ivan Avakumovic.) *The Doukhobors.* London: Faber and Faber, 1968. Toronto: Oxford University Press, 1968. Reprinted with a new introduction by the authors. Toronto: McClelland & Stewart, 1977.

(Ed.) *The Egoist* by George Meredith. Harmondsworth: Penguin Books, 1968.

The British in the Far East. London: Weidenfeld & Nicolson, 1969. New York: Atheneum, 1969.

Henry Walter Bates: Naturalist of the Amazons. London: Faber and Faber, 1969.

Hugh MacLennan. Toronto: Copp Clark, 1969.

(Ed.) *The Sixties: Canadian Writers and Writing of the Decade.* Vancouver: University of British Columbia Publications Centre, 1969.

Canada and the Canadians. London: Faber and Faber, 1970. Reprint. London: Faber and Faber, 1973, revised. Toronto: Oxford University Press, 1970. Reprint. Toronto: Macmillan of Canada, 1973, revised.

The Hudson's Bay Company. New York: Crowell-Collier Press, 1970.

Odysseus Ever Returning: Essays on Canadian Writers and Writing. Toronto: McClelland & Stewart, 1970.

(Ed.) *A Tale of Two Cities* by Charles Dickens. Harmondsworth: Penguin Books, 1970.

(Ed.) *What Is Property?* by P. J. Proudhon. New York: Dover Publications, 1970.

Into Tibet: The Early British Explorers. London: Faber and Faber, 1971.

(Ed.) *Malcolm Lowry: The Man and His Work.* Vancouver: University of British Columbia Press, 1971.

Mohandas Gandhi. New York: Vintage, 1971. Reprinted as *Gandhi.* London: Fontana/Collins, 1972.

Mordecai Richler. Toronto: McClelland & Stewart, 1971.

Victoria: Photo-Essay by Ingeborg and George Woodcock. Victoria: Morriss Printing, 1971.

(Ed.) *Wyndham Lewis in Canada.* Vancouver: University of British Columbia Publications Centre, 1971.

Dawn and the Darkest Hour: A Study of Aldous Huxley. London: Faber and Faber, 1972. New York: Viking Press, 1972.

Herbert Read: The Stream and the Source. London: Faber and Faber, 1972.

The Rejection of Politics and Other Essays on Canada, Canadians, Anarchism and the World. Toronto: new press, 1972.

(Ed.) *Typee,* by Herman Melville. Harmondsworth: Penguin Books, 1972.

(Ed.) *Colony and Confederation: Early Canadian Poets and Their Background.* Vancouver: University of British Columbia Press, 1974.

(Ed.) *Poets and Critics: Essays from Canadian Literature 1966–1974.* Toronto: Oxford University Press, 1974.

Who Killed the British Empire? An Inquest. London: Jonathan Cape, 1974. New York: Quadrangle, 1974. Toronto: Fitzhenry & Whiteside, 1974.

Amor De Cosmos: Journalist and Reformer. Toronto: Oxford University Press, 1975.

(Ed.) *The Canadian Novel in the Twentieth Century: Essays from Canadian Literature.* Toronto: McClelland & Stewart, 1975.

Gabriel Dumont: The Métis Chief and His Lost World. Edmonton: Hurtig, 1975.

Notes on Visitations: Poems 1936–75. Toronto: Anansi, 1975.

Canadian Poets 1960–1973: A Checklist. Ottawa: Golden Dog Press, 1976.

Gabriel Dumont and the Northwest Rebellion. Toronto: Playwrights Co-op, 1976.

South Sea Journey. London: Faber and Faber, 1976. Don Mills: Fitzhenry & Whiteside, 1978.

(Ed.) *The Anarchist Reader.* London: Fontana, 1977.

Anima, or, Swann Grown Old: A Cycle of Poems by George Woodcock. Windsor, Ontario: Black Moss Press, 1977.

Peoples of the Coast: The Indians of the Pacific Northwest. Edmonton: Hurtig, 1977.

Two Plays: The Island of Demons [and] Six Dry Cakes for the Hunted. Vancouver: Talonbooks, 1977.

Faces from History: Canadian Portraits and Profiles. Edmonton: Hurtig, 1978.

Gabriel Dumont. Toronto: Fitzhenry & Whiteside, 1978.

The Kestrel and Other Poems of Past and Present. Sunderland, Durham: Coelfrith Press, 1978.

(Trans.) *Phaedra* by Jean Racine. Victoria: Contemporary Literature in Translation, 1978.

(Ed.) *The Return of the Native* by Thomas Hardy. Harmondsworth: Penguin Books, 1978.

Thomas Merton, Monk and Poet: A Critical Study. Vancouver: Douglas & McIntyre, 1978. Seattle: University of Washington Press, 1978.

The Canadians. Don Mills: Fitzhenry & Whiteside, 1979. Cambridge: Harvard University Press, 1979. London: Athlone Press, 1979. St Lucia, Australia: University of Queensland Press, 1979.

A George Woodcock Reader edited by Douglas Fetherling. Ottawa: Deneau & Greenberg, 1980.

The Mountain Road. Fredericton: Fiddlehead Poetry Books, 1980.

100 Great Canadians. Edmonton: Hurtig, 1980.

A Picture History of British Columbia. Edmonton: Hurtig, 1980.

The World of Canadian Writing: Critiques and Recollections. Vancouver: Douglas & McIntyre, 1980. Seattle: University of Washington Press, 1980.

Confederation Betrayed! Vancouver: Harbour Publishing, 1981.

Ivan Eyre. Don Mills: Fitzhenry & Whiteside, 1981. Also published in a boxed limited edition of 150 copies signed and numbered by the artist, with an Eyre print and a signed poem by GW laid in.

The Meeting of Time and Space: Regionalism in Canadian Literature. Edmonton: NeWest Institute for Western Canadian Studies, 1981.

Taking it to the Letter. Dunvegan, Ontario: Quadrant Editions, 1981.

The Benefactor. Lantzville, B.C.: Oolichan Books, 1982.

Letter to the Past: An Autobiography. Don Mills: Fitzhenry & Whiteside, 1982.

Letters from Sooke: A Correspondence between Sir Herbert Read and George Woodcock. Victoria: Victoria Book Arts Club, 1982.

Northern Spring: The Flowering of Canadian Literature in English. Washington: Canadian Embassy, 1982.

(Ed.) *Canadian Writers and Their Works.* Toronto: ECW Press, 1983–92. Twenty volumes.

Collected Poems. Victoria: Sono Nis Press, 1983.

(Ed.) *A Place to Stand On: Essays by and about Margaret Laurence.* Edmonton: NeWest Publishers, 1983.

Orwell's Message: 1984 and the Present. Vancouver: Harbour Publishing, 1984.

Patrick Lane and His Works. Toronto: ECW Press, 1984.

Strange Bedfellows: The State and the Arts in Canada. Vancouver: Douglas & McIntyre, 1985.

(With Toni Onley.) *The Walls of India.* Toronto: Lester & Orpen Dennys, 1985.

British Columbia: A Celebration. Edmonton: Hurtig, 1986.

(Trans.) *The Métis in the Canadian West* by Marcel Giraud. Edmonton: University of Alberta Press, 1986. Two volumes.

(With Tim Fitzharris.) *The University of British Columbia: A Souvenir.* Toronto: Oxford University Press, 1986.

Beyond the Blue Mountains: An Autobiography. Markham: Fitzhenry & Whiteside, 1987.

Leo Tolstoi: Ein gewaltfreier Anarchist. Germany: Edition flugschriften, 1987.

Northern Spring: The Flowering of Canadian Literature. Vancouver: Douglas & McIntrye, 1987.

Caves in the Desert: Travels in China. Vancouver: Douglas & McIntyre, 1988.

Charles Heavysege and His Works. Toronto: ECW Press, 1988.

(Trans.) *The Geography of Freedom* by Marie Fleming. Montreal: Black Rose Books, 1988.

Matt Cohen and His Works. Toronto: ECW Press, 1988.

The People We Help and Why. Vancouver: Canada-India Village Aid, 1988.

The Purdy-Woodcock Letters: Selected Correspondence 1964–1984, edited by George Galt. Toronto: ECW Press, 1988.

A Social History of Canada. Markham: Penguin Books, 1988.

Traditionen der Freiheit: Essays zureversonuntide libertaren Transformation der Gesellschaft. Mulheim, Germany: Trafik, 1988.

The Century That Made Us: Canada 1814–1914. Toronto: Oxford University Press, 1989.

(Ed.) *Collected Works of Peter Kropotkin.* Montreal: Black Rose Books, 1989–95. Eleven volumes.

Dry Wells of India: An Anthology against Thirst. Vancouver: Harbour Publishing, 1989.

(Ed.) *Fanny Hill* by John Cleland. Markham: Fitzhenry & Whiteside, 1989.

Introducing Hugh MacLennan's Barometer Rising: *A Reader's Guide.* Toronto: ECW Press, 1989.

Introducing Margaret Laurence's The Stone Angel: *A Reader's Guide.* Toronto: ECW Press, 1989.

The Marvelous Century: Archaic Man and the Awakening of Reason. Markham: Fitzhenry & Whiteside, 1989.

Onley's Arctic: Diaries and Paintings of the High Arctic by Toni Onley. Vancouver, Douglas & McIntyre, 1989.

Powers of Observation. Kingston: Quarry Press, 1989.

British Columbia, A History of the Province. Vancouver: Douglas & McIntyre, 1990.

Introducing Margaret Atwood's Surfacing: *A Reader's Guide.* Toronto: ECW Press, 1990.

Introducing Mordecai Richler's The Apprenticeship of Duddy Kravitz: *A Reader's Guide.* Toronto: ECW Press, 1990.

Introducing Sinclair Ross's As For Me and My House: *A Reader's Guide.* Toronto: ECW Press, 1990.

(Ed.) *The Great Canadian Anecdote Contest.* Vancouver: Harbour Publishing, 1991.

Tolstoy at Yasnaya Polyana & Other Poems. Kingston: Quarry Press, 1991.

Anarchism and Anarchists. Kingston: Quarry Press, 1992.

George Woodcock's Introduction to Canadian Fiction. Toronto: ECW Press, 1992.

George Woodcock's Introduction to Canadian Poetry. Toronto: ECW Press, 1992.

The Monk and His Message: Undermining the Myth of History. Vancouver: Douglas & McIntyre, 1992.

Power to Us All. Constitution or Social Contract? Madeira Park, B.C.: Harbour Publishing, 1992.

The Record of George Woodcock. Victoria: Reference West, 1992.

Introducing Morley Callaghan's More Joy in Heaven. Toronto: ECW Press, 1993.

Letter from the Khyber Pass and Other Travel Writing, edited by Jim Christy. Vancouver: Douglas & McIntyre, 1993.

The Cherry Tree on Cherry Street and Other Poems. Kingston: Quarry Press, 1994.

Walking through the Valley: An Autobiography. Toronto: ECW Press, 1994.

B. BOOKS, PAMPHLETS AND THESES ABOUT GEORGE WOODCOCK.

Hughes, Peter. *George Woodcock.* Toronto: McClelland & Stewart, 1974.

Nelles, Viv, and Abraham Rotstein, eds. *Nationalism and Local Control: Responses to George Woodcock.* Toronto: new press, 1973.

New, W. H., ed. *A Political Art: Essays and Images in Honour of George Wood-cock.* Vancouver: University of British Columbia Press, 1978.

Nigol, Rick. "Liberty and Community: The Political Thought of George Woodcock". M.A. thesis, Queen's University, 1985.

Robinson, Jack. "George Woodcock: Romantic Idealist". Ph.D. thesis, University of Alberta, 1983.

[Stewart, Don.] *The Works of George Woodcock.* To accompany an exhibit of his works at the George Woodcock Symposium, Simon Fraser University at Harbour Centre, May 6 and 7, 1994.

INDEX